DO NOT REMOVE
CARDS FROM POCKET

Germaine W. Shames • W. Gerald Glover

Intercultural Press, Inc.
Yarmouth, Maine

Library of Congress Catalog No. 88-045760
ISBN 0-933662-77-7
Copyright 1989 Germaine W. Shames, W. Gerald Glover
Published by Intercultural Press, Inc.
All rights reserved.
Printed in the United States of America.

For information, contact
Intercultural Press
P.O. Box 768
Yarmouth, Maine 04096

DEDICATION

To my
PARENTS
and
GRANDMOTHER—
they
never
doubted.
G.W.S.

To
JORGE
PESQUERA
for
encouraging
our
collaboration.

To
DR. OTTO
VONMERING
for his
years of
direction
and support.
W.G.G.

CONTRIBUTORS

Clive Adamson:
Received his master's degree in hotel administration from Cornell University. He has served as the training director of a major resort firm in the Caribbean, a consultant for the Educational Institute of the American Hotel and Motel Association, and was the Director of Hospitality Management at Miami Dade Community College.

Lena Ahlström:
Is the founder and head of SAS Intercultural Communication. Ms. Ahlström is a graduate of Stockholm University with a degree in international marketing. Also, she is coauthor of the book, *Att Vara Svensk Chef i Sydostasien (To Be a Swedish Manager in Southeast Asia)*.

Georgann P. Carlton:
Is currently an executive with Sun Bank after a successful eight-year career at Walt Disney World. She planned and supervised the daily operation of EPCOT's Fellowship Program during its premier year.

Roger Fennings:
Serves as Hilton International's Area Director of Public Relations for Europe, Africa and the Gulf. Previous experience includes stock car racing, ownership of a show business public relations firm, and a stint as the PR manager for *Custom Car* magazine.

Henry Ferguson:
Is a professional speaker and seminar leader on international management and is based in Albany, New York. He has been a college professor, government manager, importer/exporter, publisher and consultant. He is the author of *Tomorrow's Global Manager*.

Renaldo Flores:
Is Personnel Director at the Condado Plaza Hotel and Casino in San Juan, Puerto Rico and one of the island's leading authorities on labor-management relations.

Harris Friedman, Ph.D.:
Is a licensed psychologist in private practice in Fort Myers, Florida. He is the President of Human Systems, Inc., a consulting and management firm in the area of human resources and human services. His areas of special interest include health psychology, organizational development, and psychotherapy.

Anders Hovemyr:
Is the Training Manager of SAS Intercultural Communication. He is currently completing the work for a doctoral dissertation at the University of Uppsala.

George S. Kanahele, Ph.D.:
Received his doctorate from Cornell University. Widely recognized for his international work in entrepreneurial development and training, he is also a businessman, scholar, civic leader, and writer. He has been described by *The New Yorker* as the "spiritual father" of the Hawaiian renaissance.

David A. Kannally:
Recently formed his own company in Colorado, David Kannally & Associates, after serving as President of the Vail Resort Association. Prior experience from 1974 to 1985 was in various positions with Walt Disney World, including six years as manager of the World Showcase Fellowship Program.

David M. Klein, Ph.D.:
Currently is Vice President for Marketing and Business Development at hiMEDICS, Inc., a developmental stage pharmaceutical company. Previously he was on the marketing faculty of the University of Massachusetts and the Florida University system.

Dante Laudadio, Ph.D.:
Is the Chairman of Hospitality at Florida State University. He is a widely known consultant and educator in the service industries. He is President of Lassen Company, a hospitality consulting firm.

James Lett, Ph.D.:
Is a cultural anthropologist with extensive practical experience in tourism and broadcast journalism. He conducted research on the impact of tourism

on the British Virgin Islands and has been a television producer, reporter, and anchor for a CBS affiliate in Florida.

Robert Lewis, Ph.D.:
Is currently professor of hospitality marketing at the School of Hotel Administration, University of Massachusetts. He is widely published in such journals as the *Cornell Quarterly* and a premier authority on service marketing.

Yasuyuki Miura:
Is President of Nikko Hotels International for the U.S.A. and Canada. He has worldwide executive experience with Japan Air Lines in areas such as Asia and the Middle East.

Ned Rosen, Ph.D.:
Is a fellow of the American Psychological Association and a former professor of industrial and labor relations at Cornell University. He is President of The Teamworkers, Inc., a network of international consultants located in Washington, D.C. and Florida.

Carol Sage:
Is former Director of Training for Sheraton Hotels and is currently an international consultant to the hospitality, travel and tourism industries. Recent clients have included the governments of the People's Republic of China and Yugoslavia. She has worked extensively with travel agents, tour operators and tourism officials to raise awareness of cultural issues.

Cliff Scott, Ph.D.:
Is currently professor of marketing at California State University-Fullerton.

O. H. Michael Smith:
Is a former director of the Bahamas Hotel Training College. In that position he was involved in projects, conferences and seminars in the Caribbean, Latin America, and Europe. He has a bachelor's degree in business administration from Howard University, a master's degree in hotel and food service management from Florida International University, a diploma in tourism from Bradford University in the United Kingdom, and is currently completing his doctorate in education at Ohio State University.

Michael White:
Was General Manager of the Kannapoli Beach Hotel on Maui, an AMFAC property, and continues to manage some of the company's finest properties. He holds a degree in travel and tourism management from the University of Hawaii.

While they did not write articles, the following people made contributions of time and effort which have greatly enhanced the quality of this book.

Louis Finnamore:
General Manager of the Kahala Hilton.

Hollis Harris:
President and Chief Operating Officer of Delta Air Lines.

Richard Jones:
Recently retired Manager of Public Relations with Delta Airlines.

AUTHORS' BIOGRAPHIES

Gerald Glover, Ph.D., CHA, is Director of Hospitality Management at Appalachian State University. He has a doctorate from the University of Florida in applied anthropology, has written numerous articles, and has consulting experience in corporate culture change, service quality, and culture management. Prior to his current position, he taught at Michigan State University and The Bahamas Hotel Training College. He has worked as an executive with Trust House Forte and the Boca Raton Hotel and Club and has consulted with such companies as Hershey, Club Med, Hilton International, Sands Hotel, Harrison Conference Centers, Essex House, BahamasAir, and the Educational Institute of the American Hotel and Motel Association. As the former vice chair of the AH&MA Quality Assurance Committee, he has presented numerous seminars for the hospitality industry.

Germaine W. Shames is a human resources/service management consultant and journalist active in the international hospitality industry. Associated with Hilton International Hotels for nine years as corporate special projects manager, she championed numerous programs and policies consistent with the "world-class service" vision. She is a member of the Society for Intercultural Training, Education and Research and holds a BS degree in hotel and restaurant management and a master's in intercultural management. Her writings have appeared in such publications as the *Cornell Quarterly, International Journal of Hospitality Management* and *Restaurant Hospitality*. Her passport is travel-worn from ten years' overseas experience in various parts of Europe, the Caribbean, Latin America and the Middle East. She is currently at work on a book concerning the personal lives of global professionals.

ACKNOWLEDGEMENTS

Many individuals have offered guidance in the preparation of this book. Space permits us to name but a few.

Diane Zeller of SIETAR International has been, as always, a conduit and supporter *extraordinaire*. Clifford Clarke of IRI; Ward Heneveld, Scott Duncan and Alvino Fantini of the School for International Training; David Hoffman of Hilton International; Don Henderson, Alan Gould, Maggie Range, Patricia Holvenstot, Tuula Piispanen-Krabbe, Cynthia Fetterolf, and the staff of the Sussex County Library—all have been generous with their time and knowledge.

Special friends, Anna and Tony DelaTorre, kept a roof over Germaine's head while we wrote. On Jerry's side, manuscript typist, Deborah Culler, and proofreader, Catherine Pinson, made order out of chaos as the book took form.

This book belongs to each of our contributors as well as to our publishers— they have brought more enthusiasm and originality to the task than we could ever have hoped for.

To these and other supporters, our sincere gratitude.

INTRODUCTION

We wrote this book because we got tired of listening to people complain about service, tired of reading articles bemoaning the state of service in the U.S. and other countries, and tired of being the victims of inept, insensitive service ourselves.

The fact is, service simply isn't fulfilling the expectations of many consumers. It's not that service providers aren't aware of the problem. They *are*, and they're trying to do something about it. The problem is they're hamstrung by die-hard management notions and traditional industry cultures that just don't work anymore—if they ever did.

True, service management has for the past several years enjoyed a spurt of development as a branch of management science. What's emerging, however, is a school of service management *as if culture didn't matter*. It seems to us that service management theorists and practitioners are unwittingly doing their fellows a disservice by downplaying or ignoring the social dimension of the service experience.

If people shed their cultures when providing or consuming a service, and if the service experience transpired in a cultural vacuum, service managers could continue to manage as they have until now. The reality is, however, that the service arena is strewn with "cultural baggage," and service managers, blind to it, are tripping all over it like slapstick comics. We propose an alternative school of service management—one built on the premise that culture prescribes how we deliver and consume service.

We believe that there can be no effective service management without "culture management," and we don't just mean corporate culture. To deliver service—particularly "world-class service"—the cultures of the service providers, consumers, operating unit and community must all be considered. This is not as complicated as it may sound. Once we have taken the most important step—reshaping the traditional reactive, ill-focused culture of service management itself—the rest becomes manageable.

Let's face it, it's time to change the way we manage service. We can't continue to treat the service experience as merely a question of employee attitude or some sort of psychological ping-pong. Service is a social experience which takes place within a cultural context, as laden with promise as it is fraught with pitfalls. We're already well acquainted with the pitfalls. It's time to tap the promise.

We invite you to explore world-class service.

Introduction

A string of senators warned airlines Thursday to shape up, improve services and cut delays or face possible reregulation or heavy government-imposed penalties for shoddy operations ...complaints about airline service to the Transportation Department have soared in recent months. The cries about delays, lost baggage and poor flight selections have been loud in Congress as well, prompting the introduction of a flurry of airline passenger protection legislation...

> from "Airline Industry Told to Shape Up"
> *Miami Herald* April 23, 1987

...the hotel industry, like other industries in the service sector, is fraught with problems: one of the highest employee turnover rates of any industry, a labor shortage, and the public's perception of hotel jobs as low in pay and low in status.... If executives appear concerned about the turnover problem, it is for good reason. The level of quality service can make or break a local chain...

> from "Heartbreak Hotel"
> by Sal Vittolino
> *Human Resource Executive* July 1987

If hoteliers are to survive, whether as independent or as chain, they must think globally.

> from Editor's International Diary
> *Hotels and Restaurants International*
> August 1987

As true as woman is the future of man—if you believe a famous French singer—tourism and hospitality are without a doubt the destined future of a civilization turning more and more to leisure activities. But it is a future which must be mastered, whether by tourist offices or hotel chains.

> from the Centre International de Glion's
> Silver Jubilee Book 1987 theme
> *The Mastery of the Future*

TABLE OF CONTENTS

Chapter 1

SERVICE AS IF
CULTURE MATTERS

"At your service" has become the byword of many industries in today's global marketplace. Where it is spoken, emphasis is on performing rather than producing, serving rather than supplying. Service industries specialize in the delivery of nonmaterial commodities whose meaning and value are (ideally) agreed upon by a service provider and consumer.

World-class service is an ideal. It has implications for both international and domestic service providers, as well as for consumers. In the increasingly competitive service arena, world-class service is the "edge" that management has been seeking.

While the term *world-class service* may conjure images of pampered jet-setters on a champagne flight to an exclusive resort (and this scenario is not incompatible with the ideal we present), it is just one small chip in a massive service industry mosaic. Equally compatible and important are the service experiences of a small-town shoe salesman attending a trade show in a neighboring city or a housewife taking her five-year-old son on a bus tour.

World-class service is the consistent satisfaction of the needs and expectations of a culturally diverse public. It matches the capabilities and approach of the service provider to the needs and expectations of the service consumer. Proactive and adaptive, world-class service feels equally "right" to the Canadian lawyer flying first class as it does to the European trade unionist traveling coach on the same flight. At a minimum, it is service perceived by each customer as appropriate and adequate. At its best, it may also make the customer feel at home, among friends, or pampered. Always, it is providing what was promised by the service business.

Service, world-class or not, involves certain universals characteristic of the experience regardless of the type of industry or product, nationalities of providers and consumers, management approach, or price tag. We

1

consider these service universals vital to understanding service as a social experience.

First, *service is the attempt of a person to fulfill the perceived needs of another within a particular social environment.* By this rather broad definition, service is a phenomenon which may be observed in any society or nation. A service industry is one whose mission is to meet specific consumer needs, usually through person-to-person contact. The manner in which needs are expressed and interpreted is culturally influenced, and each service interaction unfolds within a unique milieu of perceptions.

A second universal is that *the service experience is a social experience.* As such, it involves human interaction and communication. The nature or form which this interaction takes is determined by the culture or cultures of the interacting individuals. By *culture* we mean a set of life ways and orientations (including customs, beliefs, attitudes, and out-of-awareness values and assumptions) that are learned and reinforced through group affiliation. Culture determines what the service provider and consumer perceive as needs, what and how they will communicate, what they value and how they will react to each other. The provider enters the service experience with a predisposition to certain behaviors based on his or her own national or ethnic culture as well as the culture of the service organization he or she represents. The consumer also brings "cultural baggage" to the experience, a predisposition to expect and react in culturally prescribed ways. The service experience is clearly a social meeting place, formulated and directed by the cultures of the service organization itself, that of its locale, and those of its employees and customers.

Third, *a desirable level of customer satisfaction results when the service consumer's expectations are met or exceeded.* We have already established that expectations are shaped by culture. Consumers define service and set their own service standards according to their upbringing, education and experience. Without realizing it, they demand service *on their own terms.* If their expectations are met, they pronounce the service good. Although the service organization may hold a five-star rating, if the service delivered doesn't jibe with customers' culturally shaped expectations, they will be unimpressed by and dissatisfied with the service experience and organization.

The fourth and final service universal concerns the management of its delivery: *managing a service organization involves managing people and their cultures.* We have seen that both customers and employees bring their cultural baggage to the service experience. Differences in the content of that baggage may cause miscommunication, misunderstanding and dissatisfaction. The culturally aware manager recognizes culture's impact on his work force, clientele, operation, and bottom line and doesn't leave its workings to chance. For that person, culture management is an integral and essential foundation of service management.

2

Although enlightened service managers are becoming more aware of culture's influence, few possess the wherewithal to orchestrate the productive intermingling of the various cultures that affect their organizations. Little research has as yet been done on culture's place in service delivery, and few culture management tools are used by the service manager. This book is intended as a primer in culture management for anyone involved in the delivery of service. It states a case for world-class service. Its aim is to make the service experience more satisfying and rewarding for all concerned.

Cultural Laboratory

The hospitality, travel and tourism industries provide an excellent laboratory for exploring the application and benefits of culture management to the service industries. Highly interdependent, these three industries exercise an incalculable influence on the economies, politics, self-image and worldview of many nations. At the microlevel, they showcase the service universals presented above. In the authors' opinion, there are few other industries in which the need is as great or the time as right for culture management.

The following characteristics make the hospitality, travel and tourism industries a logical proving ground for world-class service:

- Multicultural operations
- International travel patterns
- Predominantly North American and European management models in potential conflict with local value orientations, particularly in Third World nations
- Pluralistic work forces
- Culturally diverse consumers
- Destinations whose appeal is often based on their local culture
- Labor intensiveness
- Resistance to the introduction of automation at the expense of personalized service.

Above all, we chose these industries as our laboratory because of their social nature. The frequency, diversity and intensity of social interactions they generate provide an unparalleled environment for the exploration and management of culture.

Tunnel Vision

The authors believe "cultural tunnel vision" to be among the most serious and widespread managerial shortcomings in the service arena. A

3

significant number of service managers persist in setting service standards, marketing services and managing service staff without regard to cultural differences, preferences and sensitivities. These managers are not necessarily insensitive or incompetent; they may, in fact, be among the most respected leaders in their industries. Unfortunately, however, they miss opportunities, undermine their effectiveness and cost their organizations money because of their inability to see beyond their own culturally prescribed frame of reference.

Because everyone is culture-bound to some degree, culture management is a concept which few managers can be expected to fully understand at first. Cultural tunnel vision is ingrained. Most managers learn to manage just as they learn to eat or to worship: they're taught *one* culturally sanctioned way. Imperceptibly and durably woven into that one way is a myriad of cultural assumptions, values and beliefs which filter managers' perceptions and program their behavior throughout their lives. It is the exceptional manager who is motivated and able to attain sufficient cultural self-awareness to become a manager of culture (instead of being managed by culture!).

As service industries grow and cater to broader and more culturally diverse markets, cultural tunnel vision becomes more potentially damaging, and the need for culture management more pressing. The mandate for culturally aware service managers is clear.

Culture Management's Scope

Culture permeates every management function. All areas of management action call for culture management. The division of culture management into four broad areas—business strategy, marketing, human resources development and customer contact—provides a workable framework in which to illustrate and analyze the culture management concept within the service environment. You will encounter these four terms throughout the book, and this is what we mean by them:

Business strategy is an organization's master plan. Generally decided by upper management, it takes the form of strategic plans, corporate budgets and policies, and mission statements. Because an organization's business strategy takes into account and affects all of its constituents or audiences (i.e., shareholders, consumers, employees, government officials, and community members) wherever they are, it is by nature highly multicultural. Culture management is essential in the formulation of plans and policies if they are to be accepted and implemented in diverse operating environments by different kinds of people. Culture management in the formulation of mission statements and declarations of philosophy

4

enables upper management to mold an organizational culture conducive to the attainment of its long-term goals.

When we refer to *marketing*, we include the entire gamut of functions involved in designing and selling products and services, from market research to postsale customer maintenance. In essence marketing is identifying and satisfying consumer needs. Viewed in this way, the cultural implications of marketing are apparent. As needs and expectations are culturally determined, effective culture management in this area is essential. Knowledge of the culture of the customer and the locale in which the service is offered enables the manager to "package" the local culture for foreign consumption. It also helps the manager evaluate the cultural appropriateness of advertising, sales promotions and direct selling approaches.

Human resources development is the process of attracting, maximizing and maintaining a capable and motivated team of employees. More than finding the best person for the job, this function involves hiring suitable people and providing them with the tools and incentives to perform to capacity. The most people-oriented of all management functions, human resources development is also the most cultural. If employees could check their cultural baggage at the service entrance, there would be no need for culture management in this area. The reality is, however, that employees' cultural perceptions, assumptions, values and attitudes do regulate their on-the-job behavior and pose a constant challenge to the manager.

We chose the term *customer contact* to refer to the actual interaction of the service provider and consumer (or prospective consumer) before, during or after the service experience. The interaction may be face-to-face, over a telephone line, in print, or via radio or television. Regardless of the medium, customer contact involves communication between the service provider and consumer. Managers who overlook the degree to which communication is rooted in culture invite miscommunication serious enough to affect the bottom line. Particularly in the service experience where communication is often across cultures, insight into the cultural dynamics of both verbal and nonverbal communication is critical to the management of service.

Effective management of culture in these four areas will produce world-class service. Anything less will likely result in inconsistent service delivery of questionable appropriateness.

The Case of the Caribbean Resort

The authors' experience in the hospitality and tourism industries in the Caribbean serves to illustrate the need for and application of the culture management concept. One resort, which we will refer to as the Sun and Sea Hotel, is the subject of our analysis.

The Sun and Sea Hotel is a five-hundred-room, first-class hotel located on the outskirts of the capital city of a small Caribbean island nation. A former colony which has been independent for almost two decades, this developing nation faces the economic, political and social problems typically associated with rapid modernization; thus, the hotel suffers from expatriate management and absentee ownership, labor-management friction, a relatively unskilled local labor pool and rising crime rates.

As the Sun and Sea Hotel is part of a large multinational hotel chain, many of its managers come from previous assignments in Europe and the United States, where they became accustomed to managing according to the social conditions and value orientations prevalent there. Frequently, managers and their families have difficulties adjusting to life in an island society. Complaints of "rock fever" are standard cocktail conversation, and manager turnover is high. Local managers find themselves cast in the role of "culture broker" and middleman. They often feel caught between the cultures of the organization, their expatriate counterparts and their own origin. One local manager describes his frustration this way, "I feel as if I don't belong anywhere anymore. If I act like the manager my company expects me to be, my family and friends accuse me of selling out. When I act like a local, the company and expatriates say I don't have what it takes to be a good manager!"

Several different, and often competing, views of management can be observed in the hotel and its operations. The corporate office, expatriate managers, aspiring local managers, employees, and the trade union seem to be in constant disagreement. These groups each have their own perspective and agenda, and one doesn't have to look far for examples of the problems engendered by their clashes: backbiting, infighting, sabotage and demoralization.

At the corporate office, boardroom discussion of the Sun and Sea Hotel is seasoned with war stories. Corporate officers tend to blame the "difficult natives" for the hotel's inability to maintain the same standards of service as the company's properties in Europe or the United States. There is also concern about some of the expatriate managers "going native" and letting too much of the local culture seep into the hotel.

Hotel employees and trade unions share the often unstated feeling that tourism creates a sophisticated form of servility. Having only recently thrown off the yoke of colonialism, they are determined not to allow themselves to be bullied by Jack (foreign authority figures). Many employees are alienated from the organization where they work and are receptive to trade union leaders who may or may not use their support toward constructive ends.

Of course, the most obvious and costly consequence of the Sun and Sea Hotel's unmanaged clash of cultures is inconsistent guest satisfaction. Guests are often first-time visitors to the hotel and island. They are drawn by glossy brochures and exuberant travel agents who paint an unspoiled paradise peopled by smiling and carefree natives. Buoyant with anticipation, they're herded into jumbo jets where they huddle three across and count the minutes. Their expectations of "paradise" usually fizzle upon arrival at the airport, where poker-faced customs officials offer a less than cordial greeting to the island. Visitors then inch through traffic with a taxi driver who often bears an uncanny resemblance to those encountered in New York or London. By the time guests arrive at the hotel, they are sweaty and disillusioned. Nothing short of world-class service will appease them.

But service at the Sun and Sea Hotel is, at best, uneven. Dissatisfied employees treat guests with indifference. Requests are met with nonchalance; complaints are received as personal affronts. Guests may bristle at a tardy wake-up call, coffee served cold or an unscrubbed bathtub, but soon learn that expressing their displeasure does no good. The complaints that *do* reach management tend to be extreme, multiple, and accompanied by "money back" demands. Even when managers handle complaints well, the guest is usually already lost as a repeat customer.

Most guests leave the hotel somewhat less than exhilarated by their stay. They've neither experienced the local culture nor the international jet-set environment they had been sold. Many feel as if they were given a "canned" product—something diluted and mediocre. One former guest summed it up: "If I'd wanted noisy discos, hamburgers and crummy service, I could have stayed in New York."

Paradise Lost

The leaders of the Sun and Sea Hotel recognize that the property cannot long continue to show a profit, crippled as it is by operational problems and negative word-of-mouth publicity. As concerned as they might be, they defend the status quo and resist the idea that the hotel's dilemma is largely cultural.

To analyze the case, we again make use of the four broad areas of culture management, namely, business strategy, marketing, human resources development and customer contact.

Business Strategy. Although much thought and planning had been devoted to real estate development, financing, purchasing and the logistics of airline service, the hotel's leaders gave little or no consideration to fitting the hotel's social system into the community. The hotel clearly lacks a sound and flexible business strategy for operating successfully at that particular location. Management has failed to incorporate feedback from the local community, the tourist bureau, employees and customers into the design and development of their product and service delivery system. Instead they have attempted to apply a generic corporate model, much to the dissatisfaction of many natives, employees and guests. Strongly worded directives from the corporate office insisting upon strict adherence to company policies and procedures are a constant irritant to on-location managers. A diffused and counterproductive corporate culture makes implementation of *any* directive difficult, let alone directives which are culturally provocative and contrary to local practices.

Marketing. The corporate office spared no expense in its initial efforts to market the Sun and Sea Hotel. Splashy advertising in top-dollar publications and aggressive sales forces peddled paradise to middle-income North Americans. As each successive wave of visitors to the island and hotel returned to the mainland, the hotel's image suffered more and more from negative word-of-mouth publicity. In an attempt to counteract the damage, the corporate office budgeted even more funds for additional advertising and the development of new markets. Without a repeat customer base, the hotel is now on a marketing treadmill, scrambling after new customers while losing market share. In its zeal to capture fresh markets, the hotel is neglecting to adjust its product and service delivery system to the unique needs and expectations of its new customers. It just goes on being the old "take it or leave it" Sun and Sea Hotel. Perhaps the most serious flaw in the hotel's marketing approach is its failure to imaginatively use the local culture as an asset. Instead, the hotel offers its guests a safe but numbing "tourist bubble" which shields them from the local community.

Human Resources Development. Strategy and marketing problems are compounded by the company's inadequate human resources development efforts. At all levels, the hotel's personnel are ill equipped to perform effectively. Expatriate managers are transferred in with little or no advance orientation to the local culture. Struggling with their own and their families' cultural adjustment, they are often rendered ineffective for extended periods of time. Managers from the country in which the hotel is located tend to become complacent after years of watching expatriates move in and out of the top positions to which the locals aspire. Management development opportunities are limited, and the few local candidates chosen for grooming are those who are willing to shed their cultures and adapt to the managerial mold favored by the company. Employees perceive managers as foreign and out of touch, regardless of nationality. An employee opinion survey revealed widespread displeasure with work climate and management practices. Consensus, feedback and training are nowhere apparent. Management-labor relations are strained by differences in cultural perceptions, values and behaviors. Little change has resulted from the findings of the employee survey and its cultural implications have still not been addressed.

Customer Contact. As the social system dictates the service experience, the stage is set for customer dissatisfaction. Employees raised to be gregarious and group-oriented are alienated by the self-serving behaviors they observe in the management and feel as if they are working in a foreign society. Untrained and managed by culturally insensitive expatriates, they are ill disposed to greet hotel guests in the same open, friendly manner with which they might greet a visitor to their home. The hotel's service environment somehow transforms friendly locals into unfriendly service providers. Sun and Sea Hotel managers have yet to learn that unhappy employees breed unhappy customers. They are quick to blame employees when guests complain, but resist examining the cultural forces behind employee behavior.

Status Quo

Our description and analysis of the Sun and Sea Hotel's problems are by no means comprehensive. Our intention is to raise the issues. If we have succeeded, you now understand some of the many ways culture can affect the operation of a service organization.

We concede that the Case of the Caribbean Resort is a slight exaggeration of the service industries' cultural status quo. It does, however, illustrate actual situations that the authors have observed in hotels in many countries—particularly Third World countries.

Cultural impediments to service delivery are by no means confined to developing nations. Pluralistic work forces and expanding markets pose challenges to service managers everywhere. The following case study deals with a hotel in a North American city.

The Case of the Grande Dame

The Palace Hotel is one of the "grande dames" of hospitality, constructed in the boom years of the 1920s in a midsized, midwestern city in the United States. Opulent, palatial and "old world," the hotel was, during its heyday, a monument to the city's prosperity and *the* place to see and be seen. A curious marriage of midwestern informality and European elegance, the hotel captivated the affluent but unsophisticated locals for several decades.

During her "fat" years, the hotel enjoyed carefree profits, laissez-faire management and little competition. As the hotel's owner grew richer and more smug, he allowed the hotel to manage itself while he enjoyed the lifestyle of a benevolent monarch within her walls. The hotel's staff grew accustomed to high tips, familiar faces, and a fatherly owner-manager.

When an international hotel corporation took over the hotel in the mid-1980s, they found a badly decayed physical plant, aged work force, and personalized but plodding service. While the Palace had languished, many of her original patrons remained faithful, but they were now as old and tired as she was. Competitors had wooed away the younger set with discotheques, trendy decor and faster service. The Palace's patrons nursed their daily glass of sherry amidst decaying splendor as the hotel slipped farther and farther into the red. The city's movers and shakers, in the meantime, spent freely on happy hours, meetings and parties at the slick, new hotel up the street. Visitors to the city were lured to the new hotel by aggressive and proactive marketing bolstered by snowballing word-of-mouth publicity. The Palace totally lacked the former and had gradually lost the latter. By the time of the takeover, her occupancy hovered lamely between 50 and 55 percent.

The takeover was received with skepticism and hostility by patrons and staff alike. Both had their reasons for resisting change. The patrons feared that their "comfy" second home would come to resemble the new hotel up the street, and worse, their favorite bartender might be let go. The employees resented the intrusion of outsiders (some with funny names and accents) into their family, and they feared for their jobs.

The new general manager and his executive assistant were respected and fully enculturated members of the U.S.-based multinational company they represented. They believed in working long hours, running a tight ship, setting and enforcing the highest standards of service, and doing it all with their eyes fixed on the bottom line. They were appalled by the state in which they found the property and made no attempt to conceal their displeasure. To their way of thinking, the employees and managers were all lazy, the food inedible, and the service abominable.

The new management's first major initiative was to "encourage" all retirement-age employees to leave. Two-thirds of the hotel's department heads were replaced by company people. Many middle managers followed their bosses to other hotels or opted for early retirement. The formerly docile union instantly became a menacing and relentless presence in the hotel. *Strike* entered the vocabularies of the remaining workers; dozens of age and race discrimination suits were filed.

New department heads converged on the conflict-ridden grande dame from hotels in Europe, Canada and Australia. The general manager had intentionally selected managers with a reputation for being solid company men—ambitious and tough. They lived up to their reputations. This was war! The company's policies and systems were imposed and sabotaged; the union and management locked horns on everything from severance pay to the employee cafeteria.

As the corporation poured tens of millions of dollars into renovating the hotel's physical plant and developing new markets, service standards declined. Although management went all out to recruit and train fresh talent, the hotel's climate crippled their performance and they soon became demoralized. The hotel's management team, discouraged by their lack of progress and under pressure from the general manager, began to fight among themselves. Interdepartmental conflicts caused further service problems. Neither the hotel's old patrons nor her first-time guests were satisfied: the former were put out by the new faces, changed decor, and strange menu items; the latter complained of poor housekeeping, temperamental employees and substandard service.

Corporate officers became regular visitors to the troubled property. Operating results were far below projections, and what had appeared on paper to be a prime opportunity was becoming a drain on corporate reserves, if not a nightmare. Those who had masterminded the takeover began the hunt for a scapegoat. No one was surprised when the general manager was prematurely transferred. The more savvy among them were also not surprised when service continued to decline and the hotel continued to lose money.

From Palace to Poorhouse

Renovation of the hotel is now "on hold" while the corporation reconsiders its decision to revive the ailing grande dame. Management is beginning to wonder if the hotel will ever be able to meet its competition and satisfy the expectations of the company's discerning international clientele. They know they have a serious problem but blame it on the former owner's negligence and the old guard employees' obstinacy. The more money they lose, the more blind they become to the cultural factors influencing the hotel's downward spiral.

Upon analysis, the Palace's dilemma becomes a textbook case of cultures in collision.

Business Strategy. The corporation, eager to expand its operations in the United States, was well disposed toward the acquisition of a hotel with an established name and elegant facade. The feasibility study which was conducted considered such factors as the state of the hotel's physical plant and the outlook for the local economy. No one seemed to take much notice of the employees (other than the fact that they were past their prime) or longtime patrons (other than the fact that they weren't consuming enough). In fact the corporation approached the takeover as they would an opening, as if they were starting from scratch. They didn't consider that in its sixty-five years of operating, for better or worse, the Palace had developed a well-defined and change-resistant culture, where everyone knew everyone and everyone was someone. Both the patrons and employees liked it that way and were prepared to fight to preserve the culture they had helped to create. To them and to the community, the Palace was more than a dollars-and-cents business; it was an object of civic pride and a place that enhanced the identity of thousands of people. The corporation's plan failed because it was not compatible with the hotel's existing culture and was executed with a heavy hand that alienated the people whose support it required to succeed.

Marketing. During its first fifty years, the Palace had no need of a sales department and simply didn't have one. Prestige and personalized attention had sold the hotel. When times began to change and the competition launched an active and successful campaign to dominate the market, pride and inertia kept the Palace from responding with anything but dignified resignation. The new company's management, however, wasted no time in installing a twelve-person sales team with a handsome budget in a posh office suite. They brought in one of their most seasoned marketing directors to run the department, and they engaged a top-notch ad agency. The Palace's sales effort boasted five-color brochures, full-page ads, slick video presentations and preppy, smooth salespersons—but it was a flop. The hotel simply couldn't deliver what their salespeople were selling. Because the sales staff was seen by mainstream hotel employees as an "out group" of upstart elite, their pleas for cooperation were scoffed at. Indeed, many employees enjoyed giving the salespeople a hard time and making them look bad. As a result, the salespeople ventured out of their posh office suite less and less. Forced into marginality by a mainstream culture resentful of their imposition and privilege, they became more and more out of touch with the constraints and realities of the hotel's operating environment.

Human Resources Development. At the time of the takeover, many of the hotel's employees had thirty or more years of service and were past the conventional retirement age. They were tightly bonded to their supervisors, coworkers and patrons. Age, seniority and job security were revered in the Palace culture, and older workers had been doted upon by management during the old regime. A number of them were recognized as informal leaders and teachers. Under the new regime, many of these respected elders were forced to retire. The new management fired up new employees with promises of job advancement and tacitly encouraged them to upstage their older, less ambitious coworkers. The old guard responded to this insidious campaign with righteous indignation, union and legal actions, and internal sabotage. Though they might not have explained their actions as such, they were in fact fighting to preserve a culture. The new ways that were being imposed upon them by outsiders violated their value system by placing upward mobility before loyalty and aggressiveness before experience. The result was intense, internal discord, which was crippling to service.

Customer Contact. The Palace's reputation had been built upon the quality of its service. Employees took pride in the hotel and its clientele and extended service willingly. The Palace's service style before the takeover could best be described as warm and personalized—perhaps a bit familiar and not a paragon of efficiency, but always gracious and genuine. This service style was highly appropriate, satisfying the needs and expectations of Palace patrons and bringing them back again and again. After the takeover, however, the composition of the hotel's clientele changed dramatically. The employees continued to treat old patrons like dear old friends of the family. The new customers, however, were a puzzlement and, at times, an irritant. As if it weren't bad enough that these strangers spoke unintelligible languages and made odd requests, they even complained to management about employees! Management reacted with the standard "band-aids": training blitzes, procedures manuals and warning notices. None of these measures, of course, dealt with the real issue—cultural differences. Differences between the old and new management, the old and new work force, and the old and new clientele all called for a multicultural approach to service management. The Palace's new leaders, however, responded with reactive, culture-bound formulas that accomplished nothing but the further polarization of the hotel's unmanaged cultures.

What's the Bottom Line?

Again, the Palace Hotel is a composite of a number of hotels of this kind which the authors have studied. Granted, her situation is more grave than the norm, but her problems are not uncommon. Unlike the case of the Sun and Sea, the issues raised by the Palace's dilemma do not revolve around the nationalities of managers and employees. The Palace's problems are rooted in less obvious cultural differences—clashing corporate cultures, generation gaps, and differing perspectives (parochial versus cosmopolitan).

Perhaps the term which best describes the social systems of the Sun and Sea and Palace hotels is *reactive*. Reactive social systems are typically closed to feedback from consumers and employees and have unilateral decision-making and authoritarian management practices. Their systems are class-structured, with workers, and even managers, frequently alienated from the organization. "We-they" distinctions are common among employees, managers, unions, corporate offices and consumers. Work environments are stressful and volatile, and the turnover of personnel is high. Efficiency and number crunching take priority over effectiveness and quality assurance. Is it any wonder that the failure rate among reactive organizations is high?

The dilemmas illustrated by these two case studies were aggravated and perpetuated by reactive programming. How many of their problems could have been avoided or resolved through effective culture management? In the opinion of the authors, nearly *all* of them. As a tool in long-term planning, quality assurance, conflict resolution, advertising, public relations, and customer service, culture management is as practical as it is versatile.

The reader may ask, "If culture management is such a powerful tool, why don't more managers use it?" The authors' experience suggests several reasons. As the body of knowledge and skills pertaining to culture management has not traditionally been part of the service manager's education, many managers may recognize its potential yet feel ill equipped to implement it. Other managers treat culture management as one of those soft disciplines that are assigned a low priority and kept perpetually on a back burner. The overriding reason, however, is to be found in industry culture: there is in the service industries an ingrained reactiveness which predisposes service managers to favor familiar if shortsighted quick fixes over less familiar, more integrated approaches.

This book will demonstrate how managing culture can improve service quality. Our contributors provide real-life illustrations of the difference culture management makes, the benefits of which include the following:

- Reduction of operational costs resulting from an ineffectively managed social system
- Fewer costly early returns of expatriate managers
- Increased productivity and improved customer relations resulting from a more satisfied staff
- Higher sales and/or occupancy because of more consistent customer satisfaction
- Savings in advertising and sales promotion costs due to increased repeat business and positive word-of-mouth publicity.

We are saying the improved management of culture is not just an enlightened thing to do; it is also a sound path to increased productivity, quality, customer satisfaction and profitability.

Service organizations that deliver world-class service have a strategic advantage in the global marketplace, and the service managers who know how to manage culture are the driving force behind their success.

Chapter 2 will trace the evolution of service management, explore the dynamics of a traditional service organization, and challenge the reader to break through to an alternative perspective on both.

Chapter 2

SERVICE MANAGEMENT AND CULTURE: A CONCEPTUAL FRAMEWORK

Service and culture are fundamentally and inextricably linked. Because culture prescribes how we deliver and consume service, one cannot manage service without managing culture.

Yet, few service managers consider culture manageable. To most, culture is an enigma—not a factor of production and even less an asset. Misconceptions and stigmas about culture and its study are prevalent among service managers. The following comment by a hospitality manager to an anthropologist working in business is fairly typical: "Why are you in midtown Manhattan boardrooms instead of in the wilds of New Guinea or the Amazon? What do old bones have to do with running a business anyway?"

This chapter will illustrate the importance of culture to service management and give readers the conceptual tools to use culture with greater understanding and confidence in their daily management challenges.

Culture, Organizations and Adaptation

It is culture—which may be briefly defined as the way a group adapts to its environment—that has made us human as we know and define humanity, and it is culture that has enabled humans to survive to the service age. Without adaptation, mankind could not exist, let alone exchange services, propagate a global economy, and explore outer space.

Human societies, first tribes and then civilizations, have been the culturally prescribed instruments by which we have organized ourselves in order to overcome the limitations of our natural environment and realize our potential. Organization is the essence of human culture. It provides the framework for cooperation, communication, technology and, of course,

15

service. Productivity, an achievement of human organizations, has varied depending upon the effectiveness and efficiency of each organization's social system.

Organizations bond humans in their collective, cooperative efforts to adapt to whatever physical and social environments they find themselves in. There is considerable evidence to suggest that in the early development of mankind, the social organizations which were the most adaptive were also the most productive. We would contend that the same is true today. The complex organizations of the modern world, particularly corporations, are productive and competitive only to the extent that they are able to use culture to adapt to their environments.

Service organizations face a particularly strong adaptive challenge. Service managers are finding that traditional management skills and notions just don't work anymore. What business school didn't teach them was that a corporation is a *social* organization, and the service experience, a *social* interaction. Culture prescribes how we deliver and consume service. Unfortunately, cultural myopia is limiting the ability of service organizations to adapt.

The adaptive service organization is one with a *managed* social system programmed for proactivity, that is, there is a structure and process that fosters forward-looking action rather than reaction. Its leaders use culture to plan, market and deliver world-class service. They are knowledgeable of and at ease with diversity, and they operate confidently in the global marketplace.

A number of adaptive service organizations set examples within the hospitality, travel and tourism industries (many of the most noteworthy are represented in this book). These companies enjoy long-term profitability and relative invulnerability in a field where blitz bankruptcies and hostile takeovers are increasingly prevalent. They are characterized by service-appropriate corporate cultures that travel well. As industry leaders, they are changing the culture of service delivery.

The Service Manager's Inheritance

The hospitality, travel and tourism industries are operating in almost every corner of the world. At first glance, the casual observer might surmise that many different corporate cultures and management approaches exist in this global operating environment, but that is not the case. What exists—with some exceptions—is a tired, generic pattern of reactive organizations regulated by a disjointed array of Western management principles borrowed from nonservice industries. The industry culture that has resulted is distinctly nonadaptive in a world in which diversity is the keynote. Yet, hotel and tourism schools, management

16

development programs, and industry reward systems all tend to reinforce this dysfunctional culture and the management approach that spawned it.

Our Sun and Sea and Palace hotels are classic illustrations of reactive corporate cultures. The managers of these fictionalized hotels and their real-life counterparts did not invent their closed systems, rigid corporate models, and cultural insensitivity—they are part of the service manager's inheritance.

Roots of Contemporary Service Management

Although today's service managers may pride themselves on keeping up with state-of-the-art management, many current approaches and practices are actually hand-me-downs from nonservice industries (only recently has an indigenous service management school begun to emerge). This legacy has its roots in "foreign" settings like the old plantation and the traditional factory, and in abstract "isms" like capitalism, socialism, and behaviorism. Like pieces of a puzzle, the service manager's inheritance is a bewildering collection of fragments. Most managers spend their careers struggling to put the puzzle together. Here's the catch: the pieces don't fit. And some are still missing.

Following are the most influential fragments of management thought which misguide service managers today.

Keeping Them Down on the Farm

The colonial era, with its plantation model of agricultural management, has had a greater influence on how corporations organize for production than most managers realize or care to admit. We have inherited a class structure with distant (literally and/or figuratively) owners, workers with little or no influence, and overseers (managers, supervisors) in the middle. This class system forms the basis for recognition and reward, use of company resources, and daily interactions.

In the authors' opinion, such a system creates a climate ill suited to service delivery. Consider the managerial status systems in many service organizations. As managers advance up the career ladder, the distances and barriers between them and the service environment increase. How many general managers locate their offices in a highly trafficked customer and employee area of the operation? We don't know of any. In fact there seems to be an unwritten rule that the farther one's desk is from the firing line, the more prestige and status that individual is accorded. Such conspicuous displays of status tend to reinforce "us versus them" perceptions and breed out-of-touch, inaccessible service managers.

Modern Times

In this classic silent movie, Charlie Chaplin played the role of a factory worker who became as mechanical as the job tasks he performed. This poignant and searing indictment of the Fayol and Taylor model of efficient factory production vividly dramatized the human costs of scientific management—a management philosophy which does not give adequate attention to cultural influences and that has had as much influence on the service industries as it has had on manufacturing. It can be seen in the overemphasis on efficiency evident in many service companies.

Unfortunately, efficiency does not guarantee appropriate, consistent service delivery. Serving "x" meals to a group of guests in "x" minutes using "x" amount of staff is not enough—particularly if your employees exhibit any of Chaplin's robot-like behaviors while serving.

Red Tape

The bureaucratic ideal Max Weber first proposed as a management alternative to the nepotistic, autocratic norm, redressed a number of the management abuses and shortcomings of its day. Within the social environment and economic order of nineteenth-century Europe, bureaucracy worked. Over time and across cultures, however, it has become synonymous with red tape, indifference to customers, and rigid procedures.

Clearly, Weber's brainchild has outlived its viability and has no place in the Service Age. With the growth in scale and complexity of service corporations has come increased paperwork, controls and uniformity. This institutionalization of behaviors tends to introduce "customer unfriendly" elements into service systems.

At least part of what the customer is buying is the helpfulness and warmth of the service employee. True, a certain amount of structure is necessary to properly deliver the service. However, rigid, stilted service environments in which the customer is subjected to statements like "Sorry, but that's our policy," are inexcusable.

Karl Who?

In a book written by capitalists about essentially capitalistic industries, the reader may not expect to hear about the influence of Karl Marx. But the perceptive service manager may see, in the day-to-day operation of a service organization, an example or two of the clash of social classes for control of the means of production.

"Haves" and "have-nots" are typically found in service organizations.

So are trade unions. Conflicts over resources, power and status are standard fare at union-management meetings, and the traditional adversarial relationship between management and labor has been slow to change.

Stimulus, but No Response

The human relations school of management attempted to make the service organization a more humane and pleasant place wherein workers would serve willingly. Motivating workers was explained as a simple matter of understanding their needs as individuals and providing positive reinforcements. If you wanted your employees to smile at the customer, you patted them on the back each time they did. This management approach, appealing in its simplicity, has proven inadequate.

Unfortunately, managing people is a bit more complicated than the behaviorists originally believed. First, employees must be studied within the context of a social system, both as individuals and as group members. Then their unique cultural backgrounds must be considered. A typical service organization brings together a diverse collection of groups, each with a unique cultural composition. Service managers dispensing pats on the back may not only be wasting their time, but piquing cultural sensitivities.

Given that the productivity and profitability of service companies depends upon the organization's ability to adapt to varied and changing environments and that the service manager's inheritance is rife with maladaptive influences, the person who aspires to deliver world-class service must look beyond traditional management wisdom and resources.

Recent Developments in Management Thought

Contemporary management theorists and practitioners have moved away from formulas for producing "widgets" and are increasingly focusing attention on culture and service. The service manager no longer has to contrive applications of manufacturing practices to service situations where they stubbornly resist application. In fact manufacturing now looks to service management literature for answers to its marketing and quality problems. A social science perspective is prominent in this new wave of management thought. So is an increased willingness to learn from the successes of companies from all parts of the world.

Following are some of the recent developments which have paved the way for constructive change in the service sector.

Made in Japan?

As Japan's productivity and profile in the global marketplace continue to grow, Western managers look to the East for managerial wisdom. William Ouchi, the first management writer to popularize Japanese management practice for a Western audience, took readers to the threshold of understanding productivity and business success as a function of social system effectiveness.

One of the most controversial and least understood elements of Japanese management is total quality control (TQC), a participative means of continually upgrading performance standards through consensus. Although an American (Edward Deming) is given credit for having developed the TQC concept, nowhere has it reached the level of refinement and boasted as many success stories as in Japan. In fact competition for the coveted Deming Prize for quality has become a nationwide corporate passion in Japan.

One service industry Deming Prize winner actually converted a depleted coal mine into a highly profitable tourist complex, and former coal miners into model hosts, waiters and showmen. This success story illustrates with particular clarity TQC's power to reshape organizational cultures. Unfortunately, TQC's promise as a tool for reshaping the culture of Western service industries has barely begun to be tapped.

Still Searching

When Peters and Waterman set out on their search for excellence, the management world, scrambling for a competitive edge, was receptive to new avenues of thought. The excellence movement sparked popular interest in corporate culture and customer service. Because its founders pointed to profitable companies to drive home their points, managers listened.

For the purposes of our analysis, the most significant contribution of the excellence movement was establishing the link between corporate culture and service delivery. However, because it did so only briefly and moved on, barely leaving a mark, service managers' search for the missing puzzle piece continues.

Moments of Truth

Management opportunists Albrecht and Zemke recognized the need for a new, popular model of management that would distinguish service management from just plain old management. In Scandinavian Airlines System's multibillion dollar resurgence they found a success story (and—

in company CEO Jan Carlzon—a charismatic role model) to spearhead their campaign. Service managers were urged to shift their focus from the boardroom to the "moments of truth" (when customers enter into contact with the organization's service providers). In SAS organization charts flattened and chains of command blurred.*

Every upheaval has its sacrificial lamb; in this case it was middle management. Carlson did not effectively integrate them into the new organization. Because top managers seldom understand the cultural dynamics of their organizations, they may fail to anticipate the repercussions of their interventions on their organizations' social system. Unless this new school of service management comes to recognize culture's place in service delivery, its postulates will foster only partial successes, and its credibility will gradually erode.

Anatomy of a Service Organization

Service organizations may be depicted schematically as organization charts or facility blueprints, sales graphs or work-flow diagrams, depending on the eye of the beholder. Service managers' education, training and development shape their perceptions of the service organization. The chief engineer and director of marketing may occupy adjoining offices, yet be worlds apart perceptually. To the engineer, the business is a comfortable physical plant and the equipment, staff and maintenance procedures that keep it in good working order. The director of marketing sees the same business as a perishable product, geared to selected markets, which must be sold or lost. As the social sciences have not traditionally been applied in the training of service managers, they are typically not inclined to view their hotel or airline as a social system. The concepts of social structure, social networks, values and beliefs, or ethnocentrism hold little meaning for most service managers. Yet, their raison d'etre—service—is a social phenomenon. Surely there are valuable insights to be gained by looking at the service organization through the eyes of the social scientist.

Although anthropologists and sociologists have been pondering culture's impact on social systems for over a century, managers have "discovered" culture only within the past decade. While anthropologists have become an increasingly influential presence in corporate boardrooms, their long-term impact on attitudes and approaches to service management is yet to be assessed. To date, service-specific applications of management and the social sciences have been slow to evolve.

---

*Far less publicized, yet equally important to the success of Scandinavian Airlines Systems, is the company's cutting-edge approach to managing cultural differences, which is discussed in chapter 4.

Social Systems Primer

Social systems are frameworks for human interaction. They provide for meaning and order in daily activities. Predisposed and driven by culture, they regulate behavior and make life a little more predictable.

Because they are open to their environments, social systems are alive and in constant flux. Both their structure and dynamics change as the culture that drives them evolves. They may, however, be conceptualized as comprising three subsystems: beliefs, social structure and technology.

Beliefs

Human beings learn beliefs and values through participation in a specific human organization or, in today's complex societies, a number of organizations. In addition to the workplace, other organizations such as family, schools, peer groups, and churches exercise a profound effect on an individual's belief system. Beliefs predispose their holders to think and behave in circumscribed ways. Their influence accounts for many of the behaviors, differences and conflicts present in organizations.

How do belief systems influence behavior in the service environment? Here are some examples: the expatriate manager who bemoans the fact that the local workers don't share his work ethic, the executive who insists that subordinates call him by his first name, the consumer who refuses to travel to a destination where a socialist or communist government rules. Work ethics, management and consumer philosophies, and personal and professional codes of behavior are all products of a belief system. The degree to which managers, employees and consumers hold similar or different sets of beliefs will influence their interaction within the service experience.

The school of "rational" management has shaped Western management's core values since the industrial revolution. Reactive management and authoritarian leadership are products of this school's belief system. Any significant change in organizational social systems calls for a reexamination of the beliefs upon which they are founded. An alternative ideology is suggested later in this chapter.

Social Structure

The social subsystem encompasses the positions individuals hold within the organization along with the prestige, power and resources associated with them. It is regulated by both implicit and explicit cultural rules that dictate member behavior and interaction. One's position in a social system determines the role or roles one is expected to play, much as a script prescribes behavior for an actor or actress. Both formal and informal leaders may wield influence in shaping subsystem rules and assigning roles.

Every member of an organization has a place in its social system and is expected to fit in. Newcomers unfamiliar with a particular social system, however, may have difficulty finding their place and understanding what is expected of them. Socialization of newcomers may occur through structured activities designed to align members' interests with those of the organization or through random incidents and peer pressure. The former method generally results in a sense of belonging in members, predisposing them to work with others for the common good; the latter tends to result in alienation and encouragement to cluster in cliques and work at cross purposes.

Social structures may take various forms, from hierarchical to egalitarian, rigid to fluid. The social structure prevalent within the hospitality industry is relatively rigid and highly stratified. This fact becomes glaringly apparent at lunchtime when employees and managers head for different sections of the company cafeteria and different internal food and beverage outlets. The editors know of one hotel that has an employee cafeteria sectioned off into three compartments—one for manual workers, one for clericals and another for supervisors. Managers don't dine there at all: middle managers go to the hotel's coffee shop, department heads to the main dining room, and the general manager retires to his own apartment. Whether such an arrangement predisposes service providers to behave hospitably toward hotel guests must be questioned.

Technology

The technical component of a social system comprises all things of a material nature, including how they are used. This subsystem encompasses things that are functional, symbolic or both. Aircraft, Mickey Mouse T-shirts, computerized reservation systems, roasted peanuts in tinfoil packets, reception desks, luggage trolleys, paper umbrellas gracing mixed drinks, ski lifts and roller coasters are popular examples of the technical component of tourism.

Over the past several decades, technological innovations have had a profound impact on service environments. Indeed, within the hospitality, travel and tourism industries, it is the technological component of the organization where the most change has occurred. Whether or not these technological advances have actually improved service delivery is an open question. How many customer and employee complaints stem from encounters with "unfriendly" machines? Computers are blamed for errors of human input; machines replace or circumscribe person-to-person interaction.

The question is not whether more or less technology is better, or even which technologies are appropriate to the service environment and which are not. What service managers need to examine is whether new building designs, reservation systems or communication devices need to be accompanied by changes in the organization's belief system and social structure. Introduction of new technologies calls for planned interventions within the other two subsystems to keep the entire system an integrated whole.

Service and Holism

While the division of a social system into its ideological, social and technical components may facilitate analysis, a system is by definition an indivisible whole, whose parts are highly interrelated and interdependent. This means that what happens within or to one component will usually affect the others and will have an impact on the system's socioecological environment as well. Conversely, a change in the socioecological environment will affect the components of the social system. Thus, no input or event can be isolated from its context, and the system is never static.

Unfortunately, Western managers have not until recently been trained to see and deal with wholes. Programmed to manage by fragmenting, they unwittingly interrupt cycles and upset systems by focusing too narrowly and acting piecemeal. Their "big picture" may be general, but it falls short of being holistic.

Anthropologists have for many years analyzed cultural phenomena from a holistic perspective. They view organizations as complex, open systems of people and things held together and driven by culture and in constant flux and adaptation. This perspective is in sharp contrast to the static organization model that formed the basis for scientific management or the linear, cause-and-effect conceptualization held by behaviorists. Holistic managers are better able to predict the results and repercussions of their acts as well as anticipate the impact of external environmental changes on the organization—this is what empowers them to be proactive. They are more inclined to be aware of and to question their own assumptions and frame of reference—which is what permits them to manage culture.

At present rational, reactive managers far outnumber holistic, proactive managers in the hospitality, travel and tourism industries. Examples of the shortsighted, maladaptive practices established and perpetuated by them abound. Let's examine one of the more common.

Most hotels and resorts in the Caribbean import food and other supplies from off-island sources, mainly from North America. The reasons they cite for doing so include the unreliability of local purveyors along with the unavailability, inferior quality and occasionally higher prices of local goods. While the decision to import may at first seem logical, examination of its far-reaching and long-term repercussions reveal it to be myopic and counterproductive.

First, importation perpetuates the very problems that prompted it. Local suppliers blocked from meaningful competition have no incentive to improve their products and customer service. As long as tourism businesses present no sustained demand for goods locally, area farmers and manufacturers would be foolish to risk making them available. When, in time, governments counter importation with protectionist measures that leave managers no choice but to look to local suppliers, the changeover is usually abrupt and disruptive.

Importation also takes its toll in the community. Many island nations in the Caribbean are struggling to diversify their economies. Though owners of tourist businesses may argue that they provide hundreds of jobs to natives, their limited patronage of other industries hamstrings the efforts of local leaders to stimulate investment and combat unemployment. The unemployment rate runs as high as 30 to 40 percent in many resort areas. As slums develop and crime rates rise, resort managers may attempt to isolate the resort from the community. Guests who venture outside its grounds in search of a tourist's paradise find instead unsightly squalor, begging children and street crime. One need only travel to Haiti, Jamaica or The Bahamas for graphic examples of this phenomenon. As tourists are buying the destination, not only the resort, many will be dissatisfied regardless of the quality of service they may receive within their "tourist bubble." Their negative word-of-mouth publicity will convince friends, family and coworkers to bypass this would-be paradise.

The importation decision impacts employee relations as well. In a nationwide study of attitudes and perceptions in the tourism industry of The Bahamas (Glover and Smith, 1982), it was found that employees felt strongly that the industry should use local products whenever possible. Businesses that don't are at odds with the nationalistic beliefs of their workers and hard-pressed to win their commitment.

We could carry this example further and track the impact of a single purchase decision throughout the organization and community to the parent corporation and nation. But the point is this: the holistic perspective enables managers to make wiser decisions. The ability to see and deal with "wholes" places the manager at the helm of the social system.

Pitfalls and Alternatives

Managing a social system is not unlike piloting a sailboat. Managers, like sailors, work in harmony with environmental forces to direct their organization. The organization, like a sailboat, is inextricable from its context, in constant motion and sensitive to changing conditions. Culture propels the social system and, like wind and tides to a sailor, may abet or thwart the organization's progress along its charted course. We suggest managers look to a seasoned sailor for a role model of holism, proactivity and adaptiveness.

While we don't wish to belabor the analogy, today's global economy might be compared to the open sea. The service manager who accepts the culture management challenge should not expect smooth sailing. Culture may work for or against an organization. Undesirable by-products may seep into a social system and sap productivity: ethnocentrism, perceptual bias, miscommunication, racism, alienation, "we-they" distinctions, coercive power, and reactiveness. However, the organization needn't slacken or bog down—there are alternatives. Alert to symptoms of social system ills, the culture manager counters with timely, deliberate interventions that restore the system's adaptiveness and proactivity. This continuous tending of the social system helps maintain the organization's vitality throughout its life cycle.

Following are the most common social system pollutants and their management antidotes.

Ethnocentrism/Cultural Relativity

People are taught to believe their own culture is better than others. Western-trained managers likewise are programmed to believe their way of managing is best. Not only does it seem expedient to them to arrange jobs in pyramids and establish a chain of command, it seems inescapably logical and even natural. And why shouldn't it? This is what they were taught, what their peers reinforce, and what their organizations reward. Ironically, the very thoroughness of this enculturation may be limiting the managers' ability to move their organizations toward multiculturalism and the world-class service ideal.

There are few, if any, tourism-related organizations that do not have pluralistic work forces and consumers. Ethnocentrism and its offshoots, racism and sexism, are toxic to the service environment. In contrast, the cultural relativity alternative, a fostering of nonjudgmental recognition of cultural differences, creates a climate conducive to cooperation and service.

Perceptual Bias/Social Reality

People see their world through a cultural lens. What employees, consumers and managers perceive within the service organization is

26

screened, categorized and evaluated according to out-of-awareness norms acquired through group affiliation. But the service organization, as a cultural meeting place, intermingles diverse perceptions and realities. The quality product the manager believes he is providing may be perceived as a bad deal by one consumer and a good buy by another of a different nationality or socioeconomic bracket. Likewise, the work environment on which the benign manager prides himself may be perceived as caring or demeaning to different workers, depending upon such variables as age or education.

The challenge facing service managers as they move through the service arena's complex milieu of perceptions is to see things through the eyes of others. By confronting their own perceptual biases, they gain insight into the organization's social reality and the perceptions and expectations employees and consumers bring to the service experience.

Blocked Communication/Open Communication

The way people communicate with each other is based on cultural symbols, cues and meanings. Culture determines what, how, when, where and with whom they communicate. Obviously, language barriers partially block communication. Less obvious, cultural differences also increase the potential for miscommunication. Social systems that don't encourage the free flow of feedback exacerbate such communication problems. Social barriers to the two-way exchange of information between employees and their managers rob the organization of valuable operating information. Both miscommunication and lack of communication result in such common service errors as incorrect reservations or a steak ordered rare but served well done.

The obvious alternative to blocked communication is open communication. By building feedback loops into the social system and removing counterproductive social barriers, the manager communicates a genuine commitment to world-class service.

Alienation/Sense of Place and Belonging

People look to group affiliation to reinforce their identities and self-esteem. Employees come to identify with the organization that makes them feel important and fulfills their needs for security, intimacy and trust. In organizations that fail to fulfill these basic needs, people turn instead to the union or a group of disgruntled, alienated fellow employees for identity. High employee turnover rates contribute to employee alienation as group members' brief tenure makes bonding among them difficult.

The antidote to alienation is a family-like social system that imparts a sense of place and belonging to its members. By encouraging long-term employment and facilitating bonding, the service manager develops "representatives" whose behavior reflects organization values.

Coercion/Consensus

Culture determines how power is distributed and used, as well as how decisions are made. In traditional Western management, those who hold the power make the decisions and workers do as they are told. If the authors' observations of a cross-section of tourism businesses reflect the industry status quo, decision-making power remains concentrated in a very few hands. While employees may have lost some of the "step-and-fetch-it" docility of an earlier era, it is debatable whether they have gained significant influence within most organizations. The service industries continue to suffer the consequences of an antiquated power structure: high employee turnover, negative employee attitudes and strained management-labor relations.

Japan's productivity revolution and a number of successful transplants of Japanese management methods to other cultures suggest that participatory decision making and consensus may have a favorable impact on product quality and employee motivation. By making consensus a social system norm, managers foster a service environment where employees and managers work as a team, not at odds with each other.

Value Dissonance/Change

Values are cultural conceptions of the desirable. All individuals and organizations have them. Values find observable expression in behavior. During this decade, it has become fashionable for organizations to articulate their values. This is an interesting and useful practice as it gives employees and management consultants a chance to compare the values expressed by the organization's actions with those communicated in mission statements and declarations of management philosophy. The authors have personally detected dissonance between stated values and practiced values in a number of organizations.

One example particularly pertinent to the hospitality industry is an avowed dedication to quality in contention with a lingering penchant for rigid efficiency. When the industry entered the quality assurance movement at the beginning of the decade, this efficiency bias became a serious stumbling block. It soon became apparent that the efficiency focus was deeply ingrained in the industry's culture and that quality assurance could not take root without a major cultural change. The fact that so many hotels have aborted their quality assurance programs attests to the staying power of dysfunctional elements in an essentially reactive culture. The service manager has a choice: change or retrench.

The Mandate for World-Class Service

Once upon a time, good service was good enough. Not anymore. The hospitality, travel and tourism industries, like other service industries, have undergone a drastic transformation since the post-World War II era. Today, nothing short of world-class service will keep a company viable in the highly competitive international service arena.

Shifting and expanding markets for hospitality, travel and tourism services have created an extremely diverse consumer population. People of nearly all nations, ethnic groups and social classes are potential consumers of these services. As we stated in chapter 1, all of these consumers enter our lobbies, offices or aircraft with expectations of what the service will be like, how it should be provided, and what the quality should be to justify the price they paid. Not only are consumer expectations becoming more disparate, they are also on the rise. Increasingly, consumers are demanding service on their own terms—world-class service.

The human family is converging not only at our front door, but at our employee entrance as well. Continual flurries of migration within and among almost all continents have created multicultural work forces in most major European, African, Australian and North American cities. The hospitality industry has long been characterized by the multicultural composition of its personnel. The world-class service organization capitalizes on diversity; a multicultural work team is treated as an asset. Cultural synergy enhances the company's product and broadens its appeal.

Above all, the need for world-class service is evident in the fiercely competitive climate which propels the hospitality, travel and tourism industries. The general glut of hotel rooms and restaurants, proliferation of new travel products (clubs, charters, discounters), and postderegulation price wars and buyouts in the airline industry have managers scrambling for an edge. These former glamour industries now play hardball. They know their very survival depends on delivering service that raises them above the competition.

The Response

In recent times, a number of outstanding theorists and practitioners in the hospitality, travel and tourism industries have recognized the need and begun to lay the groundwork for world-class service. They have taken original and markedly distinct approaches to a common end.

The service managers, educators and consultants who appear in this book span the globe and represent an array of specializations, nationalities and arenas of action. But, however different their backgrounds may be, their experience in the hospitality, travel and tourism industries has led them to common ground. They share an appreciation and concern for people, culture, quality, the bottom line and the future. Unlike their tradition-bound counterparts, they think long-term, deal in wholes and act as global citizens. They have come to realize that by doing so, they best serve their organizations' interests.

Keenly aware of the need for better service, the service companies and tourism entities discussed in this book are taking steps to manage culture in order to manage service. While none may yet be exemplars of the world-class ideal, each can be considered an innovator within one or more of the areas we examine: business strategy, marketing, human resources development and customer contact.

The articles in the following four chapters speak to service managers' real-world concerns. Both practical and visionary, they challenge readers to approach familiar situations in unfamiliar ways.

Photo courtesy of Delta Air Lines, Inc.

Chapter 3

BUSINESS STRATEGY

Chapter 3 examines the role of policy, planning and mission in the attainment of world-class service.

Yasuyuki Miura, Nikko Hotels International President for the U.S.A. and Canada, opens the section with his article, "Success Strategy: Nikko Hotels International Smiles a Hearty Smile." In this view from the top, Mr. Miura speaks candidly of the challenges—both internal and external—facing a foreign service company entering a highly competitive marketplace. He recounts actual events in Nikko's U.S. initiation as well as the personal experiences arising from them. The Nikko Hotels International story holds valuable lessons for business strategists in any service organization.

"The Delta Airlines Family: A Case for Supporting Service Employees" presents the other side of the coin: the strategy of an established, U.S.-based company spreading its wings globally. Delta, widely recognized as an industry leader and service-quality role model, attributes its success at home and abroad to the motivation and dedication of its employees. This article—based on firsthand interviews with Delta corporate officers, directors, and managers as well as ground and in-flight front line staff—offers a candid portrait of an organization with a genuine commitment to the welfare of its customers and employees. At Delta, as author Gerald Glover discovered, service is the product of a carefully tended corporate culture wherein employees virtually manage themselves *and one another.*

In their article, "Tourism: Keeper of the Culture," AMFAC general manager, Michael White, and consultant, George Kanahele, use the story of the Ka'anapali Beach Hotel, to illustrate the meshing of organizational and civic objectives. The authors argue eloquently for industry involvement in preserving the basis of its prosperity—native cultures. Their own successful initiative, Project Po'okela, attests to the feasibility of promoting local culture to the mutual benefit of the community and organization.

Another prominent proponent of organization/community symbiosis, scholar Michael Smith, uses Bahamian history to explore the place of sociopolitical forces in the shaping of tourism. In his article, "Tourism in Context," Smith proposes a plan to unite all stakeholders in transcending history and shaping tourism's future. Smith again demonstrates the benefits to service companies of committed community involvement.

Success Strategy: Nikko Hotels International Smiles a Hearty Smile

by

Yasuyuki Miura

I am an airline man turned hotelier. In my twenty-seven years with Japan Air Lines (JAL), Nikko's parent company, I participated in the company's diversification and globalization. Now JAL operates the largest fleet in the world and tops the International Air Transport Association (IATA) ranking. The airline's identity is well established on both sides of the Pacific. The subsidiaries, Japan Creative Tours and Nikko Hotels International, greatly strengthen the company's marketing and financial position. We are a multinational corporation with a strong U.S. presence. More important, though, we are a company of people helping people to promote international peace and prosperity.

As Yoshio Ishikawa, our cochairman and chief executive officer for Nikko Hotels International in Tokyo, has announced to the public, we in the Nikko family have resolved to establish a worldwide network of hotels comparable in number to Hilton, Sheraton or Intercontinental, but entirely unique in quality. While closely linked to JAL's direct marketing needs, the hotel network is operated as an independent business entity. Naturally, the U.S. market is our primary target since it is the biggest and most competitive in the world where we must establish our identity and reputation.

Of course, the entry of Nikko Hotels International into the U.S. posed some interesting challenges: the transfer of a corporate culture based on Japanese values to a multicultural workplace, consistent delivery of the highest standards of quality to a highly diverse clientele, and neutralization of public opinion toward Japanese competition. Clearly, we needed a world-class business strategy.

The strategy we formulated is perhaps best illustrated by the series of multicultural encounters I am about to relate. I draw upon speeches I gave between 1985 and 1987, a critical period in Nikko's multinationalization.

Together in Harmony

In 1985 Nikko acquired the Essex House in New York City at the invitation of Mr. Bill Marriott who, as in-flight caterer for Japan Air Lines, was aware of our intent to enter the U.S. market.

Why an existing hotel of prestige? We reasoned that an existing deluxe hotel would serve as Nikko's springboard for further growth. Nikko's hospitality know-how would be tested there and then honed to the competitive and challenging requirements of the U.S. market.

When I assumed the presidency of the newly established Hotel Nikko (USA) Inc., my first act was to extend an invitation to all on-site Marriott managers and Essex House employees to stay and join the Nikko family. To my way of thinking, people were the most important part of our purchase agreement. We had paid a good price—in part, for location, land and property—but more so for the goodwill of customers and employees. In response to my invitation, I found myself with an executive team of six ex-managers—four from the Marriott, one from Four Seasons and another from Meridian. This multicultural ensemble consisted of a German general manager, a North American director of rooms, an Austrian director of food and beverage, an Irish director of human resources, a Lebanese chief engineer, and a North American director of marketing.

To further complicate the situation, I brought in a Japanese comptroller. Also, at the Nikko corporate office, the secretary-treasurer and directors of marketing and human resources are all Japanese vice presidents.

With so diverse a group I knew I needed a program of executive team building. I approached Dr. W. H. Kaven of Cornell University, a well-known lecturer within the Japanese hospitality industry. In collaboration with Dr. F. Berger, Dr. Kaven developed the "Nikko Executive Team Development Program," a course that included group leadership exercises and simulations, a review of trends within the U.S. hotel industry, and a perspective on Japanese management. The culmination of the program was the collective creation of a Nikko Mission Statement at a four-day retreat.

The retreat was in May 1985 in Ithaca, a dreamy and beautiful town. The retreat progressed nicely until we reconvened after having divided the team into small working groups. I didn't participate in the group work, as is natural for a Japanese company president. When the team reconvened, the groups began to make their presentations. Then I committed a cultural faux pas: I started commenting on the presentations in a manner that the non-Japanese executives found annoying.

"If you have already formed your own mission statement, don't waste our time and energy, just give it to us! We don't like being tested like students," they protested. "On the other hand, if you don't have one yet and would like to contribute, why didn't you join us from the start?"

Here was a major culture gap, and I was utterly taken aback. It was a few minutes before I could collect myself; then I told them, "Okay, you guys go to the student pub and keep complaining and accusing me over as much beer as you can drink. It's on me. My poor Japanese executives will accompany you and listen to you patiently. Who knows, they may even agree with you. In the meantime, I will go to my room and do my homework like a good student. First thing tomorrow, I will tell you about my career, experience, management philosophy and aspirations. If that is acceptable to you, let's begin again."

That night they drank heavily, and I worked hard. The next morning I tried to regain my credibility by speaking to my team in a frank and humble manner. I described to them how JAL had grown and prospered and how my star had risen with the company's. Then I explained why Nikko had come to the United States.

> In 1985 it became apparent that JAL would be privatized and deregulated by 1987. Nikko's entry into the U.S. is part of JAL's grand design of diversification into strategic business areas related horizontally and vertically to air transportation, so as to strengthen her total marketing and financial capability. Our understanding is that we are not merely opening a few new hotels in the United States, but creating a worldwide chain.

I concluded my speech with an appeal for cooperation.

> In North America, we invite you to join and share this exciting and ambitious dream. It has taken JAL thirty years to start from scratch and reach the top of IATA. If our company accomplished this in the airline industry, why can't we do the same in the hotel industry? Together in harmony, we may reach this dream far more quickly.

I then joined my team as a working participant to complete the Nikko Mission Statement. My main contribution consisted of relating JAL's history from a values perspective.

When JAL was established, the first CEO, Mr. Yanagita, placed great emphasis upon harmony or *wa*, since we were composed of a variety of peoples with different experiences and beliefs. This value was derived from article one of ancient Japan's only constitution: "Among a variety of virtues, take harmony and deem it the most valuable" (Prince Shotoku).

Following Mr. Yanagita, the second CEO, Mr. Matsuo, introduced Zen teachings so as to emphasize the spirit of challenge in the rapidly expanding organization: "Beyond a mountain, another mountain is to be seen. How many mountains there may be!" and "Among the sea waves, no way seen, but in every direction, free way open!"

The third JAL chief executive, Mr. Asada, adopted "we are one" as a slogan for unity. In addition, he proposed three management principles: sense of urgency, healthy discontent, and constructive criticism.

I knew in that working session we were making history as we struggled to find common ground. After heated discussions and futile attempts to reach a consensus, one Japanese executive suggested we just list the essential elements of Nikko with a descriptive adjective describing the quality of each. We arrived at dedicated employees, attentive service, and quality facilities.

One North American executive proposed that these elements must be recognized by our customers, of course. This thought yielded, "At Nikko hotels, our guests always find...".

Still, something was missing. Everyone wanted to include *wa* somewhere. At the suggestion of "united in harmony," an airline man objected, "It sounds like United Airlines." Everyone laughed, and the laughter triggered consensus. "Okay, let's settle for 'together in harmony.'" Happily, we succeeded in completing our mission statement in a most participatory manner.

At Nikko Hotels, our guests always find
- dedicated employees
- attentive service
- quality facilities
  together in harmony.

TOGETHER IN HARMONY

A bright and shining future
We're working hand-in-hand
Let's all join in together
The brotherhood of man

The challenge is before us
And friendship is the key
With hands across the ocean
We'll build our family

Top quality, and service
A tradition; East and West
We dedicate ourselves to please our guests

Top quality and service
From Nikko; East and West
We dedicate ourselves to please our guests

Together in harmony
Together in harmony
A pledge from us at Nikko
To be the best that we can be
Together in harmony

Together in harmony
Together in harmony
A pledge from us at Nikko
To be the best that we can be
At Nikko Hotels
Together in harmony

Words and Music by:
Joe Teig and Bryan Kay

Seeing is Believing

Some time after the executive team-building program, our director of human resources, David Lloyd, proposed that we organize a "seeing-is-believing" employee orientation tour to Japan. "Why not?" was my reply. I made two conditions. First, in addition to a few key executives and managers, each department was to elect its own representative in democratic fashion. Second, learning was to be two-way: if the American delegation observed something which could be improved upon, they were encouraged—indeed obligated—to point it out.

Twenty-five Essex House representatives were selected and departed, attired in Essex House T-shirts. Upon arrival at the Hotel Nikko Osaka, each was assigned an exact counterpart as host or hostess: bellman to bellman, security guard to security guard, etc. In the tradition of Japanese hospitality, the orientation included an introduction to Osaka night life.

The most remarkable episode occurred when one Essex House employee asked me if it was true that most Japanese companies have their own song. I replied, "Yes, most do—JAL has one." Then a very talented employee volunteered, "Okay, I'm going to write one for the Essex House." On the emotional occasion of our farewell party in Osaka, our team sang the new song, "Together in Harmony."

One of the by-products of the seeing-is-believing tour was a grassroots fascination with "total quality control." Upon the group's return to New York, some employees actually started their own quality circles without consulting management. Of course, we welcomed their interest and initiative but wanted to ensure its productive channeling. I spoke to David and gave him three directives: take time, don't copy Osaka's program but develop our own, and last but not least, get middle management's consensus.

We asked Dr. Gerald Glover, who at that time was teaching at Michigan State University, for his advice and proceeded under his guidance to introduce a quality assurance program. We began with a series of manager training sessions. I opened each with a brief speech. Among my comments were the following:

> First of all, let me talk about investment. Nikko has made quite an investment both money-wise and name-wise in order to develop in the U.S. market. That is beyond question. Right? How about you? You made a crucial decision to invest your professional career in Nikko and leave well-established American chains to join an unknown Japanese hotel system, didn't you? I am also committed to Nikko. Let me reconfirm for all of us that we have a common investment in Nikko. We are partners. Let me talk as your partner from now on.
>
> Have you ever heard of the four golden rules for a successful

joint venture? My friend, Jon Minikes of Jones Lang Wootton, never tires of preaching them. They are

- understand and communicate with your partner,
- respect your partner,
- be patient with your partner, and
- have enough money.

I mostly agree with Jon, but rule 4, "have enough money," is a little too direct for my taste. I suggest changing it to "keep growing." Next year Chicago, San Francisco and Mexico City will see the birth of Nikko triplets. Our family is growing. Our mission statement gives direction to this growth. If we continue to live up to its values, our future growth is assured.

"Together in harmony" means commitment to a participative style of management. The founding fathers of the USA pledged for liberty and democracy in this land of opportunity. We hope to achieve democracy in this industry. Here at Essex, we are committed to participation at all levels: our quality assurance program for employees, management by goal for executives, and the productivity improvement program for you, our middle managers.

Permit me, in closing, to indulge myself in quoting from Confucian Analects. This saying holds a special meaning for me, since I named my son, Tomo Yuki (know it), after it.

The Master said, "Yu, shall I teach you what knowledge is? When you know a thing, to hold that you know it; and when you do not know a thing, to allow that you do not know it; this is knowledge."

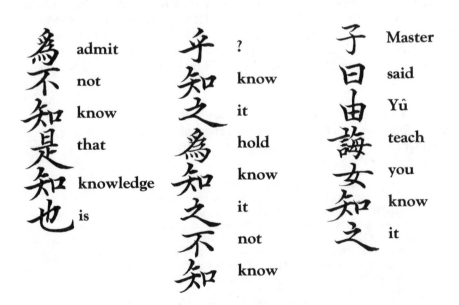

As David Lloyd, Dr. Glover and I set about building a foundation for quality assurance, twenty-five enthusiastic and vocal proponents helped us gain employee support. Our Essex House reps who had been to Nikko Osaka believed in the program because they had *seen* it in action. Truly, seeing is learning and believing.

Not Invasion, but Invitation

In 1987 I received an invitation from UCLA to talk about Nikko at the Hotel Industry Investment Conference. Before accepting, I asked who my fellow panelists would be. The answer was Regent International, Accor North America, Intercontinental and Portman Hotels. Greatly flattered to share the panel with such distinguished friends, I readily accepted—and neglected to ask the subject we were to address.

The program arrived by mail and took me by surprise. It read, "The Invasion of Foreign Hotel Companies." This was a rather awkward moment—the Japanese Prime Minister Nakasone was due to arrive in Washington at the invitation of President Reagan.

The situation reminded me of a joke. Last time they met, Prime Minister Yas told President Ron that the yen had gone up enough and the goal had been reached. Surprised, Ron fell from his chair to the floor of the Oval Office. Then, recovered, Ron told Yas that Japan's efforts had to result in the actual reduction of the trade deficit and the goal had yet to be reached. Yas was so surprised that he jumped from his chair and hit the ceiling of the White House. Such are our cultural differences: falling down versus jumping up.

We were not at all sure if the prime minister would be successful in easing the emotion of the trade war. I felt a great pressure upon me.

The opening of my slide presentation went like this: "The topic of this panel is the invasion and I'm supposed to be an invader. According to the best tradition of Hollywood movie-making, an invader needs the darkness to make an appearance. So, if I may have the lights dimmed, I will be ready to start."

The tension dissipated and I proceeded to tell my audience about JAL's collection of fine hotels. Then I returned undaunted to the topic of "the invasion." First I quoted Edwin O. Reischauer, an ex-ambassador to Japan: "The United States in 1853 dispatched about a quarter of its Navy, under the command of Commodore Perry, to force the Japanese to give American ships access to their ports. The Japanese had to bow to force majeure." Then I continued:

So, Commodore Perry, 110 years ago, invaded Tokyo Bay
by passing the Miura peninsula, where my family comes

from. Up until Perry's invasion, we Japanese had enjoyed 250 years of peace and seclusion. During this period, our hospitality tradition blossomed. Under the Shogun reign, feudal lords were required to leave their families in Tokyo and return to their territories on alternate years. Just imagine, each of more than three hundred lords had to lead a procession of hundreds of samurai every two years. It was a big market for the lodging industry, and fifty-three guest houses or *honjin* were established between Osaka and Tokyo.

Market segmentation appeared early. Road salesmen formed the business market, hot spa goers the pleasure market, and Shinto and Buddhist pilgrims the religious market.

In these good old days, kimono-clad maids brought hot water in a bucket and washed travellers' tired feet upon arrival (it is a pity that service is gone now!). After that, you were shown to your room and served hot green tea with pickled plums. This would kill the germs you picked up walking along the dirt road. Then the front desk manager would come and register you right in your own room. Wasn't that nice?

Today, 110 years after Perry's invasion forced the modernization of Japan, modern hotels exist side by side with traditional *ryokan*. *Ryokan* are characterized by communal hot baths, extensive room service, and a room maid assigned to the total care of the guest. The Tokyo Hilton was the original model for modern hotels in Japan. Japanese hotels are like Honda: their basic technology is North American in origin, but their refinement is Japanese. Unlike Honda, Japanese hotel companies are a bit hesitant to come out and join the world market because they are not confident that they will be able to maintain their high quality of service with employees who are not Japanese. As a hotel subsidiary of JAL operating in more than fifty countries, we at Nikko have no such hesitancy.

Yesterday, Mr. Hank A. Perry, grandnephew of the famous commodore, met me at the airport and drove me in his Mercedes to the Four Seasons Hotel in Newport Beach, which recently joined our Nikko membership. In retrospect Perry's entry into Japan was not an invasion at all but an *invitation* for us to come out and find the new world. That is my conclusion. I hope I have successfully changed today's theme from invasion to invitation. So, please accept my invitation to stay with us at Nikko Hotels. You will find there something refreshingly unique.

Something of Value

In the USA, Nikko is aiming at a guest ratio of 85 percent North American to 15 percent international. Accordingly, our objective is to blend American technology with the Japanese tradition of hospitality, a strategy JAL applied with particular success in marketing its Jumbo Garden Jet ("the calm beauty of Japan at almost the speed of sound"). Our quality facilities are basically American style—beds and rooms of the highest technical quality but with touches of contemporary Japanese design. As amenities, we offer Japanese gardens and restaurants. In service we strive for a *ryokan* feeling by combining functions and entrusting them to dedicated employees who serve our guests attentively and on a person-to-person basis.

It is too early to claim success. What I can claim at this point in time is that we, as multinationals, are honestly trying to achieve uniquely multicultural operations in a participatory manner. Having witnessed the miracle that democracy brought to postwar Japan, I am confident that through internal democracy, Nikko will meet her international development goals. I believe Japan has something of value to contribute to the international hospitality and travel industries. We Japanese may humbly state that we have somehow learned to live together in harmony. As we multinationalize, we strive to maintain harmony while embracing multicultural ideologies.

When we add the suffix "ly" after Nikko, our name becomes in translation "smiling a hearty smile." At Nikko, anywhere in the world, we need happy people to make people happy.

The Delta Air Lines Family: A Case for Supporting Service Employees

by

Gerald Glover

Four hundred thousand miles in just over two years! That's a long time to spend in the air with one airline. Nevertheless, that's what my frequent flier report verified to me recently. I began to think back on all the trips, both business and pleasure, that I had taken on Delta during the past two years. Visions of Hawaii, San Juan, New York, Las Vegas, Europe, and California emerged as I recalled my travel experiences. Perhaps because I have been so deeply involved with studying service quality in recent years, I began to try to recall if I had ever been given poor service or treated rudely by a Delta employee. I was surprised to realize that I couldn't recall a single instance.

I thought about experiences with other airlines and remembered lost luggage, rude ticket agents, and flight attendants who had practically made me beg for a whole can of Coke or to use the lavatory when they had the service cart blocking the aisle. It would be unfair to say that all my experiences with all the other airlines were less than world-class, but I had not experienced the consistency of quality service that Delta provided when traveling on the others. Delta's corporate culture and management approach provide insights that help us understand what has made the service environment and service experience so consistent. I conducted interviews with both executives and employees, probing the culture and observing. My intent was an analysis of the possible influence, or influences, on this service consistency.

In a segment of the economy—service industries—which has been subject to increasing scrutiny, criticism, and professional and consumer discussion, I discovered some relatively striking, documented facts about Delta's successful track record. Most notable are these:

- Profitable operations in sixteen of the past seventeen years
- The lowest consumer complaint ratios with the FAA

- A staff turnover rate of less than 1 percent for over 45,000 employees
- A Boeing 767 aircraft which was purchased by Delta's employees for "their airline"
- A record of not laying off a single full-time employee in the past twenty-five years
- Over one thousand applicants for every job opening
- Nonexistent unions, except for the pilots
- A history of relatively painless mergers and expansion into new domestic and international markets
- Consumers and employees who are extremely vocal about their loyalty to Delta

These facts are more significant if one realizes that the airline industry in recent years has been faced with deregulation, strikes, consumer dissatisfaction, heavy operating losses and the rise and fall of numerous airline companies.

How Does Delta Do It?

There are no secrets to Delta's success, just what can be fairly labeled as sound, responsive, proactive management. The Delta corporate culture is an expression of this positive and profitable management strategy. Delta executives admit to a conscious effort on their parts to maintain the culture which has evolved during the company's sixty-year history. Delta's founder, C. E. Woolman, is a cultural hero in the company and is given credit for being the people-oriented leader who originally established the Delta family. *Family* is the term most often used to refer to the company and its people. In some organizations the term *family* is used in a superficial manner to describe the social system. In Delta Air Lines the reference to family is a sincere and genuine expression of the most critical influence on the company's successful track record.

Elements of a Service Family

Delta's expression of corporate culture, its family, predisposes members to deliver outstanding service. The Delta family is primarily a mechanism for creating a competitive edge for the company by developing the following social conditions:

- Trust and sincerity
- Loyalty and identity
- Responsiveness and adaptability
- Consistent quality service

- Peer influence which supports management
- Recognition and pride
- Security and stability
- Reciprocal communication

These conditions are critical to effective culture management in any company and Delta's results attest to their potential. Executives are fortunate that this social system has been a characteristic of the company for decades. While many leaders of other service corporations seek means to develop proactive cultures, Delta's leaders wish only to maintain the one they have inherited from their predecessors.

Trust and Sincerity

According to Ouchi in *Theory Z*, one of the important influences on Japanese management success is trust. A rare degree of trust exists in Delta's work force and management group. "We-they" distinctions are not apparent, and an attitude of "we are all in this together" seems to be widespread. Delta executives state emphatically that their strategy is to create positive conditions for employees so they will take the best care of customers. "Our people are our number one asset" is given more than lip service. This philosophy is an operational strategy openly discussed by Delta management and observable in the day-to-day activities of the company.

The airline's record of not laying off a single employee in twenty-five years appears to have benefitted the company substantially. Even in 1983, when all airlines were experiencing operating losses, Delta did not adopt the short-term layoff strategy of their competitors. The impact on employee loyalty is still apparent. Ask a Delta employee about 1983 and you can assess the return the company got from its decision.

Loyalty and Identity

Delta employees consider the airline to be *their* company and identify their personal goals with their company's success. Several factors have contributed to this social condition. One is the company's long-standing promotion-from-within policy. All the Delta executives and managers with whom I conducted interviews proudly pointed out that they had been ramp workers, gate agents, or in some comparable job when they began their Delta career. By the time employees reach higer-level positions, they understand the needs of other employees because they have been one of them.

Delta employees stay with the company, which is proven by its less than 1 percent turnover rate. One reservations clerk apologized in her interview, "I've only been with Delta for ten years." Long-term, if not lifetime, employment is common at Delta. Each employee with twenty years experience is flown (with family) that year and every five years thereafter to corporate headquarters for a celebration with top executives. Last year over four thousand employees celebrated their membership in the "family" at company expense.

Responsiveness and Adaptability

The Delta organization is best characterized by the following: (1) proactiveness, (2) a relative absence of short-term, crisis decision making, (3) executives who listen to employees and consumers, and (4) a customer-friendly service environment.

Clearly, customers benefit from an adaptable family of employees whose primary mission is to care for their needs in the service environment. As a Delta executive summarized this approach, "We have policies and rules for dealing with customers. However, those policies and rules don't dictate the employee-customer interaction. Customer service and their satisfaction is what dictates policy." In other words, employees are not likely to respond to customer requests with an answer often heard from employees of other companies, "Sorry but that's company policy." An example is the application of the boarding-by-rows procedure. On several other airlines passengers trying to board before their row is called are told to sit down and wait their turn to board. Delta employees encourage boarding by numbers, but do not stop a passenger whose row hasn't been called. Nor do they lecture. I tested this twenty times and never experienced a problem with Delta. With three of four other airlines I was scolded or told to wait.

At Delta "the system" is friendly.

Consistent Quality Service

By maintaining a family ethos, Delta executives have pursued an operational strategy which is most effective in assuring quality. "Happy employees create happy customers."

For over a decade Delta has had fewer customer complaints per 100,000 passengers than any of their competitors. Consumers testify to Delta's quality service. It's not unusual to overhear Delta passengers bragging about the airline during a flight.

If Delta receives an outstanding compliment about an employee from a passenger, the employee is likely to get a letter from management. The letter passes on the compliment, congratulates the employee, and includes a certificate for one share of Delta stock. The symbolism is quite significant. "You are a part of our company" is the message.

Delta executives insist that they are quite willing to cut fares to compete but will not reduce the quality of service to make up the money. Recent air fare wars have found Delta sticking by this philosophy and service strategy. The customers still get the fare break, but they also get the same service as before (no cattle-herding scenes at check in, no loading your own luggage, and no need to bring your lunch on the flight).

Peer Influence Which Supports Management

Peer influence is perhaps the least understood social condition in American organizations. It usually works against management goals and is commonly expressed in union resistance, we-they distinctions, and employee alienation. At Delta one manager explained that employees help to manage their peers who get out of line. Peers work together with managers in keeping the focus on the company goals of developing human resources and serving the customer.

Training new employees is important at Delta. But training is not enough. Supervisors and experienced employees closely monitor new employee performance to help him or her meet Delta service standards. Also, supportive peer influence and examples help the new employee to develop the needed skills, values, and behaviors which reflect Delta's customer-responsive service environment. This approach is considerably different from many other service companies whose managers do not have time to train and whose employees provide negative role models for newcomers. In socializing new employees to be effective service providers, Delta does not leave their development to chance or trial and error. Peer influence and management attitudes are in harmony, not in conflict.

New employees, or veteran employees with problems, can expect support from the family. The nonunion environment is enhanced by a spirit of cooperation. Peers don't work against management. Status barriers exist as they would in any complex organization, but positive labor-management relations have apparently negated their impact and inhibited employee alienation. One employee of eighteen years explained the good management-employee relations as the reason he and others have stayed with the company for so long.

Recognition and Pride

Delta employees actually bought a Boeing 767 aircraft for their company. Organized totally by employees, this event serves as a symbolic statement of the Delta family concept.

All employees involved in 1982 with the 767 purchase have a picture of the plane and a piece of red ribbon from the ceremony. Pride and recognition are closely associated with family membership. With peer influence we can also observe the importance of peer recognition and pride in group and company successes.

Perhaps the essence of the Delta family is best illustrated by a passenger service agent of nineteen years, whom I interviewed in Atlanta. After completing our interview, I thanked him for taking time away from his job that morning. He explained that he was on vacation that week but had come in from Miami just to tell me about "his airline."

Security and Stability

"Security is what management provides for employees at Delta," stated one executive when asked what the key to understanding the family might be. The conventional wisdom among employees is that a job with Delta is a lifetime career. The one-in-a-thousand person hired by Delta for a job has been carefully screened. Once on board, few choose to leave.

Security is enhanced by responsive compensation, company profitability, and steady, planned growth. Sound fiscal management compliments sound people management. In a period when other service corporations are complaining about shortages in the labor supply, Delta is *the* place to work. Even in low performance situations, Delta employees are given every consideration and chance to improve. But the real benefit is the security felt by employees who know they are not suddenly going to be without a job one day.

Reciprocal Communication

Delta's "open door" policy often results in mechanics and ramp workers walking into the president's office. Employees have open channels to express ideas or problems at any level or location in the company.

Also, corporate executives conduct station visits and talk sessions every year at each operating city. Employees and managers are urged to discuss issues openly. The current practice of collecting boarding passes at the ramp gate door instead of at the counter or on the plane (which is relatively common now among all airlines) was suggested at one such meeting by a flight attendant. This has not only made boarding more orderly, it has reduced waiting time in long lines for customers in hot or cold jetways.

The family, as a social system, provides for proactive, two-way communication focused on input from managers, employees and customers. The responsiveness and adaptability of the Delta culture are enhanced by the effectiveness of family communication. The relative absence of barriers, such as we-they distinctions, between managers and employees is largely responsible.

The Delta Service Environment

Delays happen, mistakes are made, and problems occur. In fact, Delta executives are the first to admit that their operation isn't always perfect. However, the family is responsive to the service environment and usually finds a way to satisfy the consumer.

The Delta family has been around for years and its proactive applications are well established in the company. Delta's current primary challenge is to remain flexible and responsive to work force and marketplace changes. Mergers, such as with Western Air Lines, are carefully orchestrated so the Delta family tradition integrates the new employees into the company. Likewise, new domestic and international markets are developed with an eye to the local culture. In any of the above circumstances, culture management is the key to success.

Tourism: Keeper of the Culture

by

Michael White and George S. Kanahele

When it comes to tourism and native cultures, many people in and outside the visitor industry agree that the relationship has not had an entirely happy history. From Bali to Katmandu, from Majorca to Hawai'i, boats and planeloads of gawking visitors encounter hotels built on sacred sites, native performances turned into Las Vegas-type spectacles, shoddy stores where junk souvenirs have displaced local handicrafts, smoking tour buses which clog roads built for bicycles, and rising crime rates amid the influx of tourist gold.

Of course, tourism does not go where it is unwanted. Governments and communities may welcome a new hotel or airport because it brings in visitors who spend money, creating jobs and other opportunities. In many places hotels or packaged tours are considered preferable to steel plants or chemical factories with their attendant pollution.

Yet, while tourism may not always pollute the physical environment, it can pollute the cultural environment. Like droplets of water falling on a stone, over time it can erode even the strongest of cultures.

Although tourism provides many educational and psychological benefits to the visitor, any time that large groups of people descend on another people to observe them as curiosities it is an intrusion, no matter how innocent their motives. When tourism condones the unthinking exploitation of the native culture, the result is resentment and sometimes even violence toward innocent visitors. The irony is that, in the process, tourism may destroy its very reason for being: the uniqueness of the native culture and its people.

From its beginnings more than a hundred years ago, Hawai'i's tourism has been based on essentially one thing: the lure of the native culture, land and people. The symbols that have been used to create the magic of "paradise" have been Hawaiian—from the lei to the hula girl to the strains of the steel guitar. To be sure, the ads sell its beaches, water, scenery and climate, but if these were all that Hawai'i offered, travelers could go elsewhere and find the same or even better—and at cheaper rates.

Ultimately, what makes Hawai'i different from any other tourist area in the world is Hawaiian culture and people. Obviously, the same can be said of most other tourist destinations. The point is this: there is no other industry as dependent on the existence and survival of indigenous culture as tourism. Nor is there another industry as capable of preserving native culture with access to the kinds of resources available to the tourist industry. It is the number one industry in Hawai'i with approximately $6 billion in annual income.

The industry provides jobs to native Hawaiian musicians, hula dancers, artisans, and many others. It therefore may claim that it contributes to the preservation of the culture. But these jobs are strictly business. Cultural preservation, if it happens, is an unintended by-product, left to fend for itself.

The fact is that the industry, as represented by its organized associations and business entities, has done relatively little to protect and preserve its most important resource. Take, for example, the hotel associations. While they have made significant charitable contributions through their annual sponsorship of "charity walks," they have contributed almost nothing to Hawaiian cultural organizations.

The one notable exception is the Office of Visitor Satisfaction of the Hawaii Visitors Bureau. Essentially a marketing agency funded by state and industry money, it has conducted programs for educating tour drivers and other industry employees on Hawaiian culture and history and sponsored other culture-related activities.

Aware of this benign neglect, in 1981 the Office of Hawaiian Affairs, a state agency, asked the industry to contribute to a proposed Cultural Restoration and Preservation Fund. The agency reasoned that since "Hawaiian culture has been the major element in the rapid growth and promotion of tourism...the tourist industry should therefore assume some of the responsibility and financial burden of uplifting Hawaiian culture. What is at stake is the survival of the spiritual well-being of Hawai'i's native people. Much of Hawaiian culture is already lost in terms of land and lifestyle. What little remains is guarded with indiscriminate care."

The request was an earnest one that represented the feelings of many responsible native Hawaiians who could and did appreciate the social and economic benefits of tourism.

Perhaps the Office of Hawaiian Affairs did not press hard enough, but the tourist industry ignored its plea. This failure to respond was unfortunate because the industry lost a wonderful opportunity to redress some legitimate Hawaiian grievances. Instead of winning friends, it made bitter and unforgiving enemies among many Hawaiians.

Other Hawaiian, as well as non-Hawaiian organizations and individuals, have made the same kind of plea. Indeed, forward-looking supporters of the industry and the culture have been saying the same things for decades.

Why has the industry, through its organizations, failed time and again to respond? Because, in the authors' opinion, the prevalent attitude is that, in effect, the industry has no responsibility for what happens to the culture. That is the government's or, better yet, the native people's own responsibility. The industry's first obligation is to its customers, employees, owners, or stockholders.

We and others in the state believe that preserving the culture is one of the most important issues facing Hawai'i's tourist industry today; for if the culture goes, the industry will not be too far behind, and all the millions spent marketing a mirage will not bring it back.

What we propose—and urge—is that the tourist industry accept the premise that *tourism is the keeper of the culture*. By this we mean that the industry should assume the role of protector and steward of the native culture, both as an end in itself and as a strategic business decision.

We realize that achieving this aim will be easier said than done. The new role requires the industry to make a 360-degree turn in both its attitudes and policies. First, attitudes must change from indifference to responsibility, from neglect to attentiveness, from arrogance to understanding and respect. Perhaps most difficult of all, long-held prejudices against native peoples and cultures must end. Admittedly, even if the industry were able to make these changes, there would be no guarantee that a suspicious native community would automatically believe or accept any professions of repentance, but attitudinal changes go hand in hand with changes in policies and practices. The need for policy changes is especially evident at the hotel/resort level and involves community relations: hiring of native service personnel; engaging native artists and musicians; and using native materials, motifs, etc., in architecture, interior designs, advertising, marketing, and a host of other things. The implementation of these policies and practices may be almost as difficult as making attitudinal changes because they call for managerial, organizational, and financial commitments that owners and investors are (for the most part) not willing to make.

The question then becomes: is the notion of being the "keeper of the culture" viable? Quite apart from its philosophical merits, is it financially, managerially and organizationally feasible? Our answer is Project *Po'okela*.

Project Po'okela

Project Po'okela (the Hawaiian word for "excellence") was started at the Ka'anapali Beach Hotel on Maui in May 1986 by Michael White, its general manager. The hotel is a low-rise structure, built in 1962 on eleven acres fronting a white sandy beach. It has 431 rooms with rates ranging from $105 to $175 for regular rooms and $160 to $300 for suites. The hotel employs 280 persons and is managed by Amfac Resorts.

White's purpose in starting the project was to preserve the culture. Born and raised in Honolulu as a member of a *kamaaina* ("oldtimer") family, he was sensitive to the Hawaiian culture. Though he has no Hawaiian blood, he feels close to Hawaiian culture because "that is the culture I grew up with and the one I know better than any other." Like many kamaaina residents, he has also felt guilty about the devastating impact foreign cultures have had on the native culture and its people. He determined that he and his hotel should and could be "the keeper of the culture."

Coincidentally, when White took over the Ka'anapali Beach Hotel, he also embraced the hotel's old slogan: "We are the most Hawaiian hotel." Within a year Project Po'okela was to turn a mere slogan into a living commitment.

To design and implement the project, White engaged Dr. George Kanahele, a Hawaiian who combined a knowledge of Hawaiian culture and history with extensive business and training experience. The timing of the project was fortuitous as Kanahele had just published his study of Hawaiian culture, *Ku Kanaka—Stand Tall, A Search for Hawaiian Values.*

The project was divided into two parts: the first involved the formulation of a mission statement and the second, the long process of internalizing the values and ideals contained in the mission statement.

Mission statements have traditionally been dictated by owners or the top echelon of management and handed down to employees for their endorsement and compliance—which has often been difficult to get for the very fact that they have been handed down from on high. When, on the other hand, employees are given a chance to participate in formulating the mission statement, compliance follows much more easily because they have a sense of ownership.

The decision was made to involve *every* employee in the formulation process, beginning with management. Although many had questions about the project, they seemed supportive. The fact that General Manager White was totally committed to it undoubtedly influenced them. But they were also excited at the prospect of pioneering something that no one else had done before in Hawai'i, or probably anywhere else.

In the initial workshop for managers, lasting eight hours, the purpose and benefits of a mission statement were discussed, along with the general nature of values. The latter included the identification and discussion of certain specific Hawaiian values in anticipation of their inclusion in the mission statement.

In the meantime, a series of similar but shorter (four-hour) workshops was held for the other employees, all of whom were required to attend during working hours. The average workshop included about twenty participants, small enough to allow for active discussion. It took a week of two workshops a day to get everybody through.

Workshop evaluation sheets indicated that the great majority found the workshop beneficial and interesting. Employees appreciated the opportunity to help formulate their own version of the mission statement. Many also appreciated the chance to identify and discuss their personal values. Only a handful felt the workshop had not fulfilled their expectations, and just one thought it was a waste of his time.

From each of the workshop groups a representative was elected to be on the employees' drafting committee. The committee performed the same function as its management counterpart, drafting its own mission statement, then circulating it among all employees for their feedback, a process that was repeated a number of times before the final statement was completed. This kind of involvement seemed to work well in eliciting a feeling of ownership in the mission statement.

One incident that demonstrated how well it did work occurred during the final stages of the process. Kanahele, who was guiding the effort along, received from the drafting committee a copy of the final draft of the statement and proceeded to make a few stylistic and grammatical changes in it. When the committee saw his changes, members complained to the general manager about Kanahele's tampering with *their* mission statement. And when he suggested adopting an amendment procedure in case the statement needed changing in the future, they would not hear of it. Even before the ink was dry, the mission statement had become sacred property.

Eventually, the two drafting committees met, exchanged drafts, offered suggestions and revisions, and, taking the best of each, completed one overall mission statement. It took three months to reach this point.

To celebrate the completion of the mission statement, a meeting of all employees was held. Prominent figures from government, education, and the visitor industry were invited to the affair. In typically Hawaiian fashion, there was a good deal of ceremony, including a chant (composed for the event) and accompanying hula, designed to impress upon everyone the significance of the occasion. Two employees spoke so poignantly about their part in drafting the statement that several people in the audience were moved to tears.

The approximately six-hundred-word mission statement begins: "At the Ka'anapali Beach Hotel, we embody the Hawaiian meaning of hospitality, *ho'okipa*, and we share the aloha spirit with our guests while providing quality service...." It goes on to say, "We...strive for excellence—po-okela—in everything we do. We are professionals and treat each other with respect, courtesy, and honesty. We believe in informality which encourages open and direct communication." The stress on informality is a particularly important part of the temperament of island residents.

The next paragraph is as eloquent a statement of employee aspirations as expressed anywhere:

> We cherish a happy place where we have fun and smile both in our hearts and our faces; a place where we are recognized and rewarded for our achievements; a place where we can use our creativity and our unlimited potential to become whatever we want to be; a place where we can build a career and security for our families.

The desire for achieving a sense of family is also clearly stated:

> Although we come from different places and ethnic backgrounds, our commitment to common goals and values keeps us together as a family. This strong sense of family is the pillar of our strength. We prize the traditional values of love, respect and *kokua* (one offers help to others without being asked). We demonstrate this in our willingness to help one another whenever needed. We believe that *alu like*, or working together as a family, is the basis for achieving po'okela.

The mission statement ends:

> We appreciate the beauty of our hotel and our island surroundings and we realize that we must preserve it for ourselves and our visitors. We at Ka'anapali Beach Hotel recognize the need to enhance our sense of place for the *mana* (spiritual or divine force) of the land, its Hawaiian past, present and future because this is the essence of our being the most Hawaiian hotel.

Notably absent from the mission statement is any obvious reference to profits. It is not because employees were oblivious to money but because they believed that if the organization eventually embodied the values of the mission statement, the results would show in the hotel's bottom line.

When White subsequently showed the statement to the owners of the hotel, they were ecstatic. They felt that they could not have asked for a better expression of their own values and ideals. Here was an example of Americans turning the typically American business decision-making process upside down, achieving a consensus rather than handing decisions down from the top.

The first part of the project, that is, drafting the mission statement, was easy. The second, internalization or implementation, has been more difficult. Getting employees to translate the values embodied in the mission statement into everyday behavior is an ongoing challenge.

A variety of means have been used, ranging from requiring managers to commit the statement to memory to submitting periodic reports on the steps taken to make it a reality in the workplace. But the most important was setting up an in-house educational program called *Ke Kula o K Po'okela*, or "School of Excellence," consisting of a quarterly series of culture/values workshops and various other activities.

Employee reaction to having to go back to school was not entirely positive. Employees in the housekeeping department, most of whom were immigrants from the Philippines, chose a spokesperson to speak to management about the fact that many of them were not able to understand English or had no high school education. Not only the classroom but the idea of having to learn the values of a new culture was intimidating.

Such feelings were natural and management was not surprised at the reaction. Dr. Kanahele was particularly sensitive to the fact that he would be facing a group of reluctant listeners, some of whom were still bothered by negative stereotypes of the "natives" (i.e., aboriginal Hawaiians).

Fortunately, these concerns proved to be exaggerated. The housekeepers enjoyed the first workshop called "a sense of place." In fact, what most complained about in their evaluations was that the workshop was too short.

Over the next few months, three more workshops were held: one on ancient Hawaiian mythology and religion, another on "primal technology" (including tools, structures, architecture, textiles, etc.), and the last on Hawaiian economics.

And the Results?

At the end of the first year, an assessment of the project was made by David Borden, president of the Boston-based Victoria International Corporation, whose specialty is running hotel management training programs. He felt that the program "has as much impact as any postopening training program" he has ever seen anywhere. The reasons he gave for its effectiveness were that it (1) impacts on all the measures of employee morale (such as personnel turnover, absenteeism, etc.); (2) helps people develop more pride in Hawaiian culture even if they are not of Hawaiian descent; (3) builds individual self-confidence; (4) promotes a sense of teamwork within and between departments; (5) promotes a sense of pride in the hotel, community and state; (6) has a positive impact on the management style of the hotel; (7) provides impetus for a broad-based quality control mechanism; and (8) improves guest relations and service flexibility.

Borden was particularly impressed with the way the program applies the positive aspects of a culture to the work life of the hotel. He thought the mission statement formulation process, flowing from the bottom up rather than the top down, would "make most GMs a little uncomfortable," but that it was central to the effectiveness of the project.

The success of the project, according to Borden, may be "that it challenges traditional hotel management practices, that it allows for a greater sharing of decision making, and that it holds managers and employees to the same standards or values."

There have also been some unexpected results. Compared to the previous year, sick leave abuse cases decreased by more than half; worker's compensation dollar losses were reduced by 81 percent; the worker's compensation ratio dropped from 33 to 18 percent; personnel turnover went from 29 to 21 percent; and absenteeism also dropped considerably. Other results are reflected in charitable donations and activities. Individual employee donations to the United Way increased from $14 to $59 per person, with full employee participation. This was the highest average pledge per employee in the state of Hawaii. (Generosity is one of the most important Hawaiian values.)

A real test of the program occurred in July 1987, when General Manager White left to manage another property. Since he was the central figure in the project, highly respected and well liked by the employees, there was concern about the possibly negative effect his departure would have on the program.

Nothing of the sort happened. Instead, employees rallied around the program. They asked the departing White to do what he could to keep it going for another year. A planning committee was set up to decide on future activities and goals (one of which called for greater employee participation). The strong employee support was also communicated to the owners who, in response, reaffirmed their own support for the program.

Although the project has been employee-focused from the outset, the improvement in employee attitudes and performance has overflowed into better guest service. Comments from satisfied guests come in stacks of mail. Anyone in the hospitality business knows what that means for occupancy rates, food and beverage sales, and profits.

From our own vantage point, one of the important results of the project is its strong endorsement of management-by-values. When employees and managers espouse a common set of values and systematically incorporate those values into their behavior, the hotel "soars like an eagle." As one employee put it, "I am very fortunate to be working at a hotel that uses a management style based on a values system. It makes us feel happy and proud."

Such results have led to many inquiries from hotels within and

58

outside Hawaii. The project has also been implemented at another hotel, the Hotel Hana-Maui, a small but deluxe hotel located in one of Hawai'i's last traditional Hawaiian communities. A lack of qualified trainers is the major obstacle to doing similar projects in other hotels.

Hawai'i's governor, John Waihee, along with key legislators, strongly backs the idea that tourism can and must be "the keeper of the culture." The legislature has provided funding for further development, aptly called "Project Tourism—Keeper of the Culture," to train qualified persons to deliver other Po'okela-type programs in the state.

We recall a Maori leader in New Zealand, planning to get his people active in tourism, who maintained that if they were going to succeed, they would have to preserve the integrity of the Maori culture. He said, "We have beautiful scenery and nice beaches, but what we have that nobody else has is our culture and ourselves. That is what we will offer, but that is what we must also preserve at all costs."

Programs such as Project Po'okela in Hawaii are not only feasible but imperative if the tourism industry is to protect the basis of its prosperity—native cultures.

Tourism in Context:
Understanding the Host Country Perspective on Tourism

by

O.H. Michael Smith

The Importance of History

This article will use The Bahamas, my home, to explore the impact of tourism from a host country perspective. I have cast a wide net in order to consider the positions of all stakeholders in tourism (government, owners and managers, visitors, and the general citizenry) past, present and future. The key issue, however, is the impact of tourism—positive and negative— on the country as a whole. Corporate profits are considered within the larger context of social needs. I share a vision of a new tourism beneficial both to the entire industry and to the future of the host country.

What I have to say should be of value to businesses seeking to invest outside or within their home countries and to governments and other stakeholders at the national, state or local levels who are interested in developing tourism and assessing its impact. My primary audience, however, is managers, and it is to them in particular that I address the challenge of shaping a new tourism based on an understanding of the host country's historical processes.

Tourism has had a negative impact not only in The Bahamas but also in many other countries in both the industrialized and developing worlds (Murphy, 1985; de Kadt, 1979; Turner & Ash, 1975; Bryden, 1973). Some intellectuals in these countries have, on occasion, advocated ending tourism. If this were to happen, the baby (the valuable aspects of tourism) would be thrown out with the bathwater (the cultural exploitation and disruption it sometimes causes). Thus, it is important to sensitize stakeholders to the importance of the history of a particular society or community and the role of the groups they represent in this process before any meaningful long-term change can be achieved.

60

The Tourism Ideal

Before going on to examine more closely the importance of historical processes, let's construct a "tourism ideal" and envision a tourism environment from which the nation, visitor, and entrepreneur can all equally benefit. Here are the basic elements:

> Tourism should be the celebration of a nation's culture. For the national, this fosters national pride and a sense of human dignity. For the visitor, it offers a novel and enhancing vacation experience. For the entrepreneur, there is a unique, vibrant, dynamic, and potentially profitable destination to sell.

Tourism should

1. encourage the use of native or indigenous natural, cultural, agricultural, and manufactured resources, artifacts, and products in order to reduce *imports needed to supply the tourism sector*, thereby increasing foreign exchange earnings generated by visitor spending;
2. encourage regional development and linkages with both the economic and social sectors of the country;
3. create employment opportunities, develop new technical and managerial skills, and generally raise the standard of living;
4. be carried out in an *environmentally sensitive manner* so as to enable future generations to benefit as well.

My basic premise is that tourism can indeed be a catalyst for the kind of development in which strong linkages are fostered with the other sectors of the economy, thereby increasing the options of the citizens to live productive and meaningful lives. Correspondingly, there can be a positive impact on the profitability and viability of the tourism business and on the quality of the visitor experience. Unemployed and underemployed nationals of a country may be a source of cheap labor, but they are also a potential source of crime against the very visitor the hotel is trying to attract. Such a depressed environment may encourage either apathy or militant radicalism. Neither of these alternatives fosters an enjoyable or safe tourist destination. On the other hand, a destination that is alive with other economic sector activities offers the picture of a vibrant, potentially exciting, and distinctive human scene.

A Historical Perspective

At a time of increasing unemployment and trade restrictions, many communities and countries look anew to tourism as the catalyst to fuel economic recovery. Here the interests of hoteliers and restaurateurs coincide with those of the local leadership: tourism entrepreneurs make money if they have a viable and distinctive destination that encourages people to visit; government officials remain in office if they can generate employment, cultural development and environmental enhancement. When tourism is cultivated within the context of the overall society and its needs, the general citizenry benefits as well.

Change agents within this tourism context must consider the importance of the cultural norms of the country as expressed in everyday activities of the nationals and through organizational and institutional forms, structures, and focus. Contemporary cultural expression is viewed by many as a historical process of negotiation between different groups who have unequal power relations. This process is ongoing and tension-filled and occurs at all levels of social interaction. It occurs in the family, the schools, the church, and in other organizational and institutional settings and social groups. It is furthered by the media and through legislation and other political processes. Five primary stakeholding groups are involved: (1) government, with its legislative/legal apparatus and socializing institutions, like schools; (2) owners and managers—the controllers of wealth and organizational structures; (3) the media—the keepers and dispensers of relevant information; (4) the church—the keepers of moral codes and standards of conduct and the guides to heaven; and (5) unions and social movements—the general citizenry who are the suppliers of labor and the supposed beneficiaries of this negotiation process.

Understanding the historical process within which the cultural formation of a host society occurs is vital to the tourism ideal. It is during this process that a group forms the habits, attitudes, beliefs, skills, work ethic, and general self-image which they pass on to future generations. Humans are active agents in the construction of their social reality and have the capacity to transform themselves and their social institutions in ways they deem to be in their own interest. All countries, communities, and organizations must understand these historical and cultural forces if they are to identify both the constraints and enabling factors which will either retard or enhance the realization of desired futures. The Bahamas is used here to make the case for the importance of the historical perspective, but all countries go through a similar historical process which determines in large measure what they are.

Bitter Lessons from The Bahamas

The general citizenry of The Bahamas has not benefited from tourism to the extent it could have and indeed should have. Tourism is the major industry in the country and contributes some 56 percent of the government's revenue. The Bahamas has a population of 210,000 and three million tourists (1986 figure) visit the islands annually; it should not be suffering from an unemployment rate of approximately 30 percent (the actual unemployment statistics have not been issued since the 1970s). Unfortunately, the present form of tourism is so dependent on imports— generating 65 percent of all nonfuel imports from building materials and furnishings to cuisine to cultural artifacts and souvenirs (Archer, 1976)— for its functioning that there are very few linkages with other sectors of the economy. Consequently, there is a "chicken and egg" situation in which the bulk of the government and entrepreneurial energies are focused on increasing direct tourism and related retail activities, which has led to the underdevelopment of the agriculture, manufacturing, fishing and mariculture, cottage, and souvenir industries. These less developed sectors, therefore, have not been a meaningful additional source of employment.

The objective of the leadership should be to change the current form of tourism in The Bahamas from a high-import, dependency orientation to the "tourism ideal." Before these kinds of changes can be implemented, the potential blockages should be identified and strategies devised to overcome them. It is felt that many of these blockages are to be found in current practices which are the result of a "culture of dependency" in The Bahamas. This dependency centers on two critical characteristics. The first is that a highly centralized or hierarchical form of leadership has come to be accepted as the norm. This centralization retards the development of grassroots leadership necessary for indigenous entrepreneurship or community activism. The second is the belief that anything produced outside The Bahamas is better than that which is produced locally. This view has led to a rejection of local products as being inherently inferior, though this is changing as more Bahamians begin to develop cultural, agricultural, marine, and commercial products for the local market, for tourists and for export.

But dependency, as currently observed in today's tourism-dominant economy, is not new to Bahamians.

History

A review of some of the critical events in Bahamian history will enable us both to better understand this dependency culture and to identify possible strategies for change.

While people are in large part a product of their history, it is only through an understanding of their past that they can develop the commitment to transcend it. People are able to enact or socially construct their own reality. Through individual action, organization design and focus, and community and national effort, groups are able to move beyond the constraints of a confining culture to create their own future.

Four critical historical and contemporary periods have been identified as key periods in shaping The Bahamas: (1) British Rule—1600s-1920s; (2) The Bay Street Boys—1920s-1967; (3) the Pindling Era—1967-1987; and (4) the present, or what I would identify as "New Dawn or More of the Same? 1987 and Beyond." While there is a considerable situational overlap among these periods, they are sufficiently distinct to highlight activities of the major stakeholder groups (government, owners and managers, the church, media, and citizens).

British Rule: 1600s-1920s

This first period of piracy/slavery/colonialism established the culture of dependency. All of the institutions of government, commerce and education were designed to encourage the exportation of raw materials and importation of finished products. The form of government was highly centralized, with a governor whose decision was final. There was a body of laws and a military or police force to enforce his decisions. The most senior civil servants were British. The educational system was limited; it was used primarily to create a cadre of civil servants to run the departments of government and, to a lesser extent, a small merchant class.

There was some logging of hard and dye woods but no major industrial development. Visitors to the islands were primarily those using Nassau as a stopover before or after the Atlantic passage (from the Caribbean or South America to Europe or Africa). From about the 1800s to the 1920s there was some shipbuilding. During this period agricultural products were exported, especially tomatoes, pineapples, sisal and citrus. Between the 1840s and the 1930s the sponge industry generated considerable employment. Because of its location, as the gateway to the Caribbean and in the main shipping lanes between South and North America, The Bahamas became an important center of commerce and a source of employment for Bahamians as ships' crews. This location provided additional employment opportunities and external exposure, for example, the stevedores and contract laborers in Central America during the building of the Panama Canal.

A tradition of benefiting from the misfortune of others developed around this time and continues to the present. From the late 1700s to about 1857 there was a period of piratical shipwrecking. Lanterns and buoys would be incorrectly placed so that ships would be wrecked on the coral reefs in the shallow waters. The ships would then be stripped of their merchandise and valuables. Thompson (1982) estimates that in 1856 there were some three hundred ships licensed to engage in salvage operations. Some 2,679 Bahamians held individual wrecking licenses, and business activities concerned with wrecked goods represented some 50 percent of imports and nearly two-thirds of exports.

The American Civil War offered another opportunity to benefit materially from others' difficulties. Bahamians became involved in shipping guns to the Confederate army. This was popularly known as "gunrunning" since specially built steamers would "run" the blockade of the Northern navy. It was during this time that the first true hotel, the Royal Victoria, appeared on the islands. It was built in 1861 to accommodate gun merchants who needed a place to stay when they came over to negotiate with Bahamian and Confederate dealers and gunrunners. Prior to this time there had only been guest houses and taverns.

During this period (the late nineteenth century) winter tourism (a three-month season) was developing, based on wealthy visitors from England, Canada and the New York area. A six-hundred-room establishment, the British Colonial, was built in 1900 by H. M. Flagler, a Florida real estate developer.

It is important to note that throughout the whole period of British rule, tourism activities involved primarily an expatriate elite along with a small white merchant class, who were descendants of British and American settlers. The types of business activities that were pursued were aimed at satisfying the needs of this elite. No attempt was made to develop the agricultural and fisheries industries or to foster black Bahamian ownership of productive enterprises. Government and retail commerce were the principal industries. This kind of focus is exemplified in the national seal of the period, which was on all the currency: "expulsis piratis restituta commerica"—pirates expelled, commerce restored. The majority black population, always regarded as the laboring class, were never allowed to be a part of the decision-making process. They were trained for jobs as needed and were only educated for low-level clerical, civil service and tourism positions. Most of them were still involved in subsistence-level economic activities, which were combined with sponge fishing and contract labor outside The Bahamas.

Religion during this period supported the status quo. It counseled that one must bear the burdens of this life in order to benefit in the afterlife.

The Bay Street Boys: 1920-1967

Although the colonial period lasted until 1973, a group of local white merchants known as the "Bay Street Boys" became the dominant economic and political force during the period from the 1920s to 1967. Their name is derived from the main street in Nassau, where most of their retail establishments were located. This period marked the beginning of the modern era. As retailers, their creative energies were focused on ways in which they could generate revenue by marking up existing merchandise and reselling it at a profit. The Bahamas were the ideal location to bring in English-manufactured items at preferential tariffs under the colonial administration and resell them to American visitors. This external focus of the dominant elite set the stage for the mass tourism of the 1950s, which of course did not have the interest or the needs of the majority population in mind.

The Prohibition era in the United States in the 1920s presented this merchant group with an unparalleled opportunity to make money through what became known as "rumrunning." This activity, like the gunrunning of the previous period, generated business activity on the main island, New Providence, where the capital, Nassau, is located. With the ending of prohibition in 1933 The Bahamas suffered economically.

The Bay Street merchants then turned to real estate development and offered exclusive gambling for the winter visitor. By about 1936 Nassau was established as a winter resort for wealthy American and Canadian hotel and cruise ship visitors, which stimulated a population shift from the other islands to Nassau.

The general citizenry remained apathetic until the "Burma Road Riots" in 1942. Prior to this, it had survived, as noted above, on traditional subsistence farming and fishing. With the advent of winter tourism, opportunities in construction and at the more menial levels in the hotel industry opened up. The Burma Road Riots arose over feelings of unfair treatment because higher wages were being paid to white American laborers than to Bahamians on an airport construction job for essentially the same jobs. (This demonstration represented the first collective action by the black majority and was the forerunner for the agitation in the 1950s and 1960s over political and economic rights.) In the 1950s two major political parties were formed: the United Bahamian Party, which represented the interests of the Bay Street Boys, and the Progressive Liberal Party, which represented the black majority. But it was not until 1967 that the majority party was able to gain political control.

Unions, which pressured for economic rights and better working conditions, were also formed. The independence movements in Africa and the Caribbean and the civil rights and black power movement in the United States fueled the fires of political and economic change by the black majority. Dialogue and networking were established among many of these groups. Much of the black leadership had studied law in the United Kingdom; others attended colleges and universities in the United States and at the various campuses of the University of the West Indies in Jamaica, Barbados, and Trinidad. Others studied union and political tactics in Jamaica. Some of the religious leaders who had also studied abroad became more outspoken about the inequity in this world. All of these activities converged to bring the Progressive Liberal Party into power in the election of 1967.

On the economic front considerable change was occurring as well. In banking The Bahamas was attempting to become the Switzerland of the Western Hemisphere. By the early 1960s, it was an established tax haven which attracted banking interests from around the world.

Tourism in the early 1950s under the leadership of Stafford Sands changed The Bahamas from a winter resort with a three-month season for the wealthy to a year-round egalitarian tourist destination. The Castro revolution in Cuba and the rise of Duvalier in Haiti effectively closed these countries to tourists and The Bahamas seized the opportunity to fill the gap. One result was a construction boom. A second city, Freeport, was developed on the island of Grand Bahama. The style of the tourist facilities that were developed was patterned on that of Miami Beach, with large carbon-copy hotels lining the beaches. The furnishings, the cuisine, the entertainment were American and/or European. Expatriate personnel were brought in to fill all of the managerial, administrative, and even secretarial positions. Clerical positions in the banks and at the front desks in the hotels were reserved for the local white Bahamians. The black population—the majority of Bahamians—were restricted to food service, cleaning and other menial positions. It is said that the further one went in the "back of the house" in a hotel, the darker the color of the worker became. A training institution, the Dundas Civic Center, was opened to train this cadre of domestic workers. The "straw vendors" represented the only truly indigenous entrepreneurial activity of the black majority population that benefited from tourism. Primarily women, they sold souvenir items such as handbags, baskets, floor- and placemats all made from various types of palm tree leaves which are commonly referred to as straw. Soon, however, most of the items they sold were imported from Haiti and other Caribbean islands and (through wholesale distributors in Miami) from Asia and the Pacific. So here again, the same "mark-up" mentality seen in the Bay Street Boys was evident in the new black entrepreneurial class. Profit was sought in imports rather than in local products.

This period closed with a banking industry that was still booming, a tourist destination that was exciting, and a new city. Unfortunately, the majority of the population was not the beneficiary of the boom. It had, in fact, become an alienated and embittered group. A major population shift to the two main islands left older parents and grandparents behind, causing a loss of family cohesion which, among other things, was to have a devastating effect on values in the 1980s. Even with expanding economic development, the majority of the Bahamian population continued to be second-class citizens in their own country. The type of tourism pursued was so dependent on imports and external cultural norms and patterns of behavior that these foreign norms affected the everyday life of the native population. The eating habits, modes of social interaction and life-styles of the visitors began to be mimicked by the native Bahamians, and the latest craze in the United States also became a fad in The Bahamas.

The Pindling Era: 1967-1987

The Bahamian life-style was thus changing. Concurrently, political agitation bore fruit in the election of 1967 when the Progressive Liberal Party won control of the government and Lynden Pindling became the premier. Many of the party supporters saw him as their Moses who was going to lead them to the "promised land."

The Pindling administration should be credited with three major achievements which went a long way toward redressing the inequity felt by the majority black population. The first was the implementation of a new immigration policy. The policy decreed that Bahamians should be given first preference for the jobs that existed in the country. Only in the cases where qualified Bahamians could not be identified could expatriates be employed. In such cases, training programs had to be developed for Bahamians. Exceptions were made for those who owned businesses; they were allowed to hire key personnel, like the manager and controller, of their own choosing so long as those people were not deemed undesirable. Many attempts have been made to get around the policy, such as designing job descriptions which fit particular persons, identifying Bahamians for positions for which they were not qualified, or developing training programs in which Bahamians were likely to fail. However, overall, "Bahamianization" of The Bahamas labor force has been successful. It has opened up many opportunities for Bahamians from all socioeconomic groups of both the black majority and the white minority populations. Two major training institutions, the College of The Bahamas and the Bahamas Hotel Training College, were established to develop this new Bahamian.

Making Freeport a true part of The Bahamas was the second major initiative. By the terms under which the city was originally established, embodied in The Hawksbill Creek Agreement of 1955, a virtual state within a state was created. The developers were vested with most of the powers traditionally reserved for government. Among other things, they could issue licenses to investors, charge fees (taxes), hire whomever they chose (subject to an undesirability clause), and maintain a police force. Had the development of Freeport under The Hawksbill Agreement been allowed to continue unchecked, the expatriate population would have soon outnumbered the native population. One particularly demeaning action by the original developers was the requirement that the native population leave the Freeport area at night and/or when they were through work. In both the short- and the long-term it made good political and economic sense to bring Freeport fully under the control of the Bahamian government.

The third major initiative of the Pindling era was the negotiation of the independence of The Bahamas, which was achieved in 1973. This event had a substantial emotional impact and seemed to unleash pent-up creative energies in the people, spurring a cultural flowering in song, dance, drama and art, along with a greater awareness of history and an appreciation of, and a search for, "things Bahamian" in cuisine, clothing and other aspects of everyday life.

The national emblem was changed and emblazoned with "Forward, Upward, Onward, Together." The national anthem was changed to "March on Bahamaland," which started out as follows: "Lift up your head to the rising sun Bahamaland." The new anthem speaks to the need to work together through "love and unity" to make The Bahamas a better place for all. It speaks to the desire of a people who, though they had been at the bottom of the socioeconomic heap, desire to work together to improve their lot.

Unfortunately, these aspirations have yet to be realized. Beyond the three initiatives noted, the Pindling administration was little more than a clone of the Bay Street Boys, with the same emphasis on externally focused development. Tourism and banking remained the main industries. Little meaningful internal development took place to encourage domestic growth, local ownership, and viable alternative employment opportunities within other sectors of the economy. Those who ran the Pindling government either did not have the vision or were unwilling or unable to surmount the constraints of history, structure, and beliefs that had denied the majority population a better quality of life. Other initiatives fell far short of their stated objectives. Opposition groups regarded such initiatives as mere rhetoric, slogans, and empty promises, brought forth usually just before an election. These initiatives were called variously: "Towards Self-Sufficiency and Full Employment," "Social Revolution," "Towards a New Frontier," and, relative to tourism, "It's Better in The Bahamas." With the failure of these later initiatives, the government's energies seemed to narrow down to consolidating power. The civil service became extremely politicized through patronage appointments. The government, already highly centralized in Nassau, became even more entrenched and increased its hold over the economic sector by becoming the largest employer and the dominant hotel owner in the country.

A New Dawn or More of the Same? 1987 and Beyond

From the beginning, the struggle by the Bahamian majority has been over political and economic rights. The majority have been locked out and they want in. There has never been a serious examination of the form development should take. Little substantive intellectual or political discussion and debate has taken place over such major issues as (1) the massive population shift to the two main islands, (2) the breakdown of the traditional family, (3) the belief that whatever came from outside was better, (4) the history of boom-and-bust economic cycles based on living off the misfortunes of others, or (5) the fundamental characteristic of the Bahamian mark-up, retail economy, which exists parasitically on the creative innovations of other nations.

The political fallout from this head-in-the-sand approach has been the creation of an adversarial we/they approach to social interaction. Traditional union-management relations are representative of this attitude. Economically, a very materialistic culture has emerged—whatever generates material benefits is sanctioned. For example, shipwrecking, gunrunning, and rumrunning have been succeeded by cocaine transshipment between South and North America as a major producer of income. For some time cocaine smuggling was accepted because it appeared not to be having an adverse effect on Bahamians. But now that many Bahamians have become addicted there is an increasing backlash, much of which is focused on the government—both for its inability to stop the trafficking and its alleged collusion with traffickers.

For a new dawn to have any real meaning, there has to be some critical questioning of the fundamental assumptions that have undergirded Bahamian society from its beginning and have long been accepted as the norm. Those at the top of the five stakeholding groups mentioned above will have to become "transformative" leaders, moving The Bahamas beyond the constraints of the past toward an ideal which seeks to make Bahamians masters of their own destiny.

What is advocated here is a turning inward of the society in an effort to bring out the best in its people, the stretching of its collective creative and intellectual energies in the pursuit of an ideal. It must be pointed out that tourism represents just one area of many which such transformative leadership will have to address. A basic issue, for example, is how to achieve consensus on what the Bahamaian ideal should or can be. Who will be involved and what process will gain participation from all five stakeholder groups? If an attempt is not made to involve all of the stakeholders in the process, the ideal will be little more than the self-serving goal of a dominant group or groups.

What Could Have Been

Within the Bahamaian context, hotel managers and owners have played a very active role since 1861. With one hundred and twenty-six years to grow and develop, had the industry been designed with meaning-

70

ful Bahamian involvement, the story today would have been very different. Bahamian businesses would have obtained ownership, controlling interests, or substantial partnerships at all levels of the hotel and travel industry, locally and internationally. On the visitor service side there would have been greater opportunities for ownership, management, and employment in marketing, travel planning, transportation, accommodations, entertainment and other cultural activities. On the production side, greater opportunities would have been available in architecture and construction, in the manufacture of building materials and furnishings, in urban and rural planning, in agriculture and fisheries, in clothing design and manufacture, and in the development of a world-class local cuisine and restaurant tradition.

Clearly the above scenario represents what co*uld have been* had The Bahamas had a different kind of leadership over the past hundred years. Bahamians can now either become very angry with their "oppressors," many of whom are long dead, or they can learn from the past and plan for the future. If the latter approach is adopted, this is what has to be done: after identifying a desired ideal or future state, consensus must be achieved and plans of action developed which are held up to constant critical scrutiny. The ideal is *not* a fixed state but an ongoing process of committed democratic struggle with a vision of a more desirable future for tourism in The Bahamas. It includes a cooperative synergy of concerned stakeholders with a self-sufficient tourism industry based on a holistic, socioecological operational strategy.

Transcending History

While the actual historical events discussed are unique to The Bahamas, culture formation is a generalized process which occurs in every country, community, and organization. Therefore, the discussion about The Bahamas and the processes needed to bring about change has wide relevance beyond this island nation.

I have argued for a new tourism and called upon managers to champion the cause. Change is needed in The Bahamas and elsewhere if tourism is to realize its full potential. Constraining forces exist not only in the outside environment but also in our own beliefs and assumptions about tourism and service management. The creation of the tourism ideal will require vision and transformative leadership.

Photo courtesy of Hilton International

Chapter 4

MARKETING

Chapter 4 examines the role of market research, product design, advertising, sales and internal marketing in the attainment of world-class service.

Heading the section is a contribution from Scandinavian Airlines System, the travel company that caused a virtual service revolution with its wildly successful frontline-focused approach to winning customers. "World-Class Service from a Scandinavian Perspective," by corporate representatives Lena Ahlström and Anders Hovemyr, highlights a vital but little-publicized aspect of SAS marketing strategy: cultural sensitivity. The authors describe SAS's cutting-edge intercultural education and organization development program as it relates to the company's customer-centered mission. Seasoned with the counsels of CEO Jan Carlzon and in-flight anecdotes, the article makes a convincing case for cultural adaptiveness within the marketing function.

"Global Markets, Internal Marketing and Culture," by international management consultant Henry Ferguson, proposes a practical strategy for globalizing an organization's marketing function. While recognizing the importance of the organization's larger environment, Ferguson contends that *internal* marketing is the key to success in the international service arena.

Contributors Klein, Lewis and Scott present the findings of groundbreaking research into consumption-specific values. The authors have identified what they term "service gaps," the common discrepancies between managers' and consumers' perceptions of service quality, and have developed a procedure service marketers may use to eliminate them. Their well-documented study demystifies customer expectations and better equips the service manager to satisfy a diverse clientele.

Roger Fennings' colorful, action prescription for managing public relations in developing nations completes the collection. As Hilton International's Area Director of Public Relations for Europe, Africa and the Gulf, Fennings is no stranger to cultural hurdles. In this article, he reveals "what they didn't teach you on Fleet Street or Madison Avenue" and describes some of the more creative and successful approaches he has used to establish Hilton International's image across cultures.

World-Class Service from a Scandinavian Perspective

by

Lena Ahlström and Anders Hovemyr

Introduction

The SAS approach to service management has captured the interest of the international business community. While recent management literature has spotlighted SAS's frontline focus and dynamic Chief Executive Officer, it has afforded scant coverage of a service element we consider vital: intercultural communication. SAS Intercultural Communication, a department of Scandinavian Airlines System, is a unique venture in Scandinavia, offering a wide range of services within the field of intercultural communication and international management based on a holistic approach. The overarching aim of SAS Intercultural Communication is to sharpen the competitive edge of the Scandinavian business community by means of increased knowledge and understanding of other cultures. This objective is to be reached with the same professional dedication and personal commitment to detail and service that has made SAS a trademark of quality and excellence.

SAS as an Airline, a Conglomerate, and a Partnership

Scandinavian Airlines System (SAS) was created in 1946 by joining the national airlines of Denmark, Norway, and Sweden in order to solidify intra-Scandinavian as well as international air traffic. SAS is one of the 120 members of the International Air Transport Association (IATA) and is among the six largest carriers in Europe.

To many people, SAS means "the airline," but, in fact, apart from the airline, the SAS group includes some twenty subsidiaries in the hospitality, travel, and tourism industries (among them are SAS International Hotels, SAS Service Partner, and Scanair).

The SAS partners (Denmark, Norway, and Sweden) are relatively small countries with limited natural resources. They are therefore utterly dependent on international trade. Traditionally, all three have been seafaring nations and when in the 1930s air transportation became a feasible alternative, all three were eager to explore international and intercontinental routes.

The three countries realized at an early stage that none of them had resources or population large enough to support an intercontinental route network—certainly not in competition with other large carriers. This is how the SAS concept was born—a logical and efficient way of pooling resources in creating a *Scandinavian* carrier. Today Sweden owns a little less than half of SAS, while Denmark and Norway equally split ownership of the rest. Half of the shares in each country are held by private (institutional) investors while the other half are held by the state.

SAS has just recently celebrated its fortieth birthday. Scandinavian partnership and cooperation have not been and are not (as will be discussed below) achieved effortlessly, but the vision to maintain and develop this enterprise was and still is strong.

The Challenge

The aviation industry is facing a knife-edge competition as never before. Deregulation in 1978 has altered the scene in the United States, and a similar development is likely to occur in Europe.

Airlines have often had difficulty generating operating profits when those profits are derived only from selling capacity-on-board. Early in the 1980s, SAS, like many other carriers, was forced to find ways of increasing profitability. The choice was to cut costs or to increase the income of the carrier. The crucial question was how to increase income in a stagnant market. The answer SAS gave to that problem was to become a market-oriented company by turning away from selling capacity-on-board to providing the best service in a competitive environment.

This in itself was nothing unique in the aviation industry. Most carriers realized that the key to success was to become a customer-oriented company. The crucial issue was how a unique relationship between the customer and the carrier was to be achieved. SAS opted to become "the businessman's airline." The underlying conviction was that just about any carrier can transport a passenger between points A and B, but one can rise above the competitors by giving the customers a service that meets their specific needs and expectations. It was the ambition of SAS to become the best carrier for the frequent business traveler. All resources in the company were pooled to meet the needs of the traveling businessperson. Considerable investment was made to ensure that the new product (adjusted to the needs of the business traveler and differentiated from the

76

service provided to those paying discounted fares) was competitive from an international business perspective.

It turned out to be the right strategy. In 1981 SAS was on the verge of losing $20 million. One year later it was earning in excess of $24 million, one of the reasons why the airline was awarded Air Transport World's Airline of the Year Award in 1983. Their success was achieved by coordinating the technical, financial and personnel resources of the company around three nonnegotiable standards: technology, operations, and service.

The technical and operational standards are aimed at keeping SAS among the safest carriers in the world. The service standards of SAS are directly related to the business strategy and are based on the shared values that saturate the entire company. In order to achieve a superior quality of service in various environments and circumstances, SAS identified the following prerequisites:

- Regular market research
- Steering systems to measure product quality and leadership
- Ongoing organizational and human resources development
- Decentralized decision making
- Open flow of information

Moments of Truth

SAS's goal is to meet the expectations of its customers and preferably to surpass them. Having the customer in focus implies that the greatest asset of the company is a satisfied customer. These customers all have individual needs and concerns, which, if not met, may cause the customer not to choose the services of SAS again.

In practical terms, this goal implies the following. Assuming that the ten million annual customers of SAS encounter five employees each and that every one of the encounters lasts (on an average) fifteen seconds, then it is the quality of these fifty million annual encounters (fifty million "moments of truth") that constitute the greatest asset of the company. If that is so, the final responsibility for making decisions, solving problems, etc., must rest on those who at the moment of the encounter personify SAS to the customer. A second later, when the customer has left, is too late to affect the quality of the encounter. In other words, individual decisions are to be made and responsibility assumed at the point of encounter and not far up in the organizational chart. The basis for this trust invested in the frontline people is the conviction that "giving someone the freedom to take responsibility releases resources that would otherwise remain concealed" (Carlzon, 1987; other quotations in this article are from the same source).

A natural prerequisite of this customer orientation is an open information flow: "An individual without information cannot take responsibility, an individual who is given information cannot help but take responsibility."

Consequently, it is through people (and not through equipment only) that SAS is to succeed. Jan Carlzon has put it this way: "Our customer- and market-orientation cannot be realized without a strong emphasis on the individual. It is our conviction that every single employee of SAS wants to take as large a share of responsibility as possible and do her/his uttermost to achieve customer satisfaction. The future of SAS depends on its employees' willingness to adopt the strategies and objectives of the company as their own and feel personal responsibility for achieving these aims."

SAS Intercultural Communication

SAS Intercultural Communication was founded in 1984 and, as a department in the airline, it is part of SAS's marketing strategy, providing customers with a wide variety of services tied to their travel. This so-called "service chain" is aimed at making travel with SAS practical, comfortable, pleasant, and easy through the use of SAS Destination Service, SAS Limousine Service, personal service on board, on-time departures, SAS International Hotels, express check-in, and SAS Intercultural Communication.

The objective of SAS Intercultural Communication is to create an effective intercultural atmosphere for business travelers. Its aim is to provide customers with a service that facilitates international trade and that contributes to its users' competitive strength.

SAS Intercultural Communication offers training and education aimed at creating increased knowledge and competence when dealing with foreign cultures. Its work is based on the belief that intercultural awareness and knowledge is essential in the following areas of international business:

- International ventures
- Business strategies
- Organizational and corporate culture
- Teamwork and communication
- International management styles
- International marketing
- Selection and predeparture preparation of employees and families serving abroad

World-class service has been defined in chapter 1 of this book as the consistent satisfaction of the needs and expectations of a culturally diverse public. For SAS, as a carrier with a worldwide network, such service implies a formidable task if SAS is to be a truly customer-oriented airline. SAS operates in a pervasively cross-cultural environment where it is challenged continuously to put its idea of *customer orientation* into practice. This section will discuss the areas where SAS Intercultural Communication has been of most service to SAS in achieving this aim.

Scandinavian Identity—The Challenge of Unity in Diversity

The outside world tends to regard Scandinavia and/or Scandinavians as a fairly homogeneous entity. This impression is strengthened by the fact that most Scandinavians can communicate with each other in their respective languages, and when encountering a non-Scandinavian environment, they tend to identify with each other. Most SAS flights have mixed Scandinavian crews.

This uniformity, however, is more perceived than real. Based on historical and geographic factors, the Scandinavian countries have developed three distinct but related cultural spheres within which there are wide regional variations.

The forty-year history of SAS is one long process of maintaining unity in diversity. Rather than searching for uniformity, the emphasis has been on identifying the common denominators while at the same time affirming the existence of differences. SAS Intercultural Communication has given numerous seminars, workshops, and brainstorming sessions over the years, and the very nature of the task suggests an open-ended process. The seminars bring together employees (technicians, flight crews, administrators, management groups, etc.) from the three countries so that they may learn some of the basic principles of intercultural communication and explore the differences in culture and national identity among the three Scandinavian countries. The participants then work in small groups and in joint sessions to try to find ways to turn diversity into a strategic advantage for the company.

Management looked upon the seminars as a contribution to an ongoing process and expected few immediate concrete results from these seminars. It was, consequently, all the more gratifying to find that the seminars yielded valuable results. The participants of one of these seminars worked out an action plan to alter the entire service concept on board intra-Scandinavian flights so as to reflect, for example, the countries' different culinary traditions. The action plan gained approval and has been implemented. Another result, though somewhat indirect, is that these seminars encourage academic research in the field as well as provide Scandinavian scholars—who give lectures to the participants on the anthropological, historical, ethnological, and other aspects of the subject—with a platform outside the academic environment.

Culture Management in Scandinavia

A few years ago, the following incident occurred at Copenhagen Airport. An SAS flight was about to depart for Tokyo. The passengers were boarding the aircraft. The service manager at the gate noted that because of last-minute changes in bookings, some tourist class passengers were to be upgraded to first business class. The service managers' manuals list the criteria for deciding who is going to be upgraded. Consequently, with all discretion, the service manager called aside a middle-aged Japanese businessman (among others) and handed him a blue boarding card that entitled him to a seat in first business class. Upon being informed of the upgrading, the Japanese businessman firmly declined the privilege. After much hesitation, the Japanese businessman explained he was traveling in company with his immediate superior who was already seated in first business class. As a subordinate, this passenger felt that being upgraded was inappropriate—considering the circumstances. Fortunately, SAS has three classes of service to Tokyo, and thus the resourceful service manager suggested that the businessman's superior could be upgraded to first class, thereby saving face (giving respect) and being sensitive to the needs of those involved. It would have been a perfect solution had not the superior's superior, the vice president of the Japanese company in question, already been comfortably seated in the first-class compartment!

This is just one of the many occasions when SAS staff in Scandinavia are called upon to demonstrate intercultural sensitivity. Consequently, providing training for these frontline employees has been a vital concern for SAS Intercultural Communication.

Culture Management on Board

SAS operates daily flights between Singapore/Bangkok and Scandinavia. The flight to Europe during the night hours is nonstop, giving the passengers some seven hours to rest or sleep. When approaching Scandinavia, all passengers are awakened with a hot towel to refresh themselves before breakfast is served. Normally, unless otherwise stated, those passengers who are still asleep are touched gently and then the towel is handed to them. This, of course, is more problematic if the passenger in question is a Thai Buddhist monk or an Islamic religious leader from Malaysia, both of whom would consider such physical contact with a member of the opposite sex a serious affront. In situations like these, good intentions may just not be enough.

For about a year, flight attendants on SAS's long-haul flights have been attending intensive courses whose aim *is not* to provide lists of "dos" and "don'ts" but, rather, to introduce the participants to the cultural, ethnic, religious, and social background of the passengers they encounter on board. Rather than giving specific instructions that will apply in only a limited number of cases, the teachers' intent is to enable the flight attendants to serve the passengers with intercultural sensitivity in all kinds of situations. Consequently, chances are that the next time the above described situation occurs, the flight attendant will be sensitive to the conventions about physical contact between the sexes in Southeast Asia and will be able to choose an appropriate alternative method of awakening such passengers.

One of the most exciting issues that surfaces during these courses is the definition of "service on board." To most flight attendants, service, in the Scandinavian context, implies being caring, considerate, and attentive but does not suggest being servile or obsequious. The entire concept of service is also intimately tied up with the notion of unconditional commitment to one's promises. The ideal is to refrain from promising what cannot be achieved. Honesty, one of the most important Scandinavian cultural values, strongly influences this pattern of behavior. The real challenge for these frontline people is to provide Scandinavian service and care even in environments and circumstances where service is defined in another way—and still satisfy the customer. This, possibly, is what world-class service is all about.

Culture Management Abroad

There are some three hundred employees from the SAS conglomerate on assignment abroad. According to a rotation system, most stay for about three years and then return to Scandinavia or take up a new assignment overseas. Since 1984, SAS Intercultural Communication has played an integral role in their predeparture preparation and reentry adjustment.

In all SAS offices around the world there are locally recruited employees, most of whom are non-Scandinavians. The challenge for SAS is to enable these employees to understand and appreciate the SAS corporate culture (and thus, by extension, the Scandinavian culture) while at the same time remaining firmly rooted in their respective cultures. This has not been fully achieved yet, but it is high on the list of future priorities at SAS Intercultural Communication.

Customer Orientation

In the course of the past few years, SAS Intercultural Communication has identified a number of areas where it can be directly of service to SAS in implementing and strengthening the businessman's airline concept.

A number of years ago a Central Europe-based airline was transporting some fragile goods between Zaire and Switzerland. The crates the goods were packed in absolutely had to be placed upright in the cargo compartment of the aircraft. In order to assure proper positioning, large red arrows were painted all over the crates. Nonetheless, the crates arrived in Zurich in a horizontal position, causing serious damage to the goods as well as to other items in the cargo compartment. The ensuing investigation, carried out by the airline, ended with the questioning of the loading personnel at Kinshasa airport. When asked why the crates, with the large red arrows painted on them, were turned horizontally, an African employee gave the following utterly logical answer: "Sir, everyone knows that arrows fly horizontally, never vertically."

In international business culturally conditioned assumptions are one of the most common sources of ineffectiveness and lost productivity. Increased knowledge and understanding of these cultural elements, however, may enable the organizations/corporations working interculturally to develop the ability to manage culture, rather than being managed by it. With this point in mind, SAS Intercultural Communication developed the following customer orientation services.

International Business Seminars. These two-day seminars, offered to frequent business travelers, focus on different countries and world regions (e.g., Japan, China, Latin America). After the seminar the participants are expected to be able to

- demonstrate sensitivity to cultural differences,
- understand the core values in the foreign culture and how these values affect typical business situations (e.g., decision making, negotiating, problem solving, etc.), and
- show increased business efficiency abroad.

It is the long-term strategy of SAS Intercultural Communication to make these seminars an essential component of all Scandinavian business travel.

One participant, reflecting on the usefulness of these seminars, put it this way: "To expect a profitable outcome from a business trip without first acquiring intercultural knowledge and awareness is like trying to catch fish with bare hands. A prerequisite for every business trip should be passport, money, ticket and the SAS International Business Seminar."

Another form of SAS's Intercultural Communication assistance to the Scandinavian business community is specially designed workshops and consultations. Recently a series of such seminars was conducted in Bergen, Norway. The customer in question was a large shipping company, which was recruiting the top officers (captains, first and second officers) from Norway and the rest of the crew from the Philippines. While, by and large, this arrangement had worked quite well, in the course of the past couple of years, incidents occurred on board these ships which seriously hampered effectiveness and productivity. Most of these incidents were clearly caused by cross-cultural misunderstanding.

The seminars gave an introduction to intercultural communication, a survey of the history and culture of the Filipino people, and then focused on a number of case studies selected from those incidents that had occurred on board. The participants were helped to identify the most crucial components of the intercultural encounter and were asked to suggest more effective and sensitive ways of dealing with such incidents.

Predeparture Seminars. Thorough predeparture preparation of families leaving for assignments abroad is another area where SAS Intercultural Communication strengthens "The Businessman's Airline" concept. Through its vast international network, with representatives at some 150 sites around the world, SAS offers up-to-date information concerning the practical issues of living abroad. This is a unique asset and thus it is not surprising that clients represent some of the largest Scandinavian corporations (e.g., Pharmacia, Jotun, SKF, VOLVO) and the Swedish Ministry of Foreign Affairs. Some of these corporations have entrusted SAS with the predeparture preparations of all their personnel stationed abroad.

Consultation to International Corporations. As a long-term commitment to Scandinavian trade and industry, SAS Intercultural Communication offers consultation to companies going international with joint ventures, acquisitions, or subsidiaries. The consultations emphasize the following:

- Research projects to investigate and compare the corporate cultures of Scandinavian businesses and organizations abroad
- Research projects to assess intercultural productivity of multicultural personnel working together
- Transition planning for developing new synergistic corporate cultures
- Training interventions (assessment, design, implementation, evaluation) for developing international managers for multicultural assignments

As an integral part of these services, close cooperation has been established with foreign experts in the field of intercultural studies (e.g., IRI International of Redwood City, California, USA).

A Holistic View

SAS Intercultural Communication is quite alone in Scandinavia in providing such a comprehensive service. It is SAS's holistic vision, however, that won it the Air Transport World's award for Best Passenger Service in 1986 and constitutes its uniqueness. As an integral part of the SAS service chain, SAS Intercultural Communication enhances intercultural sensitivity in the different dimensions of SAS's service and at the same time contributes to the international competitive strength of the Scandinavian business community.

Global Markets, Internal Marketing and Culture

by

Henry Ferguson

Internal marketing? What's going on here? The *outside* market is where we're meant to be delivering our services and products. Target markets and market segments—out there—are meant to be our overriding concern as service marketers.

What does *internal* marketing have to do with global marketing? And what does culture have to do with either? Service industries are typically highly interactive with customers or clients. Recent advances in marketing science have emphasized a close connection between the strategic marketing function of service businesses and the behavior of their employees. We are seeing, therefore, the spread of marketing sensitivity beyond the sales and marketing office, even beyond the penthouse suite. Marketing of services now focuses on the behavior of each individual employee. How each person does the job is effectively a marketing matter.

Internal strategic marketing vision focuses on employee job satisfaction. High employee job satisfaction yields high employee motivation. High motivation yields higher levels of service quality and therefore customer satisfaction. Greater customer satisfaction yields an increased volume of business. The broader the employee-customer contacts, the more precisely this formula works in either domestic or international service business.

For exports, we have to take the formula a step further. I developed "Theory Q" to apply to industries selling overseas. Theory Q makes the point that it is not so much the marketing of a product or service overseas as the export of the corporate culture that will determine offshore success:

> Theory Q sees management as a cultural phenomenon and therefore responsive to changes in the cultural surroundings in which business is conducted. To manage in a globalized marketplace, therefore, requires (1) that the culture of the company's origin be understood, (2) that the

85

corporate culture of the company be understood and (3) that the corporate culture be manipulated and altered to fit changed or different cultural contexts in which the company must operate, without yielding ground on the company's basic mission (Ferguson, 1988).

As global economic trends open up vast opportunities for service industries, corporations are going to have to learn Theory Q and then restructure their marketing to meet its principles. Sales and marketing executives who plan now for growth into global markets by developing an aggressive international marketing strategy will be the winners in the not-too-distant future. Their first step must be to develop an internal strategic vision that will make it possible to sell the company's services in foreign markets and to market to international customers and clients. Then they must develop internal marketing operations to match that vision.

Here are some critical elements:

- Global strategy
- Motivation
- Client expectations
- Entry strategy—marketing to groups
- Long-term payoff—corporate patience
- Market research
- Communication
- Negotiations

Let's take them in order.

Global Strategy. A commitment to international marketing must be part of the entire marketing strategy, not just an add-on. Undertaken as a frill or a supplement, offshore marketing is likely to suffer when there are changes in personnel or budgets.

The following story *may* be apocryphal, but since it was related by a very senior travel industry executive, it is likely true. In reviewing market segments to pursue in the next year's strategy, the general manager of a hotel agreed to allot 6 percent of available space to international guests, both business groups and tour groups. The marketing department eagerly went to work and successfully booked a group from the Japan Tourist Bureau (JTB). No sooner was the booking made than one of the Fortune 500 decided to hold a meeting at the property at the same time the Japanese group was to be there. The general manager, abandoning the 6 percent target and thinking only of courting lucrative domestic business, instructed the marketing department to change the Japanese group's dates or, failing that, to cancel.

That hotel is no longer on the list patronized by the JTB. To the general manager, the 6 percent figure had been just an add-on, not an integral part of the strategy. Hidden behind the decision to cancel the Japanese booking may have lurked the general manager's attitude that doing business with any U.S. clientele is superior to even the best international business.

More significant, however, was the absence of both an external and internal marketing strategy. If the hotel had carefully worked out a corporate strategy for international marketing and backed it up with a specific plan, the hotel would now be earning repeat business from the Japanese. Failure to match operations to the plan reflects a lack of commitment to the plan.

Strategic planning is only as good as its ability to draw into the planning process the people who will have to implement the plans. It is only as good as its understanding of the corporate culture and its willingness to see it change and grow. In planning an international strategy, financial and operational issues have to be reviewed across the board to identify changes that will be necessary in order to serve the international market. In a hotel, for instance, foreign guests (especially travel and conference groups) will need special services in dining rooms and meeting rooms as well as special concierge services.

Culture impinges on strategy in three directions. First, the company must know its own corporate culture if it is to enter foreign markets. Second, the management and staff must be both knowledgeable about and sensitive to the cultural dimensions of the interface between the company and its international clients and customers. Third, management and staff must regard international business as an *opportunity*, not a threat. Too many U.S. companies ignore international markets because they are uncomfortable with foreigners personally and are professionally fearful of the unknown, the uncertain, or the ambiguous.

Motivation. Involving managers at all levels in global planning will only succeed if other staff feel that they have been involved as well. Putting the strategy into operation requires motivated employees whose dedication will not falter.

Theory Q, as mentioned earlier, suggests that international marketing is more a question of exporting the corporate culture to an unfamiliar cultural setting than it is the export of a service or product. That means that management and staff must understand the corporate culture in its own, more general cultural context. Understanding the corporate culture is not an academic exercise, but the first step in a concerted internal marketing campaign. Knowing the corporate culture is as important for the employee as "know thyself" is for the individual human.

What then is corporate culture? It is a set of expectations or basic assumptions that, consciously or unconsciously, guide behavior in an organization. A corporate culture evolves from the first ideas of the company founder and is molded and redirected by the environment of the marketplace, the competition, the government, and—most of all—the daily activities of the people within the company.

The basic assumptions or expectations of a company's culture are most obvious to the bewildered new employee. Even coming from a similar company, the new member can suffer significant disorientation until he or she has learned or been taught the basic assumptions of the new group. These assumptions, of course, are derived from the parent culture in which the company was founded. There is something German about a German company. No one can mistake a Japanese company. Yet within the national ethos, each separate company evolves its own culture, based on assumptions and values directed toward making the company operate to meet its goals, not the least of which is corporate survival in its external environment.

The assumptions and values of the company culture affect day-to-day relationships between employees and, particularly, decision making, especially decisions affecting the marketing operation. Perceptions—determined or at least significantly influenced by the corporate culture—of customers and clients, the adaptability of product or service, the internal relations between individuals and departments, and many other things affect how well targeted the marketing effort is and how effectively the company's resources are directed toward expansion into a new market. But most important here is the connection between corporate culture and motivation. At the bottom line is the imperative that employees be motivated to deliver high quality service at the lowest possible cost. But motivation to do so cannot be imposed. Management can only create the environment in which employees generate their own motivation. That environment is the corporate culture.

In the vast literature on employee motivation, one conclusion seems unavoidable: the synchronization of employee aspirations with corporate culture yields motivation. Research efforts to discover what makes employees work has, from Maslow to MacGregor,* effectively uncovered much about human psychology in an organizational setting. Effective corporate motivation programs have recognized that no one can motivate an employee. The challenge is to match employee expectations with corporate expectations.

The autoworker who feels that he is just a part of the machinery is apt to be the Monday morning absentee. The same worker, in the new Ford Taurus structure, has a key role in decision making on the assembly line, where quality as well as productivity is a high priority. The ability to stop

---

*Abraham Maslow and Douglas MacGregor are well-known psychologists whose theories have been applied at times to organizational development.

the line because something doesn't meet quality standards has not only produced a better car, it has rendered harder-working, more loyal Ford employees. In restructuring the manufacturing process in the Taurus plant, Ford deliberately set out to match company goals with employee expectations. It is this kind of synchronization that is essential to international marketing, where the cross-cultural factor has to be added to the equation.

Take hotels as an example. Front door, front desk and telephone problems with foreign guests who speak little or no English are commonplace in the industry today. Responses vary from the superaccommodating to the resolutely uncompromising. In one major downtown Washington hotel I saw a reception clerk demand a $100 deposit from an elderly Japanese gentleman to cover his phone calls back to Japan. Any elderly Japanese male traveling to the U.S., attended by two younger U.S.-resident Japanese males, was almost certainly a top executive of a major corporation. That fact had not entered into the calculations of the manager, who had set up the process that led to the international call cash deposit. There was no Japanese-speaking clerk or assistant manager available to help. Can you imagine how Toyota (or Honda or Sony) might feel if its CEO was the man required to make a deposit, and how they would later view a sales approach from that hotel's marketing executive seeking a trade show or major meeting?

I recently stayed in a hotel in New York City, which though pleasant enough, had smallish rooms and had generally seen better days, but the lobby was crammed full of well-heeled Japanese. Why? Because the front desk and the telephones were at all times covered by a Japanese-speaking staff member. That hotel's marketing in Japan by now rests almost entirely on word-of-mouth, the kind of advertising money can't buy.

Consciousness of the corporate culture has to permeate to every level of the organization, where it must be projected to the customer or client by motivated employees who are capable of doing so in the context of the cultural expectations of these clients.

Client Expectations. The successful company is prepared to be sensitive to the different expectations and perceptions of their customers. With three companions, I once arrived hot and tired at a traveler's bungalow in Hassan, India, expecting a relatively clean room, bedclothes, toilet paper in the WC and an early, hot dinner. The manager expected travelers who brought their own bedrolls, knew how to use a cup of water to perform personal ablutions, and were prepared to ante up enough rupees for him to go out and buy dinner ingredients before the cookfire was lighted. That the stay was a pleasant adventure speaks to the manager's ready smile and willingness to accept his strange guests' expectations and alien perceptions.

The same must be true of the entire staff of a hotel, but the marketing department has to be especially alert. We have taken a sales department's usual sales checklist and expanded it to illustrate cultural dimensions that are important to consider (see form on the next page). The implications for internal marketing are clear. Staff attitudes have to be open enough to respond to the international guest's behavior with respect, attention and helpfulness rather than with laughter, shrugs or winks. Those smirking, shrugging winks are what later direct the guest to another hotel or even another region of the U.S.A. Who hasn't heard international friends comment on the taxi drivers at Kennedy airport and the waiters in New York restaurants? They constitute a national embarrassment on one level, but on the marketing level they represent a real attack on the bottom line.

Entry Strategy—Marketing to Groups. Offshore markets mean selling to groups. A major financial services company has announced a plan to begin marketing its services abroad. Its entry strategy makes good sense: it will start by selling financial services to groups through existing associations and organizations. How much easier it is for the firm exporting services to target groups than to try to tackle individual sales, where the individual is hidden behind a curtain of cultural predispositions unknown or unfamiliar to the company's American marketing staff.

There are good economic reasons for seeking group sales. For example, a customer attending an international congress or meeting pays the hotel three times the amount of the average domestic guest, a good reason for courting such customers.

Marketing to international groups makes good sense because employees are used to dealing with group sales and delivering services to American groups; but it does, however, raise more cultural challenges than individual sales, requiring attention to internal marketing. Dealing with a group requires more sales contact than dealing with an individual. Catering and banquet managers, conference managers and others must become sensitive to the cultural challenges the group is going to present and must, in turn, sensitize personnel who will be involved in actual operations such as desk clerks, telephone operators, and waiters and waitresses.

But again, differences in perception present unique problems. For Europeans and Asians, for instance, the convention or trade show is a very different phenomenon from what it is to Americans. The meetings last longer—up to a couple of weeks—and they tend to be aimed at a broader audience, so there's a lot more local traffic. That means developing different expectations among employees from the usual fast-paced U.S. convention pattern. Long exposure to an international conference may accentuate culture conflicts as American employees grow impatient with the unusual demands of the guests.

Working with groups will also probably require the development of

INTERNATIONAL GROUP NAME _____

Contact Name _____Phone _____Telex _____

Contact's Organization/Tour Operator _____

Address_____Suite # _____

City _____Province/State _____Country ____Postal Code ____

Circle potential for repeat business: High   Medium   Possible   None

Dates: Arrival__/__/__ Depart__/__/__ #Nights____ #Sleep rms_____

    Cut-off Date__/__/__   Cancel w/o penalty by__/__/__   Arr US__/__/__

    Contact point betw depart home and arr here _____

People: Adult___ Male___ Female___ Spouse___ Kids___

    Handicapped___ Handicapping condition _____

Purpose: Meeting___ Tourism___ Incentive___ Other___

    Main meeting if elsewhere _____

    Air/Rail/Bus Carrier:_____Other Destinations: _____

    Daily schedule of activities _____

    _____

    Special ground tour needs: _____

    Special recreation needs: _____

    Special religious needs: _____

Catering: Number: Bkfst___ Lunch___ Banquet___ Reception___

    Special Dietary needs: _____

Other group/social functions _____

Facilities: Ballroom___ Meeting Rooms___ Theater___ Other___

    Set ups: Theater___ Classroom___ Seminar___ Conf.___

    Exhibits: Space___ x___ Description _____

Budget: $ _____Includes: _____

    Who pays overseas telephone charges? _____

Who makes decision? _____When?__/__/__ Advance visit:__/__/__

Guarantees (specify):_____

    When payments to be made: _____Cancel clause _____

    Penalty on cancellation _____

Language (specify): _____Interpreter accompanies? Yes ___ No ___

    Hotel to provide interpreter? Yes___ No___ Billable? Yes___ No___

    Circle avrg group English proficiency: High   Med   Ltd   None

    Circle avrg previous US experience: Much   Some   Ltd   None

    Other special cultural needs: _____

close relations with national air carriers based in other parts of the world and with the travel industry in the target country. Although their computers look the same and their tickets are identical, much of the way foreign counterparts do business in their own countries will be unique to them. So again, the international marketing executive will have to worry about local marketing practices and the expectations of the group sales agent or carrier.

Finally, the sales executive who markets to foreign groups should be ready for prolonged negotiations in which differences of perception and culture are likely to play a role. In meeting each of these challenges, the first step for the executive is to make certain that the home company and its culture are ready to deal with both novelty and difference. That's an internal marketing challenge.

Long-term Payoff—Corporate Patience. Patience in pursuit of corporate aims is not a pronounced characteristic of the American businessman or woman, who is accustomed to pressures for higher quarterly earnings, quick results, and easy gratification. Building corporate patience calls for changing internal expectations.

When exporting services, the company should not expect quick results. Like any export marketing program, this is a long-term commitment with a long-term payoff. American management, for a variety of reasons, tends to be much too eager for quick payback. No offshore marketing program is going to pay off quickly. It will take at least five years to reach its profit potential, though within two years there should be some increase in overseas traffic. When an international marketing thrust is incorporated into the company's overall strategic plans, the executive must be certain that the time frame for the offshore effort allows for the extra time and energy required for a successful international venture. If that commitment doesn't come in advance from top management and isn't understood at every level, then the company ought to stick to domestic markets.

Marketing to clients in other nations, then, requires a different perspective on time. Potential clients in Japan, for example, may need to negotiate over the course of many months, and it may take weeks for a consensus to emerge among those managers whose agreement will be necessary to a decision. Few other cultures have the short time horizons that speed American business. The sales executive in this context should see himself or herself as a farmer planting seed, cultivating, fertilizing and watering until the sun, rains and soil have done their job and the crop is ready.

In other markets time will be dealt with in other ways, but patience will always serve the corporate decision maker well. Staff should be helped to acquire a fresh sense of time, one more in tune with the new markets served.

Market Research. While most international marketing research must be conducted outside the company, there is still an internal marketing dimension.

American marketers have been taught in college and business school that marketing is a set of universal concepts. Maybe the professors did not intend to convey that impression, but students make that inference. Even textbooks on international marketing posit a highly verbal, look-up-the-answer-in-a-book or construct-a-survey approach which may be suitable for certain Western European markets, but hardly works beyond them. And such an approach doesn't relate to internal marketing at all.

Even if the company has done its market research homework with U.S. sources (government, library, consultants) and the marketing director and a team have explored certain markets overseas and even entered into offshore representation arrangements (an early step in expanding markets), there are still going to be major gaps between the offshore representation agent and the company represented, gaps related to differences both in national culture and in corporate culture.

Communication. The heart of international sales success is communication between the company in the U.S. and its foreign clients or customers, especially when they meet here in the United States. Being able to communicate in other languages is extremely important. Marketing staff members who are bilingual are a valuable asset. It is patent nonsense that "the universal language of business is English." More useful to remember is that "the universal language of business is the customer's language."

If the company must rely on interpreters or translators, the marketer should hire them, not trust those supplied by the prospect. The interpreter has to be trained, or at least thoroughly briefed, on the special vocabulary of both the company and its particular service industry. An interpreter can make or break a deal, and the marketer may not even be able to learn what actually soured the deal when the problem has to do with an interpreter. So wise marketers control communications by using the language themselves or by relying on a trained interpreter of provable loyalty to the business purposes (for which, in return, the interpreter will be used again and again).

How much more important communication becomes when the first trickle of foreign clients or customers begins to flow through the company's offices or properties! That is when the strength of the internal marketing is tested. Is language-proficient staff available when the foreign guest arrives at the hotel? Are interpreters on call to handle meetings, tours? Are the waiters and waitresses able to convey knowledgeable directions to the nearby attractions for guests who are eating in the hotel dining room?

But effective communication does not depend solely on language. Cultures train people in different ways of thinking, of feeling and expressing emotion, of determining right and wrong, of pursuing social and business relationships, and much more. To communicate effectively, even in English, these cultural differences must be taken into account. In negotiations, for instance, it is important to know such things as how your counterparts make decisions, who at the table has the authority, and what "yes," "no," and "maybe" *really* mean.

Negotiations. Negotiations can be the Achilles heel of America's international business; strong in-house training and planning is called for.

First, until a presence has been established in the offshore market, it is wise to send abroad the highest-ranking officer of the company to inaugurate an offshore marketing effort. If the CEO heads the first delegation to explore offshore markets, the payoff is likely to come sooner and be larger. At the very least, the key person who is sent abroad should carry the title of vice president, even if the title is awarded only for the duration of the trip. Rank means much more in most other countries than in the U.S. If a low-ranking sales person is sent, it will be interpreted as a sign that the company is not very serious about getting the business. Likewise, when a foreign conference planner comes to a hotel property, it must be the general manager or CEO who throws the party, not the sales staff.

Second, if at all possible the marketing effort offshore should be a team effort. Composition of negotiating teams will vary from company to company, but they should include a person who knows the technical details and one who knows the finances. Frequent changes in the sales or negotiating team should be avoided, especially in countries where continuity and assurance go together. A change of faces is often interpreted as a sign that a serious commitment to offshore marketing is lacking.

Third, in many if not most other countries, personal relationships between those involved commercially with each other are more important than they are in the U.S. This does not mean backslapping or other superficial kinds of familiarity, nor does it mean intimate relationships between families. It does mean having enough personal interaction to establish a kind of trust based on more than across-the-table negotiations and an ironclad contract.

In Asia, in particular, the corporate decision makers are looking for a long-term relationship, not a one-time sale. From the outset, negotiations should be aimed at demonstrating reliability and endurance, so that the Asian executives feel the U.S. company and its personnel can be counted on five, ten or thirty years into the future. This is not the approach Americans generally take in initial negotiations. They are more inclined to focus on the immediate transaction and let long-term relationships evolve later. It is crucial, therefore, that American business executives be trained in dealing effectively with the personal side of the negotiation process.

Fourth, agreements are rarely made at the first meeting—again, especially with Asians, repeated meetings spent going over details may be frustrating but are to be expected when selling abroad. Even if nothing appears to have been accomplished on the first visit, the executive should be prepared to go back again and again until he or she has demonstrated purpose and determination.

Fifth, the marketer must be prepared to bargain, but not to give away the store at the first meeting. A position of strength is one that moves from a carefully prepared and not unreasonable position toward a position which offers the prospect the best possible service at a reasonable price, yet which clearly provides a reasonable return on the seller's investment too. But just as important, American negotiators must familiarize themselves with the communication and bargaining styles of their counterparts so as not to be confused by signals that mean something different to each party.

Sixth, the use of contracts varies around the world. In come countries, formal contracts are rarely drawn up. If an Arab gives his word, it is probably as good or better than a written contract. If a Japanese firm shows reluctance to sign a contract, too much pressure may upset the personal balance. Besides, trying to enforce a contract in Japan is a tedious, expensive and generally unrewarding business. Contracts will of course be called for in many countries, but they may not always carry the same weight as they do in the U.S. In Korea, for example, contracts are normal, but changing conditions are also taken into account. One company doing business in Korea experienced considerable frustration when letters of credit, which one would assume would be tightly controlled by the contractual agreement, were reinterpreted by their Korean counterparts. Had the Americans been effectively briefed by experienced legal and cross-cultural experts, they might have experienced less frustration and derived greater profits. Briefings of this kind are another internal marketing priority in preparing for international negotiations. And it is not just those at the negotiating table who need this kind of preparation. The horror stories are legion of CEOs coming to sign an international agreement carefully engineered by his or her marketing, financial and operations managers only to scuttle the deal with some insensitive cross-cultural gaffe. Internal marketing makes certain that from the CEO on down every person having any role in the negotiations has been specially prepared for the cross-cultural encounter.

Good internal marketing—that is, the preparation of the entire company to do business in the global marketplace—is imperative to effectively going international. Employee attitudes and aspirations must be respected, but employee motivation must be channeled into addressing the special dimensions of international business and meeting the special demands of the foreign customer, client or guest. The marketing executive who plans to go international with sales must start with the corporate culture and the internal marketing challenge. In a world becoming increasingly interdependent, the marketing executive who is not seeking to enter global markets, whatever the services for sale, is missing the bet of a lifetime.

SERVICE GAPS

By

David M. Klein, Robert Lewis, and Cliff Scott

Culture is a system of solutions to problems. It defines the relationships and establishes the roles which delineate people's identities and predispose their interactions. Via these processes, culture transforms the otherwise nondescript surfaces of existence into cogs which make the wheels of society turn (Markin, 1974; Ulman, 1965). One of the ways culture acts to organize the society is by instilling a commonly held set of values. A cultural value may be thought of as a generally accepted belief that some given state is worth achieving. In other words, cultural values define the "oughts" of a society.

Western societies in the late twentieth century are increasingly concerned with the consumption of goods and services and their import and export. Therefore, within the framework of the overall value orientations of these societies there exists a subset of consumption-specific values (Vinson, Scott and Lamont, 1977). These values are of a lower order than those values more critical to the maintenance of social cohesion and reflect beliefs concerning specific consumption-related activities. Still further down the value hierarchy are product-specific values. These represent constructs used to evaluate particular product offerings. These two value sets are less crucial to the functioning of society than higher order cultural values and far more focused in their application. Accordingly, they lack the stability and universality associated with higher order values. They change more readily over time and can vary significantly across market segments. (Consumption-specific and product-specific values will hereafter be referred to as "CS/PS values.")

The nature of CS/PS values clearly has implications for marketers: (1) a comprehension of and appreciation for the CS/PS values germane to a given market segment is a prerequisite to the development of market strategies targeted at it, and (2) the potential for committing marketing faux pas increases when the marketer is not intimately knowledgeable of the market population's CS/PS values. Further, the perceived quality of service products depends on CS/PS values.

This article identifies the areas of service delivery most likely to produce conflicts between the management's and consumers' CS/PS values, what we call "service gaps," and reports on a study of one hotel that measured the gaps between manager and consumer expectations and perceptions.

What Is Quality Service?

In 1984 Gronroos developed a model of "the missing quality concept." He defines "perceived quality of service" as dependent upon the relationship between the expectations of the consumer vis-a-vis the service and the consumer's *perceptions* of the service. The outcome of the evaluation process through which the consumer automatically goes may be viewed as an operational definition of service quality. Succinctly stated by Lewis and Booms (1983), "Service quality is a measure of how well the service delivered matches customer expectations." (Editor's Note: This concept is closely related to the third universal of service presented in chapter 1.) Thus, quality is not inherent in the properties of the product or service itself, but is a function of the consumer's CS/PS values which govern expectation and perception.

Various factors may cause a service provider to fail to meet customer expectations. For example, a breakdown may occur in the chain of delivery such as a staff member neglecting his or her duties. Once detected, such a problem—because it is localized rather than a defect in the system—may be dealt with at an operational level without affecting the organization's marketing program. The more worrisome situation involves a service gap created by a mismatch of consumers' and providers' CS/PS values. This situation is characterized by management's lack of awareness of consumers' expectations, leading to a failure to provide for their fulfillment. In such an instance, the problem is not limited to those clients coming into direct contact with a single employee, but, rather, is characteristic of the entire system.

Service Gaps Model

Parasuraman, Zeithmal and Berry (1985) have developed a model of potential service gaps. Further, they have determined that these gaps have a definite impact on the customer's evaluation of service quality. The authors' own research has resulted in the modification of the service gaps model and the extension of its application. We propose, and will refer to, this adapted version:

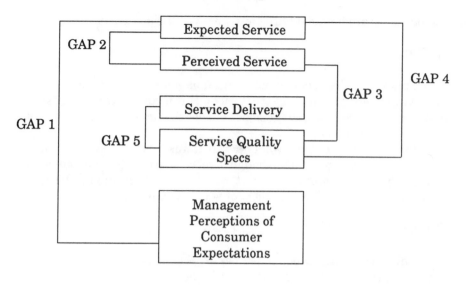

Figure 1: Service Gaps Model
(Adapted from Parasuraman, Zeithaml and Berry, 1985)

Service Gap Measurement

In order to measure discrepancies between consumers' and management's CS/PS values, the values of management must be examined as carefully as those of the consumer. The service gap analysis we are describing here involves the penetration and reconciliation of the often conflicting realities of management and consumers. When management attempts to orchestrate service delivery from the ivory tower of its own CS/PS values, the stage is set for the systematic disappointment of customers. The sources of consumer dissatisfaction are often to be found at the five critical interfaces pinpointed by the service gaps model.

The authors used this model to locate potential management-consumer value discrepancies among twenty-three upper managers and 116 guests at a four-hundred-room hotel in a large U.S. metropolis. Managers completed a questionnaire regarding what they believed customer expectations to be in selecting a hotel, what their perceptions were of their own hotel's service delivery, what they believed customers particularly liked and disliked about their hotel, and what the overall satisfaction of hotel guests was with the products and services they received. Hotel guests were asked to complete a similar questionnaire. Both groups evaluated the hotel on forty-four attributes on a 1 to 5 scale. When the authors compared their responses, a number of service gaps were readily apparent.

GAP 1

This is the discrepancy between management perceptions of guest expectations and the actual expectations of the guests. Our study shows that, for the most part, management believes that guests expect more than guests necessarily do.

In only eight out of twenty-seven items were guest expectations higher than management's, though five of these might be considered critical, that is, cleanliness, comfort of bed, quick check-in and check-out, staff friendliness, and quiet—most of which are intangibles.

GAP 2

This is the gap between consumer expectations and their perceptions of services received. In this study, service delivery exceeded guest expectations on fourteen of twenty items. Guest expectations were not met, however, on the items regarding cleanliness, comfort of bed, staff professionalism, quiet and security—once again, primarily intangibles.

GAP 3

This is the measurement of the difference between consumer perceptions of service delivery and what management believes it delivers. Considering the gaps already identified, it is not surprising to learn that management perceives their service delivery as more successful than guests perceive it to be in all items. Management is particularly oblivious to its failings in the delivery of intangibles such as management attention, security, and quiet.

GAP 4

This discrepancy reflects a comparison of what management believes it delivers to guests to what guests themselves expect to receive. The gap 3 pattern persists: management perceives service delivery to be higher than customer expectations on most items and lower than customer expectations on only two items. However, in only one of these, cleanliness, is the difference significant, clearly indicating a very high guest expectation in that area.

GAP 5

This gap measures an internal situation: does management believe it delivers as much as it believes guests expect? In this case, they clearly do believe it, with no significant exceptions.

The findings, overall, paint a picture of a hotel where management may be needlessly incurring costs to offer tangibles that guests don't necessarily expect or value, while overlooking intangibles that, unbeknownst to management, guests do expect. *Management, complacent within its own reality, is failing to understand and market to guests' culturally based CS/PS values. It is viewing the service environment through its own constructs and managing accordingly.* (Editor's note: This unfortunate phenomenon is referred to in chapter 1 as "cultural tunnel vision.") Although the study findings suggest only mild guest dissatisfaction, the case hotel is vulnerable to competition (in fact, sometime after the study was conducted, the hotel did lose a significant portion of market share to a new hotel at a nearby location).

Conclusion

Service gaps, though possibly not entirely avoidable, *are* measurable and remediable. Service marketers searching for the roots of customer dissatisfaction might begin by looking at the five critical interfaces suggested by the service gaps model.

The service gap approach to marketing underscores the impact of cultural values on service delivery. Once managers accept the premise that service quality is not in the service itself but, rather, in consumers' value-laden expectations and perceptions, their focus will shift from engineering the product to engineering the social milieu surrounding the product. The former approach almost invariably results in service gaps, the latter in service on the customers' terms and, ultimately, a more profitable business.

International Public Relations: What They Didn't Teach You on Fleet Street or Madison Avenue

By

Roger Fennings

It is an enigma, this internationalism: to provide world-class service all over the globe, while avoiding sameness; to reflect internationally accepted—and expected—levels of excellence without diluting national and ethnic individuality, specialty and character.

This is the challenge facing any organization in the international marketplace, one made even more difficult when what is being marketed is a perishable, nonmaterial product called "service"—the smile, the greeting, the handshake, the flower, the newspaper, the morning coffee, the evening drink.

The company I work for, Hilton International, has 140 hotels in forty-seven countries. It employs some fifty thousand people, nationals not only of the forty-seven countries where we operate, but of others besides. And our guests, the people we serve, come from nearly every country.

On rare occasions a guest from country A will stay in a hotel in country A and be served by a national of country A. But it is more likely that the guest from country A will stay in a hotel in country B and be greeted by a national of country C who reports to someone from country D who, in turn, reports to someone from country E. But, doesn't all this mixing of cultures invite a cross-cultural fiasco? Why, no. You see, the company's operating manuals have all the answers, and they are strictly adhered to. That may be, but those manuals were produced by the company's senior executives, and they all come from country F!

In other (less tongue-in-cheek) words, there is great potential for misunderstanding, not to mention dreadful embarrassment and errors of judgment. Such faux pas are not without consequences: substandard service, customer dissatisfaction and lost business.

Slow Learners

My own experience has taught me that culture management is essential. Unfortunately, however, it cannot be learned overnight, and the most common way of learning tends to be *cultural collision*. Intercultural training may smooth and accelerate the learning process, but neither firsthand experience nor management principles can be applied over the globe. Even that much-researched policy manual (remember the senior executive in country F?) has to be culture-flexible. And it's not just a matter of language. This overheard snippet of conversation is a reminder that adapting to culture and differing environments may be a long process.

Local: How long have you been in the Cote d'Ivoire?
Expatriate: Thirty-two years.
Local: You speak very good French.
Expatriate: I'm a slow learner.

A principal problem of cross-cultural management is communication. As public relations is both a sales and corporate communications technique, misunderstandings are frequent. It seems obvious to me that Fleet Street journalism or Madison Avenue PR will not necessarily work in Kuwait or Cairo; however, to many, that course on successful public relations to which their company sent them is the key to *all* doors.

Adaptive Strategies

World-class public relations is different from just plain public relations and it begins with a careful look at the products and services we wish to promote. Will they appeal to an international market or are they unique to one culture (for example, the Italian pizza pie vs the rather particular Korean Kinchi)? Can their appeal be broadened without unduly altering their essence? (In the case of pizza, the affirmative is evidenced in such popular and tasty adaptations as the Chicago-style pizza. In the case of Korean Kinchi, my PR sense tells me "no.") Getting the right answers to these questions early on will save a lot of time and money.

If the offering is a world-class product or service acceptable in itself or adaptable to culturally diverse audiences, the supporting public relations strategies must be equally acceptable and adaptable. I believe that to make strategies globally acceptable and effective, they should be kept as simple as possible (to avoid political, religious and cultural danger zones), and the advice of local contacts should be taken seriously. The inherent skills of the public relations practitioner working in a multinational environment will be fully called upon. And one of those skills is the ability to modify one's own modus operandi according to knowledge received through local input.

Within Hilton International, such on-site advice is readily obtained, as each hotel employs a public relations specialist either native to or thoroughly familiar with the locality. Not only are these company representatives knowledgeable about local media and mores, but about our corporate philosophy and global aims as well. They are also encouraged to play an active role within their respective operations to oversee the quality of and suggest enhancements to the products and services they are promoting.

The role of public relations varies across countries and cultures. Within the hotel industry, public relations is particularly complex and culturally charged. At my company, for example, the selling points of our 140 hotels in forty-seven countries have to be identified, interpreted and communicated to potential clients in every part of the world. Before one can understand the workings of PR in such a demanding environment, certain basics must be mastered.

PR Primer

The umbrella term, public relations, actually refers to three interrelated activities: media relations, public relations, and guest relations.

By *media relations* we mean using the printed and electronic media as the means of informing the public—our potential customer—of our service or product. Where there is a choice, the right media need to be selected to reach the right market segment, and the story (our means of delivering the message) adapted where necessary or appropriate. Where there is no choice, that story has to be carefully crafted. The result of the correct application of these skills is the positive perception of a service rendered both to the media and its audience and the resultant increased sales of the product or service.

By *public relations* we mean the employment of a wide range of methods of communicating our message to our potential buying public. Public relations has become the generic collective description of this aspect of modern marketing. Under the same heading, we can also embrace community relations, which covers the wide range of ways in which we communicate with our public other than through the media. To the imaginative practitioner, the possibilities are boundless. They might include supporting charitable or cultural institutions; sponsoring sporting or special interest activities; communicating with and participating in local organizations; and issuing newsletters to local businesses, chambers of commerce, government departments, embassies, schools, hospitals, universities, and so on. A wide variety of means can be used to create awareness and use of our organization and its facilities. It is by these methods that, in the hospitality industry, we convert the public into guests. Then we can apply *guest relations*. Guest relations is the way in which we communicate the range of services and facilities to our customer once that member of the public is either a resident or patron of our establishment. We can say with every justification that *all* service staff must practice guest relations in their day-to-day contact with the client. In addition guest magazines and newsletters might be circulated or in-house talks and tours conducted describing special offers and promotions that the guest might wish to take advantage of now or in the future. Effective guest relations are future-oriented—we want the guest to come back.

Differences

Here's where adaptiveness comes in: each of the above three activities is acceptable and successful to varying degrees at different locations and within different markets. Approaches to each may also need to be modified.

Media relations are acceptable to a greater or lesser degree in different cultures. In the Western world, they are clearly defined and well established. In many Third World countries, however, there is sometimes no relevant media, or there may be restricted access to the media. In countries of limited literacy, journalistic skills and efforts are ineffective. The PR practitioner may be well advised to turn to radio or television to communicate. But where the media is politically controlled and commercial interests are unacceptable, we have to place greater emphasis on community relations.

Clearly, the decision as to how a PR practitioner chooses specific forms of communication is not always his or hers to make. Where the media are severely restricted, for example, the practioner may have to resort to direct mailings, newsletters and organized events. Some markets may have their own media through societies and international organizations. Other markets may be accessible only through direct community involvement or paid advertising. Whatever the medium, the message must speak to the needs and values of its intended audience.

Being aware of cultural differences and constraints and being able to circumnavigate them and still reach our objective is essential. Such adaptiveness is only possible with the integration of local knowledge through the full involvement of local employees.

Alternatives

Remember our friends from the alphabet countries? The PR person in country A has a terrific product. He knows it is just right for the affluent business traveler in countries B, D and K. What he doesn't know is that his well-written, punchy press release, which he sends to his counterparts in the target countries for placement in their relevant trade and consumer journals, may never be used. Why? Because, there might be no trade media. The national or consumer media may not be used to that kind of commercial material (even if genuinely beneficial to its readers). Also, the target countries may not run a commercially oriented story without payment. Our PR man in A doesn't understand this. He can do it in his country; why can't PR people in B, D and K do it in theirs? Alternatives have to be found.

Let's look at it from the point of view of the people in E, H or S. They operate fine, successful hotels in remote places—a godsend to the international business traveler. Their owners would like to see a higher profile in the local media, and corporate headquarters would like to place internationally relevant business stories in the same local media to show they are not a one-horse operation. But these countries have, for example, a socialist government. They have, perhaps, one newspaper, and it is the voice of the government. It reflects only government policies and aspirations. There is simply no space allocated to private enterprise. Alternatives have to be found.

In one such African state, the national television station had very little money and no studio. The national TV news was broadcast from someone's apartment, frequently accompanied by the sound of ringing telephones, barking dogs and screaming babies. My colleagues and I were able to offer them a permanent room, with the result that the daily transmission from then on was broadcast "live from the Hilton Hotel."

At another location, the national TV network was well equipped with the latest British, French and German computerized mixers and other high tech equipment. But their vast studios were incredibly dreary—painted grey and without any scenery. Our hotel, in contrast, had a delightful poolside terrace surrounded by colorful tropical flowers. We offered it to the TV company for their spectaculars. Their mobile units soon moved in, a live audience eagerly attended the free shows (with refreshments), the programs again came "live from the Hilton," and everyone was happy.

In a third example, the national media would not publish business-oriented stories, but the whole country was sports-crazy. Our well-equipped hotel hosted all major national tennis and swimming championships, and the staff football team made the national league. The result: the hotel made the sports page every day.

Success

The PR practitioner working internationally constantly confronts the unexpected: cultural sensitivities, different orientations to time, unfamiliar technologies, difficulties in obtaining supplies and service, and people with their own ideas about how things should be done.

Certain personal qualities predispose a PR practitioner to succeed in a multinational environment. These include adaptability, sensitivity, flexibility, patience and tolerance. Linguistic ability is useful too. In the communication business (let us not forget that public relations is about communicating), language is our most basic, economical and powerful tool.

I have achieved more success—if I may claim any at all—not by inflicting, enforcing or imposing the corporate or so-called accepted way, but rather by adapting it to suit local conditions where existing ways and means succeed according to prevailing circumstances. Then, there has been a gradual fusion of ideas and, generally, improvement and progress.

In the multinational environment, it sometimes seems hard to know when you have succeeded, yet easy to tell when you haven't. When a tourist in Cairo asked where the River Nile got its name, she was quickly told, "It is named after the Nile Hilton." That would appear to be a success!

©1988 The Walt Disney Company

Cʜapter 5

HUMAN RESOURCES
DEVELOPMENT

Chapter 5 examines the role of proactive human resources management and development in attaining world-class service.

Walt Disney World, widely recognized for its friendly, motivated and competent service staff, faced novel challenges when the opening of its World Showcase changed the cultural composition of the theme park's work force. Unlike other Disney dreams, the Showcase is staffed almost entirely by foreign nationals who live together on-site and take part in an international work-study fellowship program. In this section's opening article, "Backstage at EPCOT Center: The World Showcase," organizer David A. Kannally and first manager Georgann P. Carlton offer a colorful description of the joys and lessons of the World Showcase Fellowship Program as well as a pragmatic prescription for harmonizing organizational and national service traditions.

"Service Quality and the Multicultural Manager," by Germaine W. Shames, demonstrates the need for and benefits to be derived from intercultural management training. Spotlighting the example of Hilton International, Shames illustrates the impact of culture on the service company and its members and argues for the development of culturally adaptive managers. Further, this article offers the reader an array of practical options for implementing intercultural training within a service organization.

In their article, "Service Managers in Developing Nations," Ned Rosen and Clive Adamson examine the impact of cultural differences and self-interest on management development. Based on a study conducted in a hotel owned by a multinational corporation in a developing country,

Rosen and Adamson's message speaks to real world issues. The authors offer acute insights into the dynamics of local citizen and expatriate manager relations and propose a strategy for complying with host government indigenization policy.

Political science scholar and labor relations practitioner, Renaldo Flores, contributes practical if sobering advice for expatriate managers of culturally different subordinates. In "Labor Relations, Culture and Service," Flores takes Puerto Rico as the example to illustrate the necessity of understanding the sociopolitical environment of local labor relations and adjusting management style to accommodate cultural differences. Speaking from experience, the author describes the management attitudes and behaviors that make the difference between success and failure.

Backstage at EPCOT Center: The World Showcase

by

David A. Kannally and Georgann P. Carlton

In the Walt Disney organization, quality service is the product of a series of dreams. Disney—the man—was a visionary who saw no reason why dreams and profits shouldn't be compatible. One particular dream, international understanding, formed the basis for the World Showcase theme park. But EPCOT Center is more than a showcase of countries and cultures; it is a model of courteous service.

When Walt Disney envisioned "EPCOT" (Experimental Prototype Community of Tomorrow) in the early sixties, his dream called for both a "permanent, international, people-to-people exchange" and a new level of entertainment and education for its guests. The project, complemented by the people who came from around the world to be a part of it, offered cultural representations more thorough and involving than possible anywhere else except in the countries themselves.

As the EPCOT concept evolved over subsequent years, though one might expect the entertainment function to become paramount, the dual purpose remained. When EPCOT Center opened on October 1, 1982, young people, mostly university students, from the nine countries then represented in the World Showcase were in residence in a designated program of education and cultural exchange called the World Showcase Fellowship Program. The countries represented were Canada, the People's Republic of China, France, West Germany, Italy, Japan, Mexico, the United Kingdom and the United States. The program consisted of a year-long regimen of study, work, living, recreation and travel experiences designed to provide participants with an overview of hospitality management, a personal involvement in cross-cultural living, and an opportunity to represent their countries' cultures to EPCOT Center's millions of visitors.

The students had to speak English fluently since 90 percent of the Center's patrons were expected to be Americans. But, more significantly, they had to learn and practice Disney-style service. Few other organizations in the country can match Disney for courteous, friendly service, and few have a more thorough program for developing quality service among their employees. Yet the Disney style of service is quintessentially American—casual, personal, and cheerful. This created two problems: (1) how would Disney-style service adapt to and remain believable within the differing cultural settings being created and (2) what would be the response of students from countries where service styles are more formal, noninvolving or subservient, and to whom the Disney style promised to be foreign.

This article will focus on a variety of measures which are taken in the selection, training and management of the multicultural work force in World Showcase to achieve the dual purpose of authentic cultural representation and Disney-style service.

Selection

Within every culture, there are individuals who are naturally more quick to smile, more at ease in conversation, and more comfortable with public contact than others. So the first step in achieving Disney-style multicultural service at EPCOT is to select participants for the Fellowship Program who have natural personality traits in keeping with the Disney image. This kind of selection happens domestically every day at the Disney employment center. But to achieve good results internationally, a substantial investment in recruitment travel for personal interviews is required.

There is no substitute for the personal interview. Disney has sworn by it for its thirty-plus years in the outdoor entertainment business and has been willing to invest in worldwide travel to continue it for the World Showcase.

The Interview

Disney recruiters learned quickly that an international interview starts at a different point than does a domestic interview. Much of the domestic common ground regarding work habits, punctuality, discipline styles, and even a fundamental understanding of the Disney parks is missing in the international interview. Also, many issues and challenges unique to the World Showcase can and have arisen. One example is a problem that occurred in the German pavilion, which is Bavarian in its architecture, food and music. Several students from northern Germany (Bavaria is in the south) found it uncomfortable to wear Bavarian costumes and difficult to feel that they were properly representing their country. This subcultural problem was addressed by centering subsequent recruiting efforts in Bavaria.

Another problem was identified when Disney recruiters found that the prospect of living, studying and working in the United States (in Florida) and with the Disney organization in particular had a strong halo effect on the students. Perceptions by students included the promise of affluence, ease of work and study, and of "ambassador status" in the representation of their countries. The cure for the halo effect was extra attention to a realistic and detailed presentation of every aspect of the program, including audiovisuals, verbal explanations, an extensive period of questions and answers, and even live testimonies by alumni of the program. Again, extra investment was required, but the savings in disillusionment have been well worth the expense.

The presentations also include reviews of Disney work values, especially the idea of the supremacy of the guest, work schedules and other potentially sensitive areas. For instance, because of durability requirements, Disney costumes contain high percentages of manmade fibers. Students from several countries found wearing manmade fabrics objectionable.

Recruiters depart quickly from structured interview techniques, moving more to informal and in-depth exchange. They ask general, open-ended questions that provide deeper insights into the students' ability to adjust to the requirements of the program. Disney has grooming standards for employees, for example, and some applicants found after an in-depth interview that they could not accept the company's right to make such demands of its "on-stage" personnel. In-depth interviews also uncover attitudes toward status, which make some individuals uncomfortable in roles which identify them with commercialism.

Criteria for final selection are surprisingly simple and consistent with most selection processes. Recruiters select those applicants who will be most successful in and rewarded by the experience offered. That may or may not be the applicant with the best family background or the best school performance (a *B* average is minimum), but rather the person with the highest degree of warmth, the greatest flexibility and the strongest spirit of teamwork.

A thorough selection process, complete with personal interviews, predisposes to success subsequent efforts in orientation, training and management.

Preorientation

Preorientation begins during the interview itself, when the interviewer discusses the company's values and expectations with the applicant in order to measure his or her ability to adapt. The process continues, by mail, during the crucial weeks between interview and arrival. During this time, newly selected students are building their anticipation and excitement about the opportunity. They are eager to read and absorb a great deal of information about their host country and company.

Disney sends several prearrival packets containing details about climate, dress, schedules, travel and so on. While much of this material is prepared for general consumption, program-specific material is carefully scrutinized for potential ambiguities or cross-cultural errors. The biggest of these errors uncovered early in the program was the use of the word *optional*, which in the United States has come to mean add-on features at extra cost. Many students interpreted the word optional to mean simply "at my discretion" and did not anticipate or intend to pay any additional fees for "optional" activities. Since the word *optional* appeared in writing, Disney found itself in several confrontations with students.

Other prearrival information includes information on community amenities, transportation, shopping, use of public telephones, postal services, banking services, etc. Students tend to study this information well before leaving home. Even so, it is important to reissue it for easy reference upon arrival.

Arrival

If the Fellowship Program has a first impression, it is the Disney kind of welcome that newcomers receive. The company makes a concerted effort to be personal and accommodating during this period. Typically, the American contingent in the program is selected from Disney's 20,000 employees. Since the American students are already on-site, they can easily participate in the welcoming process. This involvement not only makes arrival preparations easier, it builds a sense of responsibility in the "host" contingent. A welcoming party meets students at the airport, provides van transportation to the apartments, prepares the apartments with linens, and helps orient the new arrivals to their surroundings.

All students arrive on the same day to create an event for the students and for the local press. Once all flights are in, program managers throw a welcome rally in the apartment clubhouse. The fatigue and trauma of transoceanic travel quickly dissipate. Young travelers are especially vulnerable during this time, so a well-orchestrated arrival procedure is most helpful.

Next, and very important, is a rest day before the formal orientation regimen begins. This day gives the students time to get to know each other, to acquaint themselves with their apartments and the environs, and to recover from journeys that for some have been thirty hours or more in length. The day is never ill-spent, and the lack of programmed activity is appropriate.

Orientation

During the following three days, the students receive intensive orientation through classroom sessions: first American culture, then information on Florida and the region surrounding Orlando, and, finally and most specifically, the Disney organization itself. Considerable time is spent helping the students become systematically acquainted with their new home.

The Disney organization orientation, called Traditions, is a process worth detailed review. The program, designed by Walt Disney's hand-picked trainers more than thirty years ago, has been updated regularly without departure from its original strategy. It appears to translate cross-culturally very well, although it was not originally designed to do so. The Traditions program is a full-day classroom meeting/property tour that does four indispensable things:

1. It instills a sense of pride in the history and culture of the organization. Through attention-getting graphics and pertinent anecdotes, the instructor recounts the company's development from its beginnings in a Hollywood garage where the Disney brothers built their first animation stand to the multinational, multibillion dollar business that is Disney today. The story includes technological and creative milestones in many media, including film, television, merchandising, educational materials and outdoor entertainment. A pervasive sense of pride and dedication to quality knits the story into a tradition of achievement and guest satisfaction.

2. It outlines, simply and emphatically, the basic behavior required of every employee, behavior that has helped create and preserve Disney's success. Through the use of showcards and slogans such as "we know the answers" and "we work while others play," the instructor gives an elementary lesson in the basics of good guest service. The presentation is direct and completely consistent from one class to the next, from one day to the next, and from one year to the next. The "dos" and "don'ts" are offered as the formula that must be followed if the company is to continue to thrive.

3. It gives a vision of the future. Grand plans for new products and new developments have fueled enthusiasm within the Disney organization from the outset. Students in the Traditions program get a taste of the newest Disney creations through a slide presentation which shows renderings and models of the work of

115

Disney artists or "imagineers." This presentation, coupled with a tour of the Center, stimulates a feeling of confidence and optimism that comes from juxtaposing dreams already realized with others yet to come.

4. It places responsibility for the future success of the organization squarely on the shoulders of the new employees. The logical conclusion of the program is that the company's destiny is in no way guaranteed by past success but is wholly dependent upon the effectiveness of the members of the current team. Even if the new employee's job will be a small part of a large picture, every role and task is vital.

Program Overview

Study—One day per week is set aside for seminars in three disciplines:

1. International Cultural Studies. Students themselves teach these sessions, using materials and information brought from home. Topics include history, geography, politics, traditions and future goals of each country represented.

2. Future Studies. Using EPCOT Center's Future World pavilions as a point of departure, high technology firms present seminars on new developments in disciplines such as communications, transportation, energy, agriculture and computer sciences.

3. Business Management Studies. Mid- and upper-level Disney managers present seminars on the many business disciplines of Walt Disney World Company, including resort management, marketing, park operations, finance, employee relations, food and beverage management, merchandise management and support facilities management.

Work—The work setting includes the various national pavilions of World Showcase. Each pavilion is an architectural and cultural glimpse of a country, intended to entertain as well as to educate the visitor. Facades reminiscent of well-known landmarks and common building styles are combined in each pavilion to capture a feeling of each country. Traditional food and merchandise are sold in the pavilions' restaurants and shops. And through the working experience provided by the World Showcase Fellowship Program, the young representatives of each nation appear behind shop counters, at tablesides and at theater doors—welcoming, introducing, serving and selling. Fellowship students typically work thirty or thirty-two hours a week, leaving eight to ten hours a week for programmed study.

Living—Students are housed in an apartment complex adjacent to the Disney property. Roommates are selected at random, with a deliberate mix of native language and nationality (not gender!). Not surprisingly, many students rate this multicultural living experience as the most valuable part of the program.

Recreation—Students participate in intramural sports offered in the Disney employee activities program. As might be expected, soccer has joined the more traditional American sports in the intramurals since EPCOT Center opened.

Travel—During their fellowship year, students take several trips within Florida. Often these trips are coupled with Future Studies programs, taking in the sights around Kennedy Space Center and area robotics plants. At the end of the year, an excursion to Washington, D.C. and New York City is organized.

Cross-Cultural Implications of the Fellowship Program

However tempting it may be for the authors to reminisce about the trial-filled early days of the World Showcase Fellowship, it would be more useful at this juncture to itemize critical intercultural issues which surfaced as the program got underway and called for the perceptive application of cross-cultural management skills.

Power Distance, Authority and Familiarity

The Disney organization prides itself on an atmosphere of familiarity. The president of Walt Disney World wears a nametag that reads, simply, "Dick." At the same time, the chain of command is very clear. When Dick issues a directive, it never suffers from inattention just because everybody feels comfortable calling him Dick.

And so goes the Disney plan. Friendly, open-door policies encourage cooperation among management levels, while a pure, efficient hierarchy ensures the expeditious conduct of business.

Supervisors are encouraged to be coaches, not bosses. Leadership is by example. Famed for walking miles each day through the parks he supervises, vice president Bob Matheison never walks past a piece of litter without stooping to pick it up. Thus, every custodial employee knows that his or her job is important enough to warrant direct support from the vice president. (About eight thousand people report to Bob Matheison.)

But to many arriving students, it is an alien experience to see a vice president picking up trash! Is his authority not compromised through his stooping, literally, to do the work of a janitor?

Students find it even more difficult to adjust to supervisory chumminess. Suspicions arise instantly. Why is my boss trying to be my friend? Does my boss lack the authority to direct me? Does he need my friendship to gain my cooperation? Why is she seemingly friendly at one moment and directive the next? How can someone so young and with no university training be placed in such a position of responsibility?

These reactions create a credibility gap in the students' perception of their supervisors. Likewise, management resents the insubordination of students who confuse informality with anarchy and unwittingly violate the chain of command.

Training and orientation that address cultural differences are the best methods for avoiding such misunderstandings. The final solution, however, is always attributable to openness of mind.

Education vs. Competence

Disney employees advance through management ranks by demonstrating competence, loyalty, dependability and staying power. Formal education is not especially revered, nor is experience outside the organization. Employees earn acceptance and respect only in direct proportion to their contribution to the company.

Many of the Fellowship students enter the program with expectations that they will automatically receive the respect to which their home experience and status have conditioned them. Social standing, family name and university reputation may all mean something at home. Disney, however, regards these evidences of new employees' status with the reverence approximating that of a drill sergeant at boot camp.

Conversely, the students judge their supervisors by home country standards, often expecting their Disney superiors to have university diplomas and training in management theory. Coupled with the comparatively chummy management style practiced by front-line supervisors, this apparent lack of formal education in management compromises the supervisors' authority in the eyes of some of the young foreigners.

Naturally, the magnitude of this problem ranges from nonexistent in the Japan pavilion, to monumental in France and Italy.

While in some cases students have forwarded proposals for complete reorganization of the World Showcase management structure, the problem has been more realistically addressed through classic compromise. Supervisors now involve students in special projects, accepting proposals for enhancements or modifications of their work areas. Students have also come to know their supervisors as dedicated employees who earn their subordinates' respect through pure hard work, firm discipline and a ready ear.

Punctuality

The Walt Disney World Resort Complex operates on a twenty-four-hour, military-style timeclock. Work time is measured in six-minute intervals (tenths of an hour). Employees who are twelve minutes late to work are docked two-tenths of an hour's wage. Sophisticated electronic time clocks triggered by magnetically encoded time cards record each employee's arrival and departure.

Punctuality is stressed in orientation programs and strictly monitored by line supervisors. Employees are told that they are letting their fellow workers down by being late, thereby forcing their colleagues to fill in for them. The most gifted employees have learned the art of donning certain parts of their costumes while running at full speed to their work locations. (A twenty-minute "walk time" is allowed each day. Sprinting enables one to use part of that walk time for other things.)

Tardiness has been a problem with many Fellowship students. The blame falls on countless culprits. Enough alarm clocks have been alleged to be faulty to warrant a global recall by the world's timepiece industry. Waiting lines at the wardrobe window, pants that don't fit right, and bad weather have all, in their turn, been blamed for students' tardiness. But, predictably, the time clocks are oblivious to such exigencies. With certain incorrigible exceptions, the students adapt.

Intentions vs. Actions

Tardiness and other infractions of Disney policy give rise to disciplinary actions. The administration of discipline is itself governed by policy, with a succession of reprimands, first oral then written, leading to termination of employment. Using attendance as an example, a certain amount of tardiness can lead to an oral reprimand. If the situation is not corrected, a written reprimand follows (both oral and written reprimands are composed according to a prescribed format), with notification of impending termination if the infractions continue. Each step is carefully documented to ensure that the company can, if necessary, justify its case for dismissal.

The infractions are measurable and objective. Jane either shows up on time or she doesn't. There is not much room for consideration of motivation in this clear-cut procedure. It is the responsibility of the employee to arrive on time or to notify the supervisor in advance if an illness or other problem will prevent a prompt arrival.

If Jane tries to arrive on time and is sincere in her attempts to do so and even puts forth extra effort but still arrives twelve minutes late, she is docked.

Students from several of the cultures represented are accustomed to being judged—where an infraction of the rules is involved—more on intention than action. In cases in which these students make sincere efforts to abide by policy but for one reason or another do not do so, they feel insulted by a system that penalizes them without, in their view, sufficiently considering their motives. They sometimes find their disciplining supervisors to be insensitive and unbending. The supervisors, eager to fulfill their charge to be "firm, fair and consistent," do not, and in fact can not, make exceptions. The best supervisors spend enough time hearing the problem to assure the students that they are understood and then spend equal time explaining thoroughly why things have to be the way they are.

Although most students come to an intellectual acceptance of these procedures, they still sometimes find them dehumanizing. In light of its responsibility to its other twenty thousand employees, Disney does not have much room to set precedents and to depart from the mainstream of its policy. As in most other areas of cross-cultural management, the individual supervisor's patience and empathy bridge the unalterable culture gap.

Company Loyalty

Disney, and many other fine companies, work hard to build employee loyalty. For many management people in the Disney organization, a job can evolve almost into a way of life, especially during the start-up phase of a project like EPCOT Center. Far from being labeled a "company man" (or woman), a Disney manager who spends many extra hours at work and who carries out responsibility with zeal is respected and rewarded. The Japanese students find this company/employee relationship quite natural, but many Europeans feel it to be almost exploitative.

As the best Disney employees at every level go about demonstrating their worth and promotability, some students begin to question the employees' self-esteem. "How can she give so much of herself to this company? How could this job be that important to anyone?"

Without that level of devotion, the Disney organization could not be what it is. Yet, from the point of view of many students, their supervisors are being naive about their heavy investment of personal time and energy for the betterment of the company. One French student retold a story many times concerning a middle manager who found it convenient to bring a cot into the office for brief rest periods during the long days and nights prior to the opening of the Center.

But this kind of commitment, the students learn, is not peculiar to Disney. Through a future studies program, they come in contact with executives from a number of other large corporations, including Exxon, General Motors, AT&T, Kraft, Kodak, Coca-Cola and American Express, and find similar measures of company loyalty.

Fellowship students—depending on their culture's work ethic—may either find this display of corporate patriotism shocking or commendable.

Cross-Cultural Communication

Communication, a cornerstone of management, plays a particularly crucial role in the multicultural setting of the Showcase. Listening has emerged as a solution to the five previously described problems.

A case in point: Akio (from Japan) and Luc (from France) were roommates. Akio, a very traditional Japanese male, was unaccustomed to and uncomfortable with housework. Luc, in his spirit of equality, felt that precisely 50 percent of the housework was Akio's responsibility. While Luc would dutifully clean the kitchen and bathroom one day per week, Akio would often bypass his domestic chores. Their menage soon became a series of small annoyances.

The misunderstanding came to a head when Luc wrote Akio a note calling him a pig. The choice of words seemed natural enough to Luc, for, in France, the term *pig* is used quite freely to refer to someone sloppy. What Luc didn't know is that in Japan, it is difficult to find a more severe insult. Akio, incensed, appealed the case to the Fellowship Program office.

The problem was one of attribution of meaning. Was Luc aware of the severity of the word *pig* in Japanese? No. Was Akio aware that it is used frequently and casually in French? No. Was Luc aware that traditional Japanese males are uncomfortable doing housework? No. Was Akio aware that Luc perceived housework as a mutual responsibility to be divided evenly? No.

In a refereed peace talk, the young men listened to each other and came to an understanding of themselves as cultural beings. Though they may not have become the best of friends, by hearing each other out in the presence of trained cross-cultural mediators, they were able to reach agreements that allowed them to complete the Fellowship term in relative harmony.

Summary

The practical lessons of the developmental stages of the World Showcase Fellowship Program are these:

1. Select people who are predisposed to success, using in-depth interviewing techniques and fostering realistic expectations of the experience ahead.

2. Prepare participants as thoroughly as possible for the experience before arrival, taking best advantage of their prearrival eagerness for information.

3. Orient participants to the host nation, region, city and company, especially in work-related cultural values.

4. Set forth detailed expectations of performance for every participant. Assume nothing.

5. Prepare supervisors with role playing, readings and the best cross-cultural videos you can get your hands on. Allow them lead time for a learning curve once participants arrive.

6. Anticipate the classic problems outlined in all the cross-cultural management literature. You *will* have problems.

7. Listen. None of the problems will look like textbook problems when they happen. They will be immediate and personal, especially for the program participants. The lines between individual personalities and cultural behavior will be very hazy. Listen, understand and recognize common ground.

The authors wish to acknowledge the contributions of

Richard Nunis, whose unfailing belief in the intrinsic merit of the World Showcase Fellowship Program made it happen when contrary opinions might have otherwise defeated it;

Tom Eastman, who demonstrated to the authors that persistence can accomplish almost anything;

Rick Johnson, whose documentation of the collective Disney operational expertise provided the backbone of the educational program;

Kitty Holt and *Gregg Yawman*, who were the arms and legs of the program's development;

Stephen Rhinesmith, mentor, godfather and advocate;

1982-1983 Fellowship group, through whose tutelage we made it difficult for succeeding groups to get away with anything.

Disclaimer

This is a practical overview of the joys and lessons of the World Showcase Fellowship Program. Any discrepancies between what really happened and prevailing cross-cultural management theory are purely coincidental.

Service Quality and the Multicultural Manager

by

Germaine W. Shames

As hotel companies widen their scope to embrace international operations, hospitality managers face the challenges caused by cultural differences. Several of today's international hotel companies now ring the globe, and their employees regularly move from property to property and country to country. One hotel firm, Hilton International, recorded more than four hundred such employee transfers in one year. Even domestic hotel companies in many nations feel the effects of cultural differences as new ethnic groups immigrate and seek jobs in the industry. Indeed, the cultural mix in many hotels makes a stroll from the front desk to the employee cafeteria resemble a world tour. In both cases, experience has shown that unmanaged cultural differences can engender staff discord, generate service problems, and cause a manager to fail in an assignment.

The service environment requires a special type of manager—a multicultural manager who has the sensitivity and skills to orchestrate the delivery of world-class service. Multicultural managers adapt their management styles and service approaches to the cultural milieu in which they operate. They manage service as effectively in Kuala Lumpur as they do in their home towns. This article explores the role of the multicultural manager in world-class service.

Cultural Casualties

The monocultural manager operating in a multicultural workplace is severely handicapped. Let's consider the experience of two hypothetical hotel managers, one a novice expatriate, the other a national working in his/her own hometown:

Vera Silk, front office manager of the local ABC hotel,

transfers to a sister hotel in a neighboring country. Following several weeks of initial elation with her new colleagues and surroundings, she becomes increasingly irritated by certain national mannerisms, business practices and working conditions. On several occasions she has lost her temper with subordinates and even guests. Although she is working longer hours than ever before, she misses deadlines and sees little progress in her department. In fact, the number of guest complaints has nearly doubled since her arrival. Her self-confidence wavers as she struggles with service problems and her own loneliness and fatigue. She begins to regret her decision to transfer.

Vera's behavior is typical of a recently transferred manager who has passed from the honeymoon phase of cultural adjustment to culture shock, a phase characterized by irritability and hostility. Contrary to the image conjured up by its name, culture shock does not strike like a lightning bolt. Actually, the term refers to a cumulative and debilitating state of disorientation, one that builds slowly from each experience in which the sufferer encounters contrary ways of perceiving, doing and valuing things. Vera is aware that something is wrong, but she has no idea how to diagnose it or alleviate her symptoms. Her behavior may appear erratic or antagonistic to her staff and colleagues. Strained working relations aggravate her department's service problems.

Other factors may also contribute to her department's decline: her management style may be ill suited to the local work force, she may unintentionally be offending native colleagues and subordinates, her habits of grooming and dress might convey an unprofessional image, or her communication methods may be inappropriate.

The second hypothetical case is one of a manager rendered ineffective by cultural differences without ever leaving home:

> Sean Hay, food and beverage manager at the XYZ hotel, has always enjoyed the reputation of being fair with his subordinates and sensitive to their needs. Recently, a large influx of refugees from other countries has dramatically changed the composition of the community's work force. Sean willingly hires representatives of the newly arrived groups but terminates nearly all of them at the end of their probationary period. When questioned about the terminations, he explains that the new employees made his other employees uncomfortable with their "odd" behavior and that their presence began to threaten service quality.

Despite his belief in equal opportunity, Sean cannot seem to accept or manage cultural differences within his work team. The good intentions he shows by hiring the new workers are undermined by his lack of cultural awareness. He doesn't even realize he has a problem. His inability to orchestrate the multicultural work force may have various causes: discomfort with people who do not conform to his preconceptions, hastiness to judge and impose his own perspective, an inflexible management style, or poor intercultural communication skills.

Sean's monocultural orientation has already caused his company high turnover; it could also damage the hotel's competitiveness in the labor market and its image in the community. Ultimately, the hotel may become embroiled in a labor discrimination suit. All of the foregoing ills may be expected to adversely affect service quality.

Multicultural Ideal

Multiculturalism is an ideal toward which Vera and Sean would be well advised to strive. Both lack the awareness and skills to deal effectively with the cultural dimension of their jobs; both would benefit from intercultural training.

We are all culture bound to varying degrees. We view the world through the lens our culture has provided and react to it in culturally prescribed ways. Our culture is so much a part of us that its workings are outside our awareness. Our own ways of behaving seem natural, right and normal, not merely the result of cultural conditioning.

But if *our* perceptions, behaviors and patterns of thinking and communicating are natural and right, where does that leave the rest of the world—particularly our coworkers and guests from other cultures? Are they "wrong," "unnatural," and "abnormal"? Is the refugee who joins our department really behaving oddly or is he following the codes of his former culture while still in the process of learning new ones? Is the recently transferred manager moody and hostile or is she struggling with the stresses of mastering the myriad of unfamiliar cues and symbols that we may take for granted? Is the guest who complains about our service just being difficult or expressing culturally influenced expectations that may be entirely reasonable given his or her background?

Intercultural training addresses these and other issues. The rationale for such training is that people, despite basic intelligence and good intentions, are not automatically able to function effectively outside of their primary culture. People can, however, be taught how to function in different cultures and develop skills for interacting with culturally different people. By extension, they can be taught to deliver appropriate service to the culturally different customer.

In preparing a manager for expatriation or a multicultural workplace, the intercultural trainer begins by fostering cultural self-awareness and introducing general concepts that apply to any culture. While there is no absolute consensus on the exact competencies that make for success in intercultural management, variations of the following are frequently cited by intercultural specialists:

Self-awareness—the recognition of one's own values, assumptions, needs and limitations

Culture reading—the ability to find and trace the inherent logic in each culture

Multiple perspective—the ability to suspend judgment, remove one's cultural filters, and see through others' eyes

Intercultural communication skills—the ability to send and interpret verbal and nonverbal messages accurately across cultures

Gear shifting—the ability to readjust expectations, modify plans, try out new approaches and rebound from setbacks

Culture shock savvy—the ability to monitor and abet one's own progress through the cross-cultural adjustment process

Relationship-building skills—the ability to relate to and inspire confidence in all kinds of people and to maintain a solid support system

Intercultural facilitation skills—the ability to manage cultural differences and facilitate cultural synergy

Most trainers use several methods in sequence to lead trainees first to awareness, then to competence. Readings and self-assessment instruments introduce concepts and trigger insight; case studies and culture assimilators process and apply learning; and role plays and simulation games allow trainees to try out new behaviors and develop intercultural skills. To tailor such a program to the unique needs of the service manager, the trainer might include material on the service experience as a social interaction and concentrate on developing intercultural communication skills. Role plays and other exercises could simulate common customer relations situations.

Costly Faux Pas

The monetary costs of not preparing managers to manage culture are staggering; the human costs are incalculable. Cultural faux pas in business strategy, marketing, human resources development and customer relations cost a company dearly in damaged image, lost business and failed managers. Standards of service are constantly at risk where cultural competence is left to chance.

Management expertise is a highly perishable resource. A company may spend thousands of dollars recruiting, grooming and nurturing a manager, only to set him or her up unwittingly for a "cultural derailment" by neglecting the cultural dimension of management development. Intercultural training is still not included in the training programs of most hospitality companies. Transplanted managers who are otherwise effective may fail without the orientation and support to attain—as quickly as possible—an acceptable level of well-being and performance at a new location. With the increasing cultural diversification of the workplace, even stay-at-home managers lacking intercultural skills may find themselves unprepared to deal with a heterogeneous work force.

Shopping for Intercultural Training

Once convinced of the need for intercultural training, the hospitality company must determine the most cost-effective way to incorporate such training into their system. Few companies currently have qualified intercultural trainers among their staff and must either hire them or contract outside consultants. While both alternatives entail a significant expenditure, the sum is dwarfed by the prospective cost of one failed manager: an estimated $125,000 to $300,000! Let's examine several of the most viable approaches to implementing intercultural management training in a hospitality company.

One-stop shopping. Engaging outside consultants is a good option if your company can afford it and knows enough about such training to select the practitioner wisely. The number of intercultural practitioners is growing. Most are qualified professionals, but some may not have had sufficient exposure to a corporate environment to understand your company's needs and constraints. "One-stop shopping" is available through some of the more established consulting groups which offer everything from selection testing for overseas assignments to reentry counseling for returning managers and their families.

Company intercultural center. Another approach, one successfully used by Scandinavian Airlines System, is an in-house briefing and resource center. In the center, mobile employees and their families receive training and counseling in company-operated facilities from company personnel. The center also stocks relevant books and audio- and videotapes. Such a center, of course, involves considerable start-up costs and the ongoing expense of permanent staff. It also requires that the employees and their families be transported to and accommodated at the center. To justify the expense, the company's volume of interculturally mobile personnel would have to be sizable. Considering the advantages of such a center (thoroughness, customization and visible corporate commitment), however, it should not be discounted without due consideration of its feasibility.

Addition to existing management development program. If your company has already established a management development program, you may wish either to add a cultural component to each training module or to add a separate intercultural module. Such alterations or additions will probably require the services of an outside consultant, but once the new material is developed, your own trainers should be able to administer it (as they would any other portion of the program). The integration of intercultural topics with more familiar management fare aids its assimilation.

Training of trainers. Some companies may prefer to gradually prepare their own staff to assume responsibility for implementing intercultural training. Several reputable sources offer programs for training trainers, the most notable being the International Society for Intercultural Education, Training and Research (SIETAR). Workshops for beginning intercultural trainers may last from one to three weeks and provide an overview of intercultural theory and the goals, principles and methodology of intercultural training. Following such a workshop, trainers should be able to implement most off-the-shelf programs, but probably will not be ready to develop their own.

Perhaps the most expedient approach to implementing intercultural management training in a company is to use several or all of the foregoing means. Your company might draw upon the expertise of an outside specialist to assess training needs and explore the array of training options available. You may then take advantage of your own existing training framework and staff to customize and reinforce any outside training or off-the-shelf programs. By training trainers, you may gradually shift responsibility for intercultural training from outside practitioners to internal human resources managers.

Hilton International: A Case Study

Hilton International was the first of the major international hotel companies to implement a companywide program to develop multicultural managers. While the H.I. approach embraces both mobile and stay-at-home managers, particular attention is given to the orientation and support of transferees and their families. H.I.'s program takes full advantage of its existing training framework and staff. Intercultural training is increasingly appearing in the curricula of its training centers and is being referred to in the pages of its internal publications. Attendees at H.I.'s Career Development Institute participate in workshops on such topics as intercultural negotiation and cultural readjustment. Readers of corporate magazines are likely to encounter articles entitled "Intercultural Competence: Passport to the Multicultural Workplace" or "Dining Dilemmas: Defining Cultural Differences."

At the heart of Hilton International's drive toward multicultural management is a program called Meeting the Transfer Challenge. The program is a product of corporate concern for the well-being and effectiveness of its internationally mobile key personnel. Although the company's system of classifying key personnel separations has not permitted a documented count of managers leaving for reasons of cultural maladjustment in the past, perceptive human resources managers reported many such cases and attested to the gravity of the problem. Corporate decision makers were quick to lend support.

Meeting the Transfer Challenge was implemented companywide in December of 1985. Early response from a sample of human resources managers was a resounding "what took us so long!" Several well-traveled general managers wrote congratulatory letters with the line, "I wish we'd had this program back when I began my career with the company." *No one* questioned the need for such a program.

The program's formal evaluation took place eighteen months later. Again, response from program administrators and beneficiaries (transferees) was highly favorable. Upon closer analysis, however, regional patterns began to emerge. Program implementation was found to be more advanced in Asia, the Middle East and Europe than in the Americas or Australia. Likewise, the comments and suggestions of the administrators from the former areas indicated a far more penetrating understanding of the nature and impact of culture and the need for intercultural training. We deduced that the more parochial orientation of the human resources managers in the insulated Americas and Australia was impeding the program's full implementation. This unforeseen hurdle was surmounted by providing the parochial managers with cultural awareness training.

The program's success may be attributed to various factors:

• Its fit with HI's corporate culture

• Its practicality, ease of implementation and avoidance of jargon

• Its consideration of transferees' personal needs as well as their professional effectiveness

• The reinforcement provided by simultaneous introduction of intercultural training at the company's training centers and regional meetings

- Upper management's endorsement and sustained support

Although these factors may apply to the successful implementation of any corporate program, they are far more crucial to a program dealing with culture, a topic stigmatized by many as "soft," esoteric or academic. Few companies match Hilton International's level of cultural sophistication. If intercultural training found a receptive audience in Hilton International, it was because the company had long recognized and sought to capitalize on cultural diversity. Intercultural training may have a far more difficult initiation in less culture-savvy companies.

Service Age Prognosis

More than seven years ago, an article on coping with cultural differences in *The Cornell Quarterly* (Cullen, 1981) concluded with the following quotation from business scholar William Newman: "We seem to be in a twilight zone of recognizing a need, but not knowing how to deal with it." Only within the last several years has the industry shown signs of emerging from that twilight zone. Not only have champions of intercultural training initiated programs in several of the international hotel chains (Hilton International, Sheraton, Accor), but in several major university hospitality programs as well (Cornell, Michigan State, and others).

Dealing with the need for intercultural training is easier in 1988 than it was back in 1981. While the hospitality industry has been biding its time, intercultural training has enjoyed a spurt of accelerated development. Practitioners in both business and academia have learned to package and market their programs far more effectively. The ground has been broken, and educational and technical support is now readily available.

As hospitality managers exhaust their traditional service management repertoires in attempting to respond to the rising expectations of an increasingly diverse public, they may be expected to become more receptive to intercultural training. Intercultural practitioners, for their part, may be expected to respond to the service challenge with programs that add a cultural dimension to traditional customer service training. The happy result will be multicultural managers orchestrating world-class service.

Service Managers in Developing Nations

by

Ned Rosen and Clive Adamson

The hospitality, travel and tourism industries have traditionally maintained a cadre of expatriate managers who, given sufficient perks, willingly shuttle to developing nations to fill the upper ranks of their organization's offshore operations. Supporters of this practice believe the educational systems in postcolonial countries have not yet produced the trained human resources needed to run large, complex organizations profitably. While still relying heavily on imported expatriate talent, many organizations, in response to increasing government pressure and financial constraints, also invest in the development of local citizen talent.

Since most tourism-related organizations operate according to a traditional industrial Western model, the management training they afford aspiring local citizens is likewise based on imported management philosophies and methods. The training typically ignores possible differences in trainees' perceptions and values and reinforces the industry status quo.

This article describes the impact of such a training program on selected attitudes of citizen and expatriate managers employed by a large organization in a developing nation. Our study examines how well Western management training transfers across cultures and how it affects the typically strained relations between expatriate and citizen managers. The study's findings serve as a springboard for subsequent discussion of developing local talent and managing the citizen-expatriate manager relationship.

The Case of the Polarized Management Team

Our study takes place in a former colony—now an independent nation—with a service-based economy. Tourism alone accounts for two-thirds of its gross national product. Its government enforces "citizens first" employment that restricts work permits for all but upper-echelon expatriate personnel as part of an indigenization policy.

The organization studied is a large, self-contained resort employing 3,400 local citizens to tend its numerous guestrooms, food-and-beverage outlets, and banquet and meeting facilities. Its senior executive group is comprised of—with one exception—expatriates lacking formal management training. Having risen through the ranks via a food-and-beverage career path, all practice a hands-on, high intervention and directive style of management.

Many organizational and environmental conditions appear to both amplify the impact of this management approach and support its continuance:

- The low level of hourly workers' formal education

- The low level of formal training among management and supervisory staff

- Difficulty in attracting and maintaining employees with high performance potential

- The highly entrepreneurial management style of many industry executives

- The concentration of expatriate managers at the senior management level

- Expatriate managers' support of the status quo

Confusion, frustration and anxiety are endemic throughout the organization. As all matters must be referred upward for decision making, middle managers and supervisors suffer from "learned helplessness." Young talent is blocked from advancement by "here today, gone tomorrow" expatriates and by older, sometimes underqualified citizens entrenched in positions until retirement. Ill feeling exists toward expatriate managers as they are perceived by citizens as a privileged elite.

The Management Training Program

The organization's chief executive officer seemed at first to recognize the need for a change in management approach and, for this reason, authorized the implementation of a management training program. In addition to encouraging participants to reassess their management styles, the program was expected (1) to improve organization communication and climate, and (2) to foster unity between expatriate and local managers.

A dozen programs were reviewed prior to selecting one that appeared to fit the organization's needs. The CEO chose it partly because he and several colleagues had previously participated in the program while employed elsewhere and partly because it required minimal written responses, encouraged interaction and involvement by participants, and used tasks familiar to them. Accordingly, the instructional *process* at least was flexible and pitched to an appropriate educational level. Also, the same program had reportedly been applied successfully in other developing countries, although in totally different industry settings and cultures. Moreover, the program emphasized both efficiency and teamwork—concepts that, while highly desirable, the organization was perhaps not prepared to fully embrace.

Consequently, we had reason to believe at the beginning that the training intervention would be beneficial to the organization and that the executive group would be particularly supportive of the management model used in the course. However, our early optimism was not fully justified and failed to take into account all of the social and environmental factors that influenced participants' reactions. By querying course participants after each major course segment, we were able to trace their attitude toward and responses to the training.

Pretraining Status

Few differences were apparent between the expatriate and citizen trainees at the outset. We noted the expatriates were consistently more structure-oriented in their management approach than were citizens (that is, they claimed to clearly define goals and set quality standards for their subordinates). The two groups also held different positions on preferred styles of interpersonal behavior: citizens expressed softer, more understanding attitudes toward subordinates than did expatriates. Otherwise, the two groups held similar views about management and the organizational climate.

Posttraining Status

While pre- and posttraining changes were not large, some attitudinal shifts did occur. Moreover, the data suggest that the training experience and the context within which it occurred had a greater impact on expatriates than on citizens. As a group, expatriates' views became more homogeneous. Overall, however, the pattern of results indicates that training did not bring the expatriate and citizen groups closer together. In fact, it appears to have brought their differing attitudes and self-interests into sharper focus.

Findings worthy of mention include the following:

- While citizens' attitudes toward interpersonal style tended to harden, expatriates' tended to soften.

- The groups retained their original relative position on structure orientation.

- Both groups came to view their executive committees more negatively—especially the expatriates. Citizens, however, tended to develop more positive views of the organization.

The training experience appears to have served as a mild morale booster for citizen managers who may have felt they were finally being groomed to ascend to higher levels of management. Expatriate managers, on the other hand, appeared disheartened by the experience, believing their inclusion implied a lack of faith in their managerial ability on the part of senior management. The hoped-for improvement in teamwork did not result.

It should be mentioned that each training module culminated in the formation of participant task forces responsible for effecting actual changes in the operation. Predictably, none of the task forces succeeded. The expatriate and local managers worked poorly in teams and failed to win upper management's support for their proposals.

Senior management's ambivalent, noncommittal behavior following the training did nothing to either reinforce any positive changes in trainee behavior or to correct any adverse situations unintentionally fostered. Sensing that the training had been less than successful, they reneged on plans for follow-up activities and shrank from addressing the feelings and attitudes the program had forced to the surface.

Win/Win Citizen-Expatriate Manager Relations

While we do not conclude from the largely counterproductive findings of this study that management training should be abandoned, the findings do suggest that short-term interventions that do not address cultural differences and employment practices are unlikely to improve citizen-expatriate manager relations. The attitudes and issues involved in the citizen-expatriate relationship are the product of complex historical, cultural, organizational and political forces. The organization alone cannot change them.

What is needed is a broad, long-term, collective effort in which government, educational and corporate leaders join in creating a systematic procedure for the development and integration of citizen managers. The objective should be to develop appropriate relationships and teamwork among expatriate and citizen managers while simultaneously preparing citizens to assume full responsibility in their employing organizations. To accomplish this, a partnership of government manpower-control agencies, local education authorities and corporate managements must lay down a coherent strategy that considers the interests of all stakeholders, one that all can support. At a minimum, such a strategy needs to include the following action components:

The setting of targets, timetables and standards. Working together, employers and cooperating agencies should agree upon the number of local managers to be trained, selection and evaluation criteria, and training objectives and standards.

Identification of all pertinent resources. Cooperating groups should evaluate and pool the educational expertise, materials and facilities available to them.

Involvement of the right people. Not every expatriate manager is a good trainer and coach. Not every local employee who wants to be a manager is a good prospect. In both instances, candidate screening must consider not only managerial skill and potential, but attitudes and motives.

Getting the expectations straight. The responsible organizations should clarify the objectives and roles of expatriate managers and their local citizen understudies. Expatriate managers must understand that they are expected to work themselves out of a job; understudies must be willing to invest the necessary time to learn and advance.

Building in the right rewards. If a company wants to demonstrate commitment to local indigenization policy, it must reward expatriate managers who develop their subordinates and then make sure these managers can and *do* leave for greener pastures elsewhere.

Use of the right training methods and materials. Work force training will soon be one of America's greatest exports. To date, however, there is little information available to guide prospective Third World users of Western training models and materials in their selection and application. Indeed, the authors' experience suggests that many of these learning materials are being misrepresented and that without varying degrees of modification are not suitable for use in developing countries. Let the buyer beware of vendors, trainers and consultants claiming universal applicability for their products and services without even attempting to evaluate the needs of the local client or to assess the impact of cultural differences on their use.

Open discussion of indigenization policy. Built into the program, such discussions will serve to remind all parties of their respective obligations.

Promotion of the understudies and encouragement of learning from experience. Employers must be prepared to promote local understudies to full-fledged management positions within a reasonable period of time and then absorb their early mistakes. Their former mentors may remain as temporary coaches, but they must be gradually withdrawn.

Conclusion

Effective service management requires a high level of manager teamwork and goodwill. Traditional corporate employment practices and government indigenization policies have tended to worsen relations already strained by cultural differences. Traditional management training is clearly not the antidote to citizen-expatriate manager polarization. A broader-based, longer-term strategy is called for.

We do not claim that the above-proposed components constitute a comprehensive strategy for managing the citizen-expatriate interface and related development process. We do believe, however, that commitment to their substance would go a long way toward resolving major problems.

Labor Relations, Culture and Service

by

Renaldo Flores

Labor relations, organizational conflict and cultural clashes are challenges which service managers must continually address since these problems pose a threat to service quality. The environment of international service is undergoing rapid change as this segment of the economy gains in importance. Service managers feel the pressures not only of increasing competition and rising consumer expectations but of internal changes in employee expectations, management-labor relations and cultural differences as well. Even on their home turf, managers' ability to meet these challenges is a moot point. In unfamiliar settings it must be seriously questioned. This article examines labor relations and cultural issues as they affect expatriate tourism managers in my home culture, Puerto Rico.

In Puerto Rico we didn't really begin to plan or develop an infrastructure for tourism until after the Castro Revolution in Cuba in 1958. When Cuba closed its doors to tourism, Puerto Rico was suddenly an alternative Caribbean destination. As a territory of the United States, we offered the political and social stability that was missing in many other Caribbean destinations. But the problems that we faced were enormous. We did not have people trained in the service industry, so we took them off their farms and sugar and coffee plantations and converted them into bartenders, waiters, cooks, and maids. But these people, who had never worked in industry before, were fertile ground for the work of labor organizing campaigns, and, before management knew what was happening, they found themselves forced to negotiate with aggressive new labor leaders.

Evolution of Labor Relations in Puerto Rico

The Western historical and cultural heritage of Puerto Rico dates back to its discovery in the late fifteenth century. A colony of Spain for four centuries, the island's language is Spanish, its religion predominantly Catholic, and its cultural heritage heavily influenced by its connection with Spain. Though the island is linked politically to the United States, our work ethic, ways of doing things, family life, education and social relations are very different. Therefore, when people of these two distinct cultures meet and work together, there is often a direct confrontation between their differing perceptions, beliefs and attitudes.

Puerto Rico became an American territory as a result of the Spanish-American War in 1898. While there is some debate about the nature and desirability of Puerto Rico's unique political relationship with the United States, there is virtually no doubt in anyone's mind in Puerto Rico that there exist very significant cultural and social differences. These distinctions are also present in our work environment and in labor relations.

The organized labor movement in the U.S. emphasizes the obtainment of economic and social benefits for its members, and, with a few exceptions, is not greatly influenced by political ideology even though it tries to exercise political influence. The labor movement in Puerto Rico is different. While we do have labor unions that follow the pattern of their counterparts in the United States and strive exclusively for economic gains for their members, we also have unions strongly influenced by socialist ideology. These unions, though setting as their immediate objectives better salaries and working conditions, also promote class consciousness among their members for ideological reasons.

The Puerto Rican labor movement has been identified with politics since the early part of the twentieth century. Even though certain labor associations existed before the turn of the century, it was not until the arrival of the Spanish socialist (and father of the organized labor movement in Puerto Rico), Santiago Iglesias Pantin, that organized labor as we know it today emerged. To understand why the early stages of Puerto Rico's labor movement took a political direction, the reader needs to understand the circumstances under which Puerto Rico's attachment to the United States was forged.

For a short period of time prior to the Spanish-American War, Puerto Rico had obtained, through years of negotiations and hardship, political and social autonomy. By becoming a territory of the United States, we lost that autonomy and were subject to absolute military rule. At the same time, however, the military assumed a tolerant attitude towards the labor movement, allowing it to develop according to ideological tenets pervasive in the United States. This attitude motivated Santiago Iglesias to look at North America as both an economic and political model for the labor movement in Puerto Rico and to accept a close linkage between the two countries. The result of his policies, however, was a division within his own union between those who supported him and those who opposed Puerto Rico being closely associated with or, indeed, a part of the United States.

One result of this early division in the labor movement—which is reflected in Puerto Rican society to this day—and of its ideological orientation appears in Puerto Rican politics. Here, the Popular Democratic Party, which came into being in the late 1930s, adopted labor's program. Using the slogan, "Bread, Land and Liberty," the party achieved complete political control in 1952 under the leadership of Luis Munoz Marin, who became governor at that time.

The result was the weakening of the labor movement (only 6 percent of the Puerto Rican labor force was unionized) but at the same time the provision of significant protection and benefits to laborers in such areas, for instance, as maternity and sick leave, paid vacations and severance pay.

On the other hand, while the unionized labor force was small—and frequently aggressive, pursuing its goals through intimidation and violence—it was disproportionately strong in the tourist and hotel industries in Puerto Rico.

During the 1950s and 1960s the hotel industry in Puerto Rico blossomed in a typically disorganized and ill-planned manner. Hotels were built on the beaches with little or no zoning restrictions, and a steady flow of tourists came to the island and were willing to pay whatever price was necessary to get a quiet room in a peaceful setting where they could enjoy the Caribbean sun. Management during that period was not willing to risk difficulties with labor and, therefore, gave way to whatever demands the unions made in regard to salaries and fringe benefits. Management even forfeited to the union some managerial rights such as making certain operational decisions, maintaining discipline, and recruiting. As a result of these management decisions, 42 percent of the hotel employee's basic salary today is determined by contract obligations and legislative mandate.

The labor situation is aggravated by cultural issues. Expatriate managers can make little headway against disadvantageous labor arrangements as long as they are insensitive to the cultural patterns of Puerto Rican society.

Managing Culture in the Service Industry

In my years of experience I have seen many North American hospitality managers earn the love and respect of Puerto Rican workers by taking the time to understand our cultural and social environment. At the same time, I have seen executives of great technical competence literally bang their heads against a cultural wall and wind up only creating antagonism and rejection, even to the extent that the workers have actively endeavored to make the executive look bad. The formula for failure is simple: attempt to manage with the attitude of "I come from a place where things are done right and, therefore, these people have to learn to do things my way—which is the most cost-efficient and productive." Efficiency and effectiveness are two concepts that many managers who come to Puerto Rico believe are synonymous. This approach just does not work on the island. To win over a Puerto Rican, you must make him or her feel that you are—as we say in Spanish—*buena gente*, which translates into "a nice person." If we perceive that an executive is not *buena gente*, his or her problems begin.

Puerto Ricans are basically warm and sociable. We smile and will move heaven and earth for someone whom we like. Any person will receive love and loyalty from our people if he or she will express the same warmth and sociability by offering a hearty "good morning" and a smile to each member of the staff, by taking a few seconds to ask an employee, "How's the family?" and by shaking hands with everyone in sight from the front office manager to the dishwasher. The executive who sits down in the employees' cafeteria, eats one of our local dishes, and tries to speak Spanish (even though it may sound completely ridiculous) will win over the staff. But these efforts have to be sincere attempts to adapt to the rhythm and style of life on the island. On the other hand, the executive who feels that the island and its people are underdeveloped and who continuously reminds us of that will undoubtedly have difficulty in being effective. This does not mean that managers cannot create changes here. On the contrary, Puerto Rico's ability to change and adapt to different situations has created a society which enjoys the best standard of living in the Western Hemisphere outside of North America. In just twenty years Puerto Rico has made a drastic change from an economy based on agriculture to one based on manufacturing and industry. But we do not like to be told that we have to do things a certain way. We do respect and will respond to two-way communication but not to being talked at or to unilateral decision making. Even though a company may survive with that kind of organizational culture, its effectiveness will suffer. In the hospitality industry, such an organization will not be able to maintain the level of service quality necessary to remain viable.

The only way to obtain quality service is to have quality people who sincerely enjoy their work and feel some loyalty toward the organization.

Cultural Management and Labor Relations

These national or cultural characteristics of Puerto Ricans have an effect on labor relations. For instance, even though they know that they work for an organization, the perception of the Puerto Rican staff is that it works for a particular manager or person. The workers will feel loyalty directly to that person and will strive not to let him or her down. On the

141

other side of the coin, they will react negatively towards a specific manager who behaves poorly and will not necessarily blame the corporation for whatever problems are involved. In the light of these attitudes and behaviors, the importance and role of the unions is thrown into doubt. If employees feel that they can go to management (a person), be heard and have their problems solved or receive a reasonable explanation, those employees will not feel they have much use for a union.

Most expatriate managers concerned with labor relations in Puerto Rico do not distinguish between dealing with the union as an organization and dealing with the employees—who are not necessarily an active part of the union. They take the position—now that the era of giving in to unions is past—that "unions are bad for business and, therefore, management must not give in to them." They fail to realize that a poor management-labor climate is largely the product of one cardinal sin—not listening to employees. As a personnel director, when I deal with a grievance, my main function is as an intermediary between the employee and the supervisor. I become a facilitator of the bilateral communication process that supposedly should exist between the parties. This process becomes more dramatic and tense when dealing with a manager from outside Puerto Rico. Not only are expatriates often unwilling to understand this process, they may even be unwilling to sit down and talk, so certain is the individual that he or she is right. The arrogance of being the truth bearer in any cultural or social environment invites conflict. Therefore, the problem that we personnel directors face is how to balance and minimize the tension that will be created when the attitude of "my way is the best way" meets the attitude of "we have been doing our jobs *our* way for the past ten (fifteen, twenty) years and no one is going to make us change our behavior without our consent." In the long run, the latter attitude will prevail because of aggressive union activism and local labor legislation. The expatriate manager must flex or lose.

Facts of Life

Under these circumstances, some very talented expatriates become discouraged, angry, and resentful and have gone home—to the social and organizational environments where they feel comfortable and where they believe they can accomplish their personal and professional goals. On the other hand, executives who try to understand their culturally different subordinates, who are not hasty in making judgments, and who build upon the positive attributes of the local culture to obtain desired changes and behavioral modifications will get results.

Labor unions in the hospitality industry are a fact of life in Puerto Rico, as they are in most countries. A local government that historically maintains a paternalistic, protective attitude towards the worker is also a fact of life in Puerto Rico. However, it is also true that a work force can be efficient, effective and productive, even if its members don't adhere to the Protestant work ethic. An expatriate manager who comes to an unfamiliar culture and tries to understand the dynamics of the locale will have a far better chance of succeeding than one who foolishly tries to change hundreds of years of history and cultural tradition.

Photo courtesy of Hilton International

Chapter 6

CUSTOMER CONTACT

Chapter 6 examines the service environment at close range, focusing on the interaction of service provider and consumer face to face, through the printed word, and over the air waves.

In "Extending Service: Sheraton Woos the Japanese Traveller," former Director of Training, Carol Sage, offers a firsthand account of one hotel's successful effort to attract *and maintain* a foreign market. Sage's description of the joint marketing and training initiative that sent revenues from Japanese business soaring up more than 250 percent in a mere two years holds valuable lessons for any service organization.

Customer contact takes on new meaning when conceptualized as occurring in a cultural meeting place. Gerald Glover, Germaine Shames and Harris Friedman, in their article, "Service Environment as a Cultural Meeting Place," present the findings of a nationwide tourism study that spotlights culture's impact on the outcome of the service experience. Based on their research, the authors argue for responsive social systems and offer workable recommendations for facilitating the interaction of hosts and guests.

"Kahala Magic" by Gerald Glover explores the influence of guest-employee bonding in the long-term success of a resort. Repeat guests, many of whom spend as much as two or three months each year at the Kahala Hilton, and employees with years of service at the hotel were interviewed, with some striking findings. The author suggests how resorts anywhere can create an "aloha" service environment.

Dante Laudadio, in "Service Spoken Here," describes the important relationships among communication, culture, and service. He provides illustrations of the need for increased awareness of the influence of communication in service environments.

Finally, versatile anthropologist and broadcast journalist, James Lett, tells readers "How to Deal with the News Media." By understanding the culture of broadcast media, Lett contends, service managers may use television as a public relations arm of the organization. The author uses contrasting case studies and a two-headed turtle to colorfully illustrate his argument.

Extending Service: Sheraton Woos the Japanese Traveller

by

Carol Sage

A 1987 *Newsweek* cover article titled "Why is Service So Bad?" sparked national reflection on how Americans extend service. The article generated particular concern within the hospitality industry. We hear too often of surly front desk clerks, belligerent waiters, and service employees ignorant of their product and seemingly indifferent to the customer. Some customers may resign themselves to such treatment; others will turn to the competition.

In the hotel industry, the competition is increasingly foreign. Fine companies like the French Novotel and the Japanese Nikko International are vying for the markets. Hotel guests too are increasingly foreign. Canadians, Japanese and Europeans make up a significant proportion of many U.S. commercial and resort hotels' market mix.

U.S. hotel companies face a dual challenge: the need to respond to direct competition on their own turf from outstanding foreign counterparts and the need to attract and keep culturally different customers. Pressed to gain an "edge," many enlightened hoteliers are looking to culture management.

Meet the Public

As director of training of Sheraton's City Center Hotel in midtown Manhattan, I became accustomed to the challenges of helping a multicultural workforce serve a multicultural clientele. Telephone SOSs, like the following from an engineering department employee, were part of my daily routine:

> "I've got a Chinese guest in 608 who is upset about his room. Can you call him?"

"Why did you call *me?*"
"Well, I know that you've been to China and you're interested in their culture. I thought you could handle it."

Now, I don't speak Chinese, and although I do enjoy learning about Chinese culture, I'm sure the engineer or guest service agent could help a Chinese guest just as well as I might. For many Americans, however, dealing with a foreigner seems disconcerting. An unfamiliar language, custom, or appearance is to them unwieldy. Often, rather than make the extra effort, they will pass the task off on someone else who, though no better qualified to extend the service, feels less threatened by it.

Clearly, hotel employees require additional training in serving the culturally different guest if a hotel is to maintain its standards of service while tapping nondomestic markets. At Sheraton, management has determined to take a two-fold approach:

1. Foster employee cultural self-awareness and sensitivity

2. Teach employees about the hotel's customers, highlighting cultural differences

Training for World-Class Service

Sheraton's first intercultural training program was implemented in New York in 1984, to coincide with an aggressive campaign to attract the burgeoning Japanese travel market. Working closely with the hotel's Japanese sales manager, a program was designed to equip employees to meet the special needs of Japanese guests in order to improve the guests' service experience and, thus, solidify this important client base.

As with any systematic training effort, this one began with a needs assessment. We pinpointed employee perceptions as the most important factor influencing service delivery. We reasoned that how employees perceived themselves vis a vis the Japanese guest would shape their attitudes and predispose them to behaviors which would either help or hinder service.

Analysis of the findings of a recent employee opinion survey told us much about employee self-perceptions. We had included, as one of the demographic variables, the question, "Do you have a New York mentality?" Many employees responded quite definitely one way or the other. This was a first step in identifying employees' cultural affiliations and helped trainees lead the group toward cultural self-awareness.

We then spoke to the employees who had been serving our Japanese guests. A frequent comment (one we were to learn was telling though not true) was, "The Japanese are always happy—they smile a lot."

One observant coffee shop waitress commented, "Sometimes they leave their food untouched. I remember one Japanese fellow who just stared at his eggs and poked them around with his fork. He looked kind of unhappy. When I asked him if anything was wrong, he said, 'No.' But I noticed his eggs looked a little runny, so I offered to take them back to the kitchen and have them cooked a little more. He started thanking me. And when I brought those eggs back, he ate every last bite. Why don't they just complain or something!"

A room attendant noted, "They're real nice people and always polite. But, come to think of it, they seem pretty shy when they're alone. Most of the time they keep together, a whole bunch of them."

The next stop was the security department. "The Japanese have a tendency to leave their bags in the lobby and walk around," one guard said. "They're unbelievable. Don't they know this is New York City! Are they crazy!"

Similar impressions were gathered from clerks, managers, and bellmen. Most considered the Japanese traveller to be quite undemanding and easily pleased.

We then checked these impressions against actual statistics made available to us by the New York Marketing Office of New Otani Hotels. Contrary to employee perceptions, the Japanese hotel guest actually has higher expectations of service than an American guest. Indeed, service heads their list of hotel priorities. Contrast this with the priorities of U.S. clientele (see table).

We concluded from our needs assessment that, although it appeared to our employees that our Japanese guests were satisfied with our product and service, there was indeed room for improvement. We recommended to management that an intensive training program be implemented among guest-contact staff. Our plan was approved, and we proceeded.

Implementing the Program

To design and conduct the training program, we formed a team made up of two members of the training department, the Japanese sales manager and an outside consultant (although American, the consultant had lived in Tokyo, spoke Japanese, and had considerable intercultural training experience). We also hired two Japanese part-time employees to work in a dual capacity: during the training sessions, they would sit in and keep us on track; afterwards, they would work at the front desk as guest service agents.

Then we structured the program. In order to pool a variety of experiences, we formed departmentally mixed participant groups. We scheduled four sessions—to coincide with the arrival dates of major Japanese tour groups.

Session One: Looking at Ourselves

To heighten employee awareness of their own cultural idiosyncracies and of the traveller's experience in a foreign country, we asked participants, "If you were a foreigner coming to the United States for the first time, what would Americans and New Yorkers look like to you?" Employees compiled and discussed lists of physical and behavioral traits, which were then contrasted with the responses of our Japanese advisors.

The traits named for Americans were markedly different from those for New Yorkers. Americans were seen as friendly, loud, funny, casual and blonde, with big feet; New Yorkers, on the other hand, were seen as rude, loud, always in a hurry, more formal, and dark-haired. Group discussion was very lively, and many attendees remarked that this was the first time they had ever looked at themselves in a "cultural mirror."

Session Two: Looking at Another Culture

We then lead the group through various exercises focusing on cultural differences. One person would read a statement, such as, "In some cultures, it is perfectly natural to have long periods of silence between people." We would then personalize the statement for the participants and ask them to react to it. Building on the foregoing statement, we might have asked a waitress, "If you were having dinner with someone who barely spoke to you, how would you feel?" "Awful!" she would probably have replied. "I would feel like I have to fill up the dead air." We would then explain that, in Japan, silence is the norm and not at all uncomfortable for members of that culture. We would explain why this might be so and then contrast it with the corresponding cultural norm in the U.S. Finally, we would lead a discussion on how this cultural difference might affect employee interactions with our Japanese guests.

In like manner, we addressed the topics of emotional display, group harmony and indirectness. Some of the participants found the differences in values difficult to accept, but all came away with a better understanding of why we never received complaints from our Japanese guests.

HOTEL GUEST PRIORITIES: JAPANESE VS U.S.

Japanese guests value...

1) personal service/good employee attitude
2) location
3) price
4) security (as theft and assault are only minor concerns in Japan, this item may refer largely to freedom from annoyance by prostitutes and other undesirables)
5) room condition
6) health and function facilities

U.S. guests value...

1) room (including cleanliness, comfortable beds, and amenities)
2) security (from theft and assault)
3) service/employee attitude
4) location
5) price
6) facilities

Session Three: Basics of the Japanese Language

Our Japanese consultant introduced us to the sounds and rhythm of the Japanese language and taught us some simple phrases of welcome that would make our guests feel at home. He also demonstrated common physical gestures and explained their meaning.

Employees left this session better able to communicate with the Japanese guest verbally and nonverbally.

Session Four: Service Role Plays

The final session consisted of a series of realistic and provocative role plays. Included were situations like the following:

- You are a front desk clerk checking in a Japanese guest who has no credit card. You ask for cash in advance, and he doesn't understand why you can't trust his word. How would you handle the situation?

- You are a bellman standing in the lobby, and you see some Japanese tourists leave their cameras and luggage in the corner while they go off to the lounge. What would you do?

Employees rotated through the roles of guest, coworkers and self. Everyone offered suggestions for handling the situations portrayed and practiced using the Japanese phrases they had learned in the previous session. Each course participant was evaluated, and, since more Japanese tour groups were on the way, we all geared up for action.

The Big Moment

When the groups arrived, service did not miraculously change, but there was a heightened awareness and sensitivity, which our guests noticed and acknowledged in letters of appreciation and increased business. Relations with Japanese tour operators improved significantly, and we received highly favorable press coverage in *Nihon Keizai Shinbum*, a major Japanese financial newspaper. The bottom line is that our Japanese clientele grew 250 percent from 1984 to 1986.

Building on Success

Our first intercultural training initiative proved so fruitful that management decided to make this type of training a permanent feature of our in-house training program. We accomplished this by creating the "International Ambassador" series, monthly discussion sessions offering insights into serving others of our culturally different customers. Two particularly animated sessions dealt with our Italian and Chinese clients. The first included a speech by an Italian tour operator discussing the needs of her clients. Many attendees were surprised to learn that Italians often find a visit to the U.S. frustrating and even frightening. A sales manager from Inter-Pacific Tours addressed the differences and similarities between the Chinese and American traveller, and showed a slide presentation of the People's Republic of China. Attendees were encouraged to examine their culturally colored perceptions of the Chinese and to learn to differentiate among Far Eastern peoples.

Japanese language classes have also become an integral part of our in-house training program. They are held twice weekly and tailored to each department. While our coffee shop employees are learning to say, *irrashaimase* ("welcome") and *motto ikaga desuka?* ("how about some more?"), our operators are mastering *denwa bangoo o onegaishimasu* ("the number, please") and *denwa o kitte kudasai* ("please hang up"). These

152

classes get a high priority. It is important that our guests enjoy their meals and use the telephone painlessly, and we want to offer a service that our competition lacks. The classes have, therefore, been made a job requirement for guest-contact employees.

Costs

Considering the results, the program's expense has been nominal. Initially, my budget ran to $780 to train 250 employees (or roughly three dollars per employee). The program's continuation has averaged four-hundred dollars per month for translation services, instructors' fees and supplies.

As the results have become apparent, the purse strings for intercultural training have loosened. Sheraton recently sponsored the production of the Going International film series, "Valuing Diversity"—a ten-thousand-dollar investment.

Reactions

Let me share with you how our employees have reacted to intercultural training. Frankly, not all were initially "sold" on the effort. One waiter insisted, "I don't want to go to Japanese class; I treat everyone the same. I'm always polite to all our guests, and I don't see a need to change just for them." It's true that he tries to be helpful to our guests. We decided not to push him. After three classes, however, much to my surprise, he came in, sat down, and took an active part in the class. A coworker of his has never missed a class, even though it means commuting almost an hour to attend on her days off. Another devotee was the first to take an entire meal order in Japanese, a feat for which she received a hundred-dollar award from the hotel's Quality Committee. Her success and subsequent recognition have encouraged other employees to stick with it.

Managers, too, differ in the importance they attach to such training, but skeptics are fast becoming advocates. It is difficult to deny the need for intercultural training when your lobby is packed with Japanese, Italian and Chinese tour groups. And, after all, if we don't learn how to serve them, the competition will!

What Can Be Learned from Sheraton's Experience?

A 250 percent increase in a targeted market over a two-year period is no modest accomplishment. There must be a lesson or two here for other companies who aspire to enter a challenging new market. I would underline the following:

- Link the marketing effort with training of guest-contact staff. The sales manager and training director should work closely together to ascertain the needs of different market segments and equip employees to meet those needs. Make sure the training effort keeps pace with the penetration of new markets.

- Tailor the training to immediate use. Create awareness first, but move along to service specifics and real-life situations while employee interest is still high. Reward employees when they apply their learnings to improve the service experiences of their culturally different customers.

One of the most important things we can do for our organization is to foster empathy among its members. Once we're able to recognize and accept cultural differences, we're ready to take on the competition, a new market, or the world!

The Service Environment as a Cultural Meeting Place

by

Gerald Glover, Germaine W. Shames, and Harris Friedman

The general manager of a deluxe resort in the Caribbean once invited us to join him for lunch. After meeting him in his office and exchanging greetings, he confided that he was experiencing serious problems in one of the resort's restaurants. "No one will do what they are told. Most of the service staff are hostile to *everyone* with whom they come into contact. Morale is low, and, not surprisingly, guest complaints are sky high!" He went on to relate measures he had taken to remedy the situation: everything from training to firing both employees and managers. Nothing seemed to work.

We proceeded to the restaurant in question to have lunch. No sooner had we arrived at the entrance than a well-groomed and courteous native waiter welcomed us warmly and hospitably showed us to a table. He seated us, recited the day's specials from memory, and assured us he would return immediately to fill our water glasses. A touch of nervousness notwithstanding, this waiter was a very model of service. In disbelief, we turned to our friend for an explanation. "We thought you had problems here. Our waiter seems to have a great attitude and goes to extremes to provide good service. How do you account for him?" Sadly, the general manager responded, "He just started today. He hasn't had time to learn to be like all the rest of them."

We left that luncheon with the conviction that *service—good or bad— is a function of how the people expected to provide the service are organized into social systems.* In other words, that waiter had just been hired into a system and was faced with two choices: to conform to the prevailing negative culture or continue to deliver good service despite pressures to conform. Service providers *learn* to have attitudes and skills which result in happy or unhappy experiences for consumers. Our theory was confirmed when, several weeks later, the aforementioned waiter was observed to be discourteous and much less service-conscious.

155

This story is just one of many indicators we have encountered in our work which point to the need for *culture management* within the service industry. While working in The Bahamas, we began to form a cultural perspective on service management that drew upon our social science background and cast traditional management practice in a new—and not entirely favorable—light. With the support of The Bahamas' Ministry of Tourism, the Hotel Training Council, and industry leaders, we conducted a study of service within the nation's important tourism sector. This article summarizes some of the findings of that research and suggests an approach to formulating a culturally attuned business strategy for the delivery of world-class service.

The Study

The intent of the research was to investigate and suggest remedies for the so-called "attitude problem" of Bahamians working in the tourism industry. Industry executives were frequently heard to express displeasure with the service provided by hotel and restaurant employees. A Bahamian colleague, Michael Smith—the executive director of the Bahamas Hotel Training College—shared our contention that the "attitude problem" was the result of cultural influences operating in the service environment. We did not accept the conventional wisdom that Bahamians were necessarily the cause of the problem, and we were determined to uncover the true picture through a nationwide attitude- and product-evaluation study.

Research Design

Our primary goal was to create a data base for investigating this issue. We recognized early on that we were serving two masters: academicians who would examine our methods and question the study's validity and industry leaders who would expect workable answers to their day-to-day operating problems. Pleasing both would require a scientifically sound investigation leading to implementable recommendations.

The research was also logistically challenging. As The Bahamas is actually seven hundred islands—some more accessible than others—we decided to focus on six islands which were representative of the various aspects of Bahamian tourism. On these six islands, we selected twenty hotels of different sizes, price categories, and types of ownership from which to draw our survey population.

Our initial intent was to concentrate on in-depth interviews with a sample of tourists, industry managers and employees. As the scope of our project grew, however, we incorporated questionnaires as well.

Expectations

We expected our data would provide answers to three key questions:

1. Was the attitude problem a reflection of Bahamian workers' displeasure with performing jobs in organizations which were usually extensions of international corporations?

2. Did the management approach of those organizations lack cultural sensitivity, and, if so, did this factor contribute to the attitude problem?

3. How did guests perceive the attitude problem, and what effect— if any—did it have on guest satisfaction?

We further expected that the answers to these questions would convince tourism officials and businesspeople to take a fresh approach to the problem. Our intention was to help them reconceptualize the service environment as a cultural meeting place, a complex milieu of social interactions where, at any given time, various cultures are in contact. The study would, we hoped, demonstrate that *solving the attitude problem meant understanding and managing this cultural meeting place.*

The Human Element

Certain commonalities emerged among members of each population group.

Managers were generally expatriates or Bahamians who behaved as expatriates—that is, regardless of their country of origin, they behaved the way products of European and North American schools of service management behave. Even the Bahamians were often perceived as outsiders in the organization and in the community as well.

Employees were nearly all Bahamian, with strong feelings of both personal and national pride. Their parents had fished or farmed, and they were the first generation to make beds for and serve drinks to tourists (economic development through tourism came abruptly in the 1960s and 1970s). Some Bahamians saw in tourism the opportunity for a better life but resented foreigners controlling their access to it.

Guests were often first-time visitors to The Bahamas. Their expectations mirrored the carefree, picture-perfect image conveyed by glossy brochures and full-page ads. Their behavior in The Bahamas was often less inhibited and responsible than it might be back home, and they were sometimes perceived as pushy by the Bahamian employees who worked in the resorts, stores, taxis and airlines.

Attitudes

As mentioned, the study focused on attitudes. We believe that values and attitudes predetermine the behavior of all parties to the customer-employee interaction, which is the essence of service. While values are at the root of this alchemy, they are often out of awareness. Attitudes are relatively accessible to the researcher and provide a point of intervention for changing the behavior that dictates the outcome of the service experience.

Findings

Results indicated that there were indeed social and cultural influences operating in the service environment which were affecting the tourism product. Analysis of the data revealed important trends and relationships which brought the idea of tourism as a cultural meeting place into sharper focus.

Corporate Culture and Management Practices

The corporate culture and management practices of Bahamian hotels and resorts appeared to have an important influence on the attitude problem of service staff (see table 1 for a summary of responses to questions concerning "the way things are done"—and managed—taken from a sampling of staff members at twenty resorts).

Employee dissatisfaction and alienation from the company they were working for was apparently a contributing factor to poor service and attitudes. Poor management-labor relations (84 percent desiring a change), lack of cooperation (67 percent did not feel staff cooperated), management insensitivity (71 percent stated managers needed training to understand workers), and unclear or vague expectations of employees by management (60 percent claimed they were not given clear orders) were indicators of a service environment which gave Bahamian employees few reasons to have positive attitudes concerning their jobs and little motivation to serve guests properly.

In addition almost half of the employees did not believe or trust management's intentions (47 percent felt managers were not interested in their welfare) and thought that the operation of the hotel could be improved

(42 percent would make many changes and 53 percent felt management ignored problems). The lack of confidence in existing management was also an indication of strong feelings of dissatisfaction and alienation among Bahamians working in the service environments.

The staff attitudes revealed by this survey shed light on the dilemma suggested by our opening vignette. In such a low-trust, low-affiliation culture, it is hardly surprising that employees taught new employees how to do their jobs non-productively, whom to like and dislike, and how to interact with the customers. Management's efforts were apparently misguided and only served to strengthen the hostile employee-generated social system. Specifically, labor-management relations were strained, "we/they" distinctions between managers and employees were readily apparent, consensus and participation were not encouraged in setting work standards, and the managers were using skills and techniques to deal with employees that were not adaptive in the setting. In response to those conditions, employees had developed a counter-culture which gave them protection in a difficult working environment.

In hindsight, five years after the study was conducted, we are led to conclude that these problems of employee dissatisfaction are not unique to The Bahamas. Because the predominant model for managing the service environment is reactive and has its roots in the "rational" school of management, it is not surprising to find that many employees in New York City, San Juan, Caracas, or Athens are equally unhappy in service environments. Corporate culture is closely tied to management philosophy and practices in all service organizations. When that culture and management are not supportive of employees, the following influences are typically present:

- Expatriate-native competition and conflict or social class gaps between organizational levels
- Autocratic, insensitive managers
- An orientation to efficiency at the expense of effectiveness in operations
- One-way (top to bottom) communication
- Tendency to relieve the symptoms of problems rather than to solve them—or to ignore them altogether
- Failure of managers to appreciate the relationship between satisfied employees and good service

Our research may have focused on the culture of Bahamian tourism in 1981, but the results have implications for service environments everywhere. Managers learn perceptions of natives, employees, and unions from a peer culture whose members have traditionally reacted to management situations instead of adapting with a proactive style to the socioecological setting in which the business operates. World-class service requires a departure from traditional management practices. Creating a social system in which the new waiter in our story would have been encouraged to continue his positive approach is a challenge to all service managers.

TABLE 1
Corporate Culture and Management Practice

Frequency	Staff Responses
84%	A change in management-labor relations is needed.
71%	Managers need training in how to understand workers' needs.
67%	Staff do not cooperate well together.
60%	Management does not give clear orders or reveal expectations.
53%	Problems at the hotel are ignored by management.
47%	Management is not interested in their welfare.
42%	Staff would "make many changes" in the hotel if they were in charge.
40%	Employment and promotion practices are unfair.
30%	Criticism is the only type of feedback experienced.
25%	Managers are not effective motivators.

Host-Guest Interactions

The interaction of the Bahamian employee and the tourist was another area of investigation which revealed possible influences on the attitude problem (see table 2 for a summary of notable results concerning this interaction).

Although The Bahamas is an English-speaking former colony of Britain and many tourists come from North America and Britain, both guest and staff responses indicated that perceived cultural differences among them are quite pronounced.

Bahamian employees had preferences for serving tourists which were based on the nationality and cultural background of the tourist. Canadians, white Americans, and Germans were clearly the tourists preferred by Bahamian hotel and resort employees as persons they liked to serve. Least preferred were black American, British, Latin American, and French tourists.

We attempted to better understand the clear preferences cited by Bahamians by interviewing several Bahamian professionals. Canadians and white Americans, they explained, were the two largest groups of tourists, and they shared interests with the typical Bahamian worker, such as television programming, shopping in Miami and Fort Lauderdale, sports, and other culturally prescribed lifeways. Germans were not as easy to explain as preferred tourists. Perhaps they were preferred because they seldom interacted with the Bahamian service worker due to language difficulties.

Black Americans who visited The Bahamas were socially mobile, usually middle-class. Bahamians apparently resented black Americans because of the alleged patronizing manner in which they treated the staff. British tourists were not preferred, according to Bahamian staff, because they supposedly displayed "colonial" attitudes toward Bahamians, and they were often seen as symbols of colonial oppression.

TABLE 2
Host-Guest Interactions

Frequency	Staff and Guest Responses
	Hotel Guests
87%	Bahamian people are friendly, courteous (83%) and interesting (84%).
52%	They would probably not return to the same hotel (although the same sample of hotel guests responded positively regarding the courtesy (79%), helpfulness (80%), and efficiency (77%) of the hotel's staff).
	Staff
64%	Guests are sometimes difficult to serve.
60%	Bahamian customs and lifeways are not understood by guests.
56%	The customs and lifeways of guests are confusing.
46%	Social skills and cultural awareness training are needed more than technical skills.

Interactions between hosts and guests were apparently also influenced by a misunderstanding of customs: 64 percent of the staff felt guests were difficult to serve; 60 percent felt that guests did not understand Bahamians; and 56 percent felt guests' customs were confusing. Also, 46 percent of the staff felt social and cultural skills training was needed more than technical skills training (which received only an 11 percent vote).

Guest's responses revealed that they felt Bahamians working in their hotel were courteous (79 percent), helpful (80 percent), and efficient (77 percent). These guests, however, often stated they would not return to the same hotel (52 percent). Additional evidence of the guest's positive regard for Bahamians in the general community was also found: a large proportion of the guests felt Bahamians in the community to be friendly (87 percent), courteous (83 percent), and interesting (84 percent). These data appear to contradict those who argue that the "attitude" problem of Bahamians was the major reason for guest dissatisfaction and low return rates. Clearly, guests seem to have favorable impressions of Bahamian employees but less favorable impressions of the service environment at the hotel where they were staying. Also, it is somewhat misleading to assume that some of the response frequencies of guests regarding Bahamians (79, 80, 77 percent) working in the hotels are entirely favorable from a service quality perspective. Data such as these indicate that potentially one in five guests (21, 20, and 23 percent) did not think Bahamians were courteous, helpful, and efficient. Service quality cannot be measured by "bell curve" mentalities and approaches. Not very many hotel managers should be content to have one in five of their guests less than favorably impressed with service staff. We feel this unfavorable impression of employees was related to worker dissatisfaction.

The cultural differences between host and guest may have a critical influence on the satisfaction of each in the service environment. This is an area which certainly deserves more attention by managers as well as research by marketing professionals and academicians. For example, it is frequently stated by hospitality managers that Asian culture contributes significantly to the prevalence of high quality service in Asia. Conversely, people in certain other cultures are felt not to be as well suited for hospitality because of cultural predispositions. This question is one of many research possibilities which might provide profitable insights into the issues related to host-guest interaction in the service environment, particularly when the host, guest, and manager may have different cultural predispositions.

Design and Quality of the Tourism Product

Culture can be an important influence on the design and delivery of tourism products. Service, as a product involving social interaction, is evaluated by the consumer along culturally prescribed lines (see table 3 for our survey results related to these influences on the Bahamian tourism product).

Although Bahamian employees were very positive concerning tourism (92 percent felt that the local community benefited from it), they appeared not to want to change their culture (82 percent) and, in fact, felt that Bahamian culture was an asset. Eighty-eight percent preferred the use of Bahamian products instead of imported ones. Also, 70 percent felt a unique Bahamian tourism product should be developed. These results indicate that Bahamians were happy with tourism in their country but preferred it to reflect Bahamian culture.

Bahamian and guest responses to questions regarding product quality indicated an awareness of both design and quality problems. Forty percent of the staff felt that better quality service was needed and 33 percent said they would not stay at their hotel as a guest. Some guests felt the vacation was too expensive (53 percent), were unhappy with the facilities (34 percent), and were disappointed upon arrival (28 percent). Equally interesting was the fact that guests who decided to visit The Bahamas because of word-of-mouth information (32 percent) were almost as numerous as those influenced by travel agents (35 percent).

Implications of these results may be transferrable to destinations throughout the world. The central issue is this: should the approach to tourism be based on something other than a standardized, "rational" corporate model artificially imposed from some distant boardroom? How much of a tourist's motivations to visit a destination is based on a desire to experience a product different from what might be encountered elsewhere? Certainly many travelers to destinations such as China are strongly influenced by such a cultural interest. In The Bahamas the distinction may not be as clear-cut, but it is there.

Employees wanted tourism in their country to be something which had cultural relevance to them while meeting guests' needs. Tourists generally found Bahamians to be a pleasant part of the product. Although expatriate managers and Bahamian governmental officials cited Bahamian attitudes as the primary cause of tourist dissatisfaction (a 16 percent return visitor rate was reported for Nassau in 1980) and product quality problems, attitudes were apparently symptoms of more complex problems of corporate culture, management practices, host and guest cultural differences, and a failure to capitalize on Bahamian culture. Moreover, guest responses did not indicate that poor employee attitude was a primary factor in their decision not to return to the Bahamas.

Recommendations

Our recommendations made to Bahamian and expatriate tourism officials may have broad application for managing culture in the service environment.

TABLE 3
Design and Quality of the Tourism Product

Frequency **Staff and Guest Responses**
Staff

92% Tourism benefits the local community.

88% Bahamian products should be used in the hotel instead of imported products (food, straw goods, etc.).

82% The success of Bahamian tourism depends on learning more about guests' expectations, but without loss of Bahamian customs.

70% A unique Bahamian tourism product should be developed.

40% Better quality service is needed to improve the product.

33% They would not stay at the hotel where they worked if there were other opportunities.

28% Tourists are not receiving their "money's worth."

Guests

53% Their vacation was too expensive.

34% The facilities for tourism did not meet guests' expectations.

32% The decision to vacation in The Bahamas was made because of information (word-of-mouth) from friends and relatives (travel agents were cited by 35%).

28% Their experiences when first arriving in The Bahamas were disappointing.

Hotel Staff

We recommended that increased emphasis be given to creating conditions which predispose hotel staff to satisfy guest expectations. More specifically, we recommended the following steps, designed to provide management with a framework for new initiatives in culture management:

- A comprehensive program to encourage use of Bahamian products in the industry must be promoted.
- Hotel executives need to develop a managerial style which achieves high employee performance while being sensitive to local customs and needs.
- An industry-wide program to enhance staff knowledge and awareness of guests' countries and cultures should be established.

- A unique Bahamian tourist "product" which combines the best aspects of imported and domestic food, art, music, and recreation should be developed.
- Both management and union leadership should listen more carefully to the views of the workers and the expression of their needs.
- Each hotel management team should review the existing performance appraisal and communications procedures with the intent of improving management-employee relations.
- Training should be given a top priority in all hotels—with particular emphasis on standards of performance, management/supervisory competencies, social skills, and basic English.
- Product quality improvement programs which are responsive both to specific organizational characteristics and to guests' needs should be implemented in all hotels.

Hotel Guests

Although many guests had generally favorable attitudes toward the hotel product and Bahamian tourism, there were strong indications of dissatisfaction. We recommended the following actions to improve the situation reflected in the data:

- Each hotel management team should develop methods for obtaining daily information about guest satisfaction which can be used to ensure continual product improvement efforts.
- The amount of effort, resources, and incentives allocated to the purpose of assuring visitors' desire to return should be equal to that spent in getting them to come in the first place (i.e., internal marketing).
- Additional research should be conducted, both nationally and by individual hotels, to reduce the discrepancies between the images of The Bahamas projected by promotional activities and actual guest experiences.
- Programs should be initiated to make hotel guests feel at ease and happy about being in a society different from their own.
- The development of informal marketing networks, such as friends and relatives, should be given the same attention as that given to the more formal networks, such as travel agents. (Note the data indicating that word-of-mouth promotion equaled travel agent promotion in effectiveness.)

Did We Answer Our Research Questions?

Our findings provided support for our expectations regarding the three key questions posed in our research design. First, the attitude problem did appear to be influenced by a relatively high percentage of organization-related dissatisfaction among workers. Data indicate not only job dissatisfaction but also low trust levels of employees toward management (see table 1).

Regarding the second question related to management style, the findings support our contention that management style in the hotels tended to be insensitive to Bahamian culture and led to negative worker attitudes. For example, most employees felt managers needed training to better understand their workers' needs. Data also indicate the characteristics of typically reactive corporate cultures in the hotels (see table 1).

A third question (how guests perceived the attitude problem) was not as clearly answered in the data. Both guests' and employees' responses indicated a need for improved culture management in the service environment. Guest dissatisfaction, however, appeared more influenced by price and product quality than by Bahamians and their culturally influenced behaviors (see tables 2 and 3).

In Summary

Our research indicates that the manager cannot manage the service environment *without* managing the cultures in contact within it. By shaping an adaptive and responsive social system, the manager sets the stage for positive host-guest attitudes, satisfying service experiences, and repeat business.

Kahala Magic: Social Bonding and Its Influence on Successful Resort Operations

by

Gerald Glover

Several miles to the east of Waikiki, between Diamond Head and Coco Head, the Kahala Hilton has operated as a highly successful resort for over twenty-four years. Recognition of the resort's successful operation has been given in a variety of ways. "Life Styles of the Rich and Famous," a well-known television program, recently mentioned the Kahala Hilton as one of the ten best resorts in the world. More specifically, it is notable that 60 percent of the resort's guests are repeat visitors and operations have been consistently profitable for the past twenty years.

Kahala's magic is more than facts and statistics. In an era of highrises and mechanical service, the resort's physical setting and service are thought by many to be the standard for "how it should be done." Of course, everything at the Kahala Hilton is not perfect. Mishaps do happen as in other resorts. However, the service magic of the Kahala is what sets it apart from other resorts. During the past three years, with the cooperation of Louis Finnamore, Peter Forsythe, and Gaylynne Sakuda, I have used the anthropological method of participant observation to investigate the reasons behind the resort's success. Interviews with guests, employees, and executives at the Kahala revealed certain unexpected findings related to the influence of culture in successful service environments.

Kahala magic is not based on the supernatural. My investigation revealed that the Kahala's success is attributable to influences that are quite profane. These influences can be observed in the organizational culture and service environment of the resort. In fact they are long-standing elements of the social system, and their analysis can provide insights for bottom-line enhancement in any service business in which service providers and consumers have continual and/or frequent social interaction.

Ohana and Social Bonding

Observable in the Kahala Hilton culture are the two traditional Hawaiian values of *ohana* and *aloha*. These values are primary motivators for employees and managers and were frequently stated by guests as the reason why the service at the Kahala was superior to many other resorts, both in Hawaii and elsewhere.

Ohana is best described as the "family feeling" that was both reported and observed among service staff and guests. Social bonding has created an informal network of "old timers" among both employees and guests. Twenty-four years of interaction in the service environment has resulted in a feeling of a home away from home for a group of approximately fifty families who spend the winter months at the resort. Equally important to the development of ohana has been the fact that one-half of the employees have ten years' or more service with the property. This combination of long-term employees and guest families has served to bond those persons by repeated interaction and social contact. Loyal employees and loyal guests expect more than a luxury room or beautiful beach or gourmet dinner at the Kahala Hilton—they expect to meet with each other. Also, bonding among long-term employees provides for a potentially more effective service delivery system. The hotel managers exert considerable effort to maintain social bonding among employees. In addition to providing a stable and hospitable work environment, they organize numerous programs, ceremonies, and employee get-togethers to permit employees the opportunity to play, as well as work, together. Employee-to-employee, employee-to-guest, and guest-to-guest bonding create harmony in the service environment and long-term relationships.

Mr. Chu, a manager of twenty-four years, is a focal point of interest in the lobby. He knows almost every guest by name and in many cases has been an influence on their lives. One guest, a male in his twenties, considers Mr. Chu as something of an authority figure. He explained that his family has been coming there for years and that Mr. Chu kept him in line during his childhood and teen years.

Another guest described her and her husband's affection for a Kahala housekeeping employee who brings them cookies from her home during every visit. Other guests have entertained employees in their own homes in Seattle or London when the *employee* was on vacation. Numerous other employees and guests correspond between visits to Hawaii. These examples are just a few of the many stated by guests regarding their affection for Kahala employees. The ohana feeling can also be found in hotel executives who give high priority to the maintenance of this social network and consider the subsequent social bonding that ocurs in the Kahala service environment as similar in ways to an extended family system.

Aloha and Corporate Influences

Aloha is Hawaii. In many circles the two terms are synonymous with hospitality. At the Kahala Hilton aloha is a second core value found in the service environment. The managers and employees of the resort appear to share the aloha spirit. Most of the guests I interviewed mentioned the hospitality and service they received at the Kahala as being what they had imagined as the aloha spirit prior to their arrival. My investigation revealed that the organizational culture and management practices of the hotel played a significant role in maintaining this traditional Hawaiian value in its corporate environment.

This is an important point which may confirm Dr. George Kanahele's work (see chapter 3) on values and on tourism as the keeper of those values. When service businesses destroy the social values found in local communities by imposing "less than human" technical and/or financial systems on employees, the result may be contrary to guest satisfaction. Employees without a sense of place, both in their work and in their community, will be hard-pressed to maintain values like the aloha spirit. The following management practices contribute positively to the special service environment at the Kahala:

- Frequent scheduling of employee-management meetings
- Long-term employment and job security
- Immediate response to grievances
- Service training programs such as "Magic at the Last Three Feet" and "Kahala Cares"*
- A systematic procedure for inviting employee suggestions and identifying employee problems
- Effective orientation and job skills training
- Numerous employee-management social functions and ceremonies
- An extensive guest history system with a full-time employee to maintain it.

These management practices combine to foster a feeling apparent in all staff that the Kahala is someplace special. Just one of many examples of aloha happened on my first visit. After arriving in my room I decided to walk down to the beach. As I left my room and headed for the elevator, I was surprised to hear a pleasant voice from a room across the hall. "Good afternoon, Mr. Glover. Welcome to the Kahala Hilton." The voice was that of a housekeeper who had taken the time and effort to learn my name and greet me. I continued down the hallway only to notice another employee who, upon seeing me, turned abruptly and disappeared around the corner. I

* "Magic at the Last Three Feet" refers to the space in which service employees interact with guests. The training program focuses on what must occur before, during and after that interaction to make the experience "magical" for the guest. "Kahala Cares" is a program in which employees submit service-related suggestions to a management-employee group; the aim is to foster employee involvement in service management.

thought this was unusual behavior until I reached the elevator (around the corner) to find that employee holding the door to the elevator open for me!

Service management practitioners and marketing experts are often concerned with the question of why people choose to patronize a particular service business. Kahala magic provides one answer—the social bonding of guests with employees and guests with guests, a strategy that can be employed by managers at other resorts. When combined with management practices which develop the aloha and ohana feeling (or something similar to them), social bonding can provide a resort with the means of greatly enhancing guest satisfaction and boosting profits—without resorting to magic.

A Word Concerning Methods

The use of participant observation has been important to anthropological field research for a century. This qualitative research technique, when properly conducted by persons trained in the description and analysis of human social systems, yields a wealth of data which are not readily obtainable in more statistically rigorous approaches, such as written surveys. I selected participant observation as a primary data-gathering method for the Kahala Hilton for two reasons:

1. A less than quantitative analysis is necessary to study nonmaterial phenomena, such as ambiance
2. Demonstration of such a technique is of value in the understanding of service organizations

In addition other methods, including interviews, review of guest comments, focus groups, and the documentation of management practices such as the "Kahala Cares" program provided data which helped increase understanding of the resort's culture. Data was obtained in April 1985; August-September 1986; and December-January 1987-88, while I was a guest. The executive team of the Kahala was supportive of my efforts and assisted me in scheduling interviews and obtaining other data in the organization.

Service Spoken Here

by

Dante Laudadio

Communication is an essential aspect of one's participation in any social system. Meaning in any social or cultural environment is always closely linked to communication among the human beings involved. The importance of communication is particularly clear in service organizations where consumers and providers depend upon it to consummate largely nonmaterial transactions. It is my contention that, without a working knowledge of communication, service managers are at a strategic disadvantage because they lack an essential tool of culture management.

Communication can be defined as sending and receiving messages, both verbal and nonverbal, within a social system. How these messages are sent and received, as well as the social environment in which the communication takes place, depends on culture.

Perhaps the most common stumbling block to effective communication is the tendency of most people to think of their own cultural traits as human nature. They then assume that others are just like them. This erroneous assumption, termed "projective cognitive similarity," causes the sender to believe that the receiver perceives, reasons and judges the same way he or she does. Consequently, in the absence of contrary feedback, the sender will further assume that he or she has been understood when this may not be the case.

Generally, the extent to which individuals or groups understand, fail to understand, or misunderstand one another is determined by the degree to which the perspectives and frames of reference of the communicators overlap. Thus, the larger the common ground, the more likely it is for effective communication to take place. Conversely, the more the frames of reference of sender and receiver differ, the more likely misunderstandings and noncomprehension become.

The service environment as a cultural meeting place poses a communication challenge: the transfer of meaning across cultures. There are four principal culturally related factors that affect communication within a service organization:

- The cultural background of the service provider
- The cultural background of the service consumer
- The culture of the society
- The corporate culture of the service organization

All four elements have a profound impact on the nature of the service relationship and the satisfaction of the consumer.

Cultural Background of the Service Provider

An employee in any service organization at any location in the world comes to work with his or her own unique cultural baggage. Employees communicate with other employees, managers, and guests along lines prescribed by such influences as how their families taught them to behave with guests or strangers, whether or not tourism is welcomed in the community, the employees' perceptions of race, sex, and age relative to the consumer receiving the service, etc. Also, language and dialect may act as a barrier or facilitator of communication in service delivery.

The following communication scenario, common in Caribbean tourism, illustrates how cultural baggage might derail the service relationship. An American visitor to island X became very upset when he felt the local employees would not listen to him when he approached them with a legitimate complaint. Ironically, the employees were actually listening and trying to communicate exactly the sort of respectful concern that the guest was seeking, but in the manner their own culture prescribed.

Specifically, the visitor alleged that the employees looked away as he stated his complaint, which aggravated the situation by making him feel that, on top of whatever else was bothering him, he then had to deal with indifferent or rude employees. Upon analysis, the cultural roots of the miscommunication became apparent: most of the hotel's employees had been taught as children to respect authority figures by averting their gaze ("Don't look at me child when I'm talking to you!"), whereas guests had been conditioned to maintain eye contact as a sign of respect ("Look at me when I'm talking to you!"). The Caribbean children-turned-adult service providers were communicating in a manner appropriate in their homes but not at the front desk of an international hotel.

It is difficult to determine how many guests leave this hotel or other service organizations mistakenly convinced that employees are unconcerned and unresponsive to their needs. Fortunately, however, where culture is recognized and managed, differences in the background of service providers and consumers do not have to result in consumer dissatisfaction.

Cultural Background of the Consumer

The literature on the influence of culture and communication on consumer behavior is abundant. Consumer choice, perception, experience and satisfaction are all a product of the communication process.

A case in point is the experience of two American couples vacationing in the Middle East. The couples intentionally chose a small, family-run hotel in order to experience the local culture more fully. However, after three days, they prematurely checked out and transferred to a larger, American-operated resort. The reason? "We felt like our hosts were smothering us," one of the Americans explained. "Every time we'd so much as stick our head out of our guestroom, the manager or his wife would insist we join them for a cup of coffee and a chat. They may have meant well, but we wanted our privacy and wanted to feel free to do our own thing."

In this instance, the hosts, acting within the framework of an ancient and renowned hospitality tradition, attempted to send the message, "You are welcome; you are our honored guests." The message, because it disregarded the values and needs of its American receivers, miscarried.

There are as many definitions of hospitality as there are cultures. Tourists travel with cultural baggage full of expectations, values and habits; because of it, their "honeymoons" with exotic cultures are often shortlived. When receiving foreign guests, the host is often faced with the challenge of reconciling his or her hospitality tradition with consumer expectations.

Culture of the Society

Cultural customs and societal conditions send messages to the traveler. These can be very subtle or alarmingly direct. The lei and welcome to visitors arriving in Hawaii is a time-honored tradition whose message conjures up the consumer image of aloha. In other countries, machine gun-equipped soldiers may "greet" passengers on arriving flights. Their presence sends quite a different message.

Of course, not all customs or conditions send messages as purely positive and negative as the lei and machine gun respectively. Cultures tend to combine positive, negative and ambiguous elements. The tourism organization may enhance its product by highlighting the positive elements and by presenting even the less positive elements in an original and tasteful way.

Take the example of Israel. Because of this country's observance of "shabbat," the Jewish sabbath, hotels must, by law, restrict certain guest services from sundown on Friday until sundown on Saturday. Rather than resign themselves to a weekly apology, some hotel managers make an exciting event of shabbat by sending guests, in advance, an explanation of the significance of the day and an invitation to celebrate it with hotel staff. Through internal promotion, the hotel welcomes guests to a candlelighting ceremony and offers a special dinner; thus, a potential service deterrent becomes a meaningful experience for the tourist and a generator of revenue for the hotel.

The service manager who understands how the larger environment sends messages to the service consumer may be able to change some of these for the better through community involvement. Failing this, he or she can affect, through proactive communication, how service consumers perceive the environment and interpret the messages.

Corporate Culture of the Service Organization

There are many examples of corporate culture and communication affecting service delivery. In fact service quality usually depends on the philosophy and shared values of the people in the organization. It is easy to distinguish, as a consumer, if an organization truly values service. The signs are clear. Employees are well trained and eager to please. The physical facilities reflect a concern for sanitation and security. The service advertised is the service that is delivered.

A colleague who recently returned from a professional conference had the misfortune to stay at a hotel where such a commitment to service was glaringly lacking. Throughout his stay, he was confronted with ring-around-the-bathtub, cold oatmeal, and slow room service. "I could have pardoned these service flops," he commented to me, "but what I could not stomach was the 'woe is me' routine I received from employees and managers when I complained. 'We're understaffed.' 'Management knows the equipment never works right and they don't do anything about it.' 'The owners won't put up the money to remodel the kitchen.' I got so tired of listening to their problems that I took my complaints directly to the meeting planner. Fortunately, she moved next year's conference to another hotel." This corporate culture communicated the following message loud and clear: Don't bother us about service. Can't you see we have our own problems!

The point is, whatever happens in the corporate culture will influence the quality and consistency of service, and the outcome, in turn, will convey a message to consumers—for better or worse.

The Outlook

Communication, culture and service are inseparable. Increasingly, diversity is the keynote even in domestic service organizations. The common ground between service providers and consumers is, in many instances, shrinking, and organizations are confronted with the challenge of training service providers to communicate with people who perceive, think and behave differently from themselves. At the same time, managers are becoming more aware of corporate culture as a force in productivity and profitability. They are learning to use communication to shape service-centered social systems. The organizations that master these challenges will deliver world-class service.

How To Deal With The News Media

By

James Lett

If you're involved in managing a hospitality business in a multicultural setting that caters (at least in part) to a U.S. clientele, then somewhere, sometime, somehow you're going to have to deal with the American news media. That's a given. If you're like most managers, chances are you'd prefer to deal with the media by ignoring them. And that's a mistake. It's a mistake because there may be times when you won't have that option (when, for example, tragedy strikes, as it did at the Fountain Valley Club on St. Croix when tourists were shot by locals on the golf course in the late summer of 1972). Then you're going to need to know how to talk to the media. But it's also a mistake to ignore the media because not all news is bad news. And if you know how to deal with the media, you can use them to your advantage, just as you use advertising and public relations to accomplish your goals. What I want to do here is to tell you something about the organizational culture of the news media so that you'll better understand their assumptions, values, and beliefs. Then I will give you some specific advice that will help you put that understanding to good use.

First, the news media, especially the broadcast news media, play an enormously influential role in contemporary American society; you simply can't afford to ignore them. Television, in particular, reaches the largest and most diverse audience of any form of mass communication in human history. Research shows that a majority of Americans rely primarily upon television news for information about the outside world (Lett 1987b). The news media have the potential to define the public's perception of your part of the world, and that means that the news media have the potential to define the health and future of your business. The bottom line, simply, is that good media relations is one aspect of sound culture management. You need to be able to communicate effectively with the media in order to insure the vitality of your business, and you need to understand the cultural organization of the media in order to do that. So let's look at who and what the media are and why and how they do what they do.

The Culture of the Media

American journalists (both print and broadcast) are people who are aware, at least implicitly, of the concept of culture management. They see themselves as culture brokers. They realize that there are many different subcultures out there—the corporate culture, the blue-collar culture, the academic culture, the black culture, all the various educational, associational, ethnic, and socioeconomic groups that make up a diverse society—and journalists regard their role as that of interpreting one culture to another. (Ironically, this has *not* tended to give journalists a multicultural sensibility; most of them, in my view, are still distinctly ethnocentric—see Lett 1986.) The journalist's perceived audience is always an audience of lay people, an audience that doesn't share the specialized knowledge of the group which is the subject of the story, an audience that's on the outside. The problem, of course, is that journalists themselves are always on the outside; they are generalists. For the most part, they do not have specialized knowledge; indeed, most of them would regard specialized knowledge as a hindrance to their jobs. They want to see the story from the audience's point of view—from the point of view, in other words, of someone who has little or no knowledge of the subject matter. If you're the manager of a resort hotel on some Caribbean island, chances are the journalist whose attentions you've attracted will know little or nothing about the culture and history of your island. And chances are he or she will be satisfied not to know much more.

What you have to do, then, is accept the obligation to educate journalists. Don't inundate them with information—they'll just ignore most of what you offer and select only what seems important to them. Instead, your task is to determine what's likely to be important to them and then help them (subtly) select the pertinent bits of information that serve both your needs and theirs. To do that, you have to understand how journalists define *news*.

Journalists pride themselves on their ability to distinguish between what is and is not newsworthy, but in my experience very few of them are willing or able to give you a precise definition of just what news is (see Lett 1987b). To be sure, there are journalism textbooks which define the elements that contribute to making a story newsworthy, but most journalists are much more comfortable with a more intuitive and implicit definition. To paraphrase an eminent broadcast journalist, news is whatever journalists say it is, and generally they say something is news if it is characterized by *immediacy* (did it just happen?), *proximity* (did it happen close to home?), *prominence* (did it happen to someone famous?), *oddity* (does it happen often?), *conflict* (is there an inherent drama in what happened?), *significance* (does it affect the lives of a lot of people?), and/or *human interest* (is it in some way titillating?). Is there a celebrity staying at your hotel? That's news. Is there a battle going on between your expatriate managers and your indigenous staff? That's news too. Are there Scandinavian tourists bathing nude on your beach? I don't have to tell you what that is.

If you know what news is, you know what journalists are looking for—and you know what *not* to tell them about your business. Tell them something that fits their categories, not yours, because the one thing you know for sure is that they are not going to use your categories. So if you want them to select the information you would have selected (and I'm talking about factual information; it is always a bad idea to lie to the media), you have to put *your* information in *their* terms. In other words, be a culture broker. Employ the techniques of effective culture management.

Thus, when a journalist appears in your lobby and wants to ask you about your marketing strategy and why you are deliberately attracting all those hedonistic Scandinavians and offending all the pious locals, you know the journalist is looking for a story based on human interest and/or conflict—and you know you may be able to persuade the journalist to focus on the innocuous aspects of the story by providing attractive human interest details.

Damage control is hardly the only dimension to effective media management, however. There will be plenty of times when you won't want to wait for the camera crews to arrive, times when there's something prominent or unusual or interesting happening at your establishment and when you wouldn't mind the favorable publicity. If you restrict yourself to advertising or public relations to tell your story to the world, you are selling yourself short. The news media have an inexhaustible need for stories—all you have to do is convince them that your story fits their definition of news. In other words, you shouldn't hesitate to approach the media with story ideas. But when you do, you want to be sure to approach the right person, which means you need to know a little about the social structure of media organizations.

The media organization that I know best, and the one that will be most important to you, is the television station. For glamour, impact, and pervasiveness, the print media cannot compare with television; so if you are going to contact a journalist, by all means think first about contacting a television journalist. When you do so, keep in mind that television newsroom personnel are identified by a set of terms peculiar to the medium (Lett 1987b). Calling the newsroom and asking to speak to the editor, for example, will not give you the person in overall charge of the news product (as at a newspaper) or even a person who proofreads scripts. Instead, you will find yourself talking to one of several technicians responsible for the electronic assembly of the audio and video in each story, and that person won't have the authority to decide whether your story idea is worth pursuing or not. Instead, you should ask to speak to either the *assignment editor*, the *reporter*, or the *producer*, in that order of preference. The assignment editor is the person responsible for deciding which reporters and which camera crews will cover which stories on any given day. The reporter is the person who goes out in the field, conducts the interview, writes the story, and narrates the report for broadcast. The producer is the person who decides which of the day's available stories will appear in the newscast, how much time will be given to each story, and where each story will appear in the "line-up" or the "run-down." If you know and use the correct terms, you are more likely to inspire confidence, which will increase your chances that your story idea will be approved.

Just remember to describe your idea in journalistic terms, showing the assignment editors, reporters, and producers that you have something for them that serves their interests. Journalists are very quick to dismiss story proposals that appear to be transparent requests for publicity devoid of any real news value. But now that you know what news is, it should be obvious that virtually *any* story is likely to have news value if it is properly translated—and proper translation is the task you should set for yourself.

How to Be a Successful Interviewee

Eventually, whether it is your choice or the media's, you are going to find yourself being interviewed by a reporter; and it will be useful to remember that there is an art to being an interviewee just as much as there is to being an interviewer. Elsewhere (Lett 1987a:22), I've given academicians and bureaucrats advice on being interviewed, and much of that advice applies with equal force to managers. So here are a few suggestions on how to talk to the media.

The best advice I can give you can be summed up in a single sentence: *when being interviewed by a member of the broadcast media, be concise, confident, candid, and colorful.* Here's what I mean by each of those terms.

Be concise. A commercial television newscast must be fast-paced if it is to survive; the medium dictates that. The reporter is likely to ask you several questions, but chances are only one or two brief excerpts from your answers will be used (and I do mean *brief*: typically five to fifteen seconds of reply). You should always speak in simple, complete sentences. Be clear, precise, direct, and to the point.

Be confident. Speak with an assured tone, and speak with authority. Do *not* hedge your answer and do not refer the question to higher-ups in the organization. If you don't have the authority to speak for the company, get someone who does to do the interview.

Be candid. Be forthright and forthcoming. Every rule has an exception, but in general it is always a bad idea to "decline to comment." If you refuse to answer a question, the journalist will perceive that as an admission of wrongdoing, and you can be sure that perception will be conveyed to the public. It is always risky to lie to the media because they resent it very much; and they will always portray any lie, even the smallest whitest lie, as evidence of the most reprehensible character traits.

Be colorful. Television reporters and producers are always looking for the "human" element. If you are warm, witty, personable, relaxed, unguarded, and uninhibited, you have a much better chance of being aired and a much better chance of receiving a favorable response. If you can find a colorful turn of phrase, use it; if you can't find one, keep looking.

Case Study #1: The Wrong Way to Deal with the Media: The Beachfront Hotel That Lost Its Beach

Let me tell you a true story that may illustrate some of the general principles I have been talking about. On Thanksgiving in 1984 a major storm hit the southeast coast of Florida. A strong northeast wind blew furiously for thirty-six hours, causing severe coastal erosion from Miami to Daytona Beach. The worst damage was halfway between those two cities, in an area known as the Treasure Coast. One beachfront resort hotel there was particularly hard hit, losing more than twenty feet of shoreline over the holiday weekend. The lawn between the hotel and the beach simply disappeared; the advancing water exposed the entire side of the swimming pool, leaving a vertical escarpment twelve feet high. At high tide, the surf was literally breaking against the first-floor rooms, and the windblown spray from the ocean was soaking the third-floor balconies. On Thanksgiving night, when the breakers began pounding against the sliding glass doors, the hotel moved all the guests in the oceanfront rooms to the parking lot side. The next day coastal erosion experts were called in, and about half of them predicted that the building would fall into the sea within forty-eight hours.

Needless to say, all the journalists in the area thought this was great news. As far as they were concerned, the story had everything: immediacy, proximity, oddity, significance, and human interest. The hotel managers, of course, thought it was horrible news. If the surf undermined the hotel's foundations, they would be facing a catastrophic financial loss. Even if the water retreated, they could still be facing a devastating blow to their business as a result of all the publicity (who wants to go to sleep in a hotel that may not be there in the morning?).

I was a local television reporter at the time and was able to get several interviews that made for wonderful television. I talked to guests who had awakened in the night to discover the ocean much too close for comfort. I talked to marine engineers who accused the hotel management of refusing to spend the money to take the necessary steps to protect the guests (aha—conflict!). But it was a while before I talked to the hotel managers or owners. They refused at first to be interviewed. They wanted to be left alone to deal with the disaster, and they certainly didn't want the negative publicity that followed the disappearance of their beach (after all, they'd just lost their most valued and most touted attraction). So, in the initial television stories, the management looked as though it were refusing to deal with reality. The hotel's owners appeared incompetent, insensitive, and possibly culpable. When at last I was granted an interview, my interviewee was sullen, resentful, and uncommunicative. He refused to answer some of my questions, referred others to unavailable spokespersons, and presented a bitter, combative, ineffective image of the hotel's management to the world at large.

The point, of course, is that the hotel could have used the inevitable media coverage to its own advantage. The management could have portrayed itself—confidently, candidly, and colorfully—as the victim of an act of nature, but a victim who was responding competently and decisively in a time of great confusion (the marine engineers were making contradictory recommendations—anyone would have readily sympathized with the manager's plight if he had just humanized himself). The general manager could have granted an interview immediately and described in riveting terms the exciting details of the middle of that wild night when the staff was knocking on the oceanfront doors out of a preeminent concern for the guests' safety. It was naive and unrealistic to think that publicity could have been avoided. By trying to ignore the media, the management succeeded only in insuring that the inevitable publicity would have a less favorable tone.

Case Study #2: The Right Way to Deal with the Media: The Tourist Attraction with the Two-Headed Turtle

A few miles south of that unfortunate hotel on the Treasure Coast there is another beachfront tourist attraction, a small maritime museum housed in a 110-year-old building that was once a remote outpost of the U.S. Lifesaving Service. The museum features nautical memorabilia from the nineteenth century, and it also provides facilities (including salt water tanks) for an active and ongoing sea turtle research project. In the summer of 1984, the museum suddenly found that turtles could make news—big news.

An early morning beachcomber had discovered a two-headed loggerhead hatchling and delivered it to the museum. The turtle was alive, apparently healthy, and otherwise normal except for the fact that it had two fully developed, fully functioning heads. The museum's curator recognized immediately that he had news on his hands, news that he could use to promote public awareness of the museum and its programs. The story of the two-headed turtle had immediacy and proximity, and it certainly had oddity and human interest. So, the curator called the media. He called the local television stations, the radio stations and the newspapers. He called everyone who might possibly be interested in the story, and he was enthusiastic and accommodating. He persuaded the beachcomber who had found the turtle to talk to the media. He made himself available for repeated interviews, and he opened the museum to the media during off-hours.

And he was more than candid; he was also colorful. He gave the two-headed turtle a name (Captain Janus, after the Roman god with two faces), and he insisted on using the name whenever he referred to the turtle. When speaking to reporters, he was genuinely and passionately interested in the topic, and he wasn't shy about demonstrating his interest. The curator arranged to have a sea turtle expert on site to answer reporters' questions about the turtle's physiology and its chances of survival (in other words, he found someone who could speak with confidence about Captain Janus).

The story was picked up by international news services, and the museum received worldwide publicity. For weeks, until Captain Janus finally expired, visitors flocked to the beach to see the two-headed turtle in its specially constructed aquarium. The museum watched its revenues from ticket sales shoot up while doing more to familiarize the public with its sea turtle research project than it had done in a decade of advertising and public relations. Without effective media relations, however, the story could have been a disaster. Had the reporters not been fully engaged with oddity and human interest, they might very well have looked for conflict (after all, why had a respectable museum decided to open a freak show?). By actively and creatively seeking the attention of the media, the curator managed to further his museum's interests—and the fact that he also furthered the interests of the local media in the process was hardly incidental.

Conclusion

As the other articles in this volume make clear, effective culture management involves a number of variables: you have to be thoroughly familiar with the culture of your own organization and with the cultures of your staff and your customers. My point is that there is another culture you need to know, the culture of the media. In an age when the electronic mass media are enormously influential and ubiquitous, you don't have the option of ignoring them. What I've tried to do here is give you a very brief introduction to the values, beliefs, and organizational structure of television journalists and their culture. I can't promise that all your news will be good news, but I can promise that you'll enjoy better media relations if you follow the advice I've offered here. And I can promise that better media relations will mean better business.

Chapter 7

COMMON THREADS: EMERGING MODEL OF THE WORLD-CLASS SERVICE ORGANIZATION

Within the hospitality, travel and tourism industries, champions of world-class service are using culture to change organizations. Their approaches are as diverse as their constituencies. Attuned to the needs and expectations of a global market and multicultural work force, they counter ingrained reactiveness with adaptive strategies that make service everyone's business. Their vision is unobstructed by "left luggage" from the industrial era and cultural blinders from "the school of service management as if culture didn't exist." They are holistic, proactive and multicultural, and these qualities characterize the innovations they champion. By changing the very culture of the industries they serve, they lay the foundation for world-class service. The synthesis of their individual initiatives forms a model of the world-class service organization that may be applied to any tourism-related business as well as to other service industries. We will look at their contributions here from the four principal perspectives taken by this book: business strategy, marketing, human resource development and customer contact.

Business Strategy

1. *Provision of an adaptive framework that encourages creative consistency and avoids imposed sameness*
    The world-class service organization has policies, procedures, and standards just as its less successful competitors do. But in the world-class organization, these policies and procedures spell out what is *negotiable* and what is not. Wherever adaptation is permissible or desirable, guidelines rather than absolutes are provided. Day-to-day operations are largely regulated by unit-level procedures that are reexamined regularly and modified as conditions change. Realistic standards are set for each unit

184

that incorporate customer and employee input and that consider material, cultural and political constraints. Executives responsible for enforcing policy are familiar with the locations they serve, thoroughly briefed on the areas' business, political and cultural conditions, and above all, willing to listen to the on-site manager. The articles by Miura and Smith offer valuable insights on the need for adaptive policies in multinational companies that straddle East and West and developed and developing nations.

2.   *Combination of long-term planning with day-to-day flexibility*
     Western business in general and the hospitality, travel and tourism industries in particular have operated with a short-term, fiscal-year orientation whose effectiveness—even on home turf—must be questioned. A number of current and emerging players in the global marketplace, such as the Middle East, Japan and China, operate with radically different time frames. Experience has shown that the companies that fare well in such countries—and, generally, in their own as well—are those that establish long-term relationships with their customers and communities. These companies may plan ten to twenty years ahead, yet maintain the flexibility to adapt to changes in the operating environment and take advantage of opportunities. Nikko's methodical yet dynamic multinationalization pro-vides an example of this strategy. Nikko may be said to manage with its eyes on the horizon and its ears tuned in to the immediate.

3.   *A good fit within the broad context of community and national resources, priorities, values and constraints*
     Ideally the service organization nourishes and is nourished by the communities and cultures within which it operates. Potential for such a symbiotic relationship should be a feasibility criterion assessed along with the locality's economic and political outlook. Contributors White, Ka-nahele, and Smith propose strategies for meshing organizational and civic goals. Using the examples of Hawaii and The Bahamas, they demonstrate how meaningful involvement in the community goes beyond the tradi-tional solicited support of local charities or tea party-type public relations. The onus of responsibility to establish broad-based reciprocal relations with social and political groups is on the organization. The overall objective of establishing such a network is the attainment of recognition and influence as a full member of the community. To a degree, the network frees the organization from dependence on owners or partners as sources of information and support. Organization leaders gradually gain access to the whole range of resources the community has to offer. Of course, community involvement also makes demands upon the organization. However, as the future of the organization and industry is tied to that of their hosts, any contribution to the community may be viewed as an investment in the long-term viability of the organization. In the case of the

hospitality, travel and tourism industries, as White and Kanahele point out, involvement in protecting the local culture is a particularly vital investment.

4. *Mission formulation in a participatory manner*

A mission statement makes manifest the values and aspirations of an organization. As such, it is a cornerstone of the organization's culture. Where differences in national, ethnic or generational culture exist among organization members, value orientations will vary. The organization that imposes a mission statement runs the risk of piquing cultural sensitivities and alienating its members. If the mission statement is to serve as something more than filler in the annual report to shareholders, it must be an authentic reflection of the beliefs and good faith of the people— managers and employees—responsible for its implementation. Miura, White, and Kanahele describe how mission statements were drafted in a participatory manner at hotels in such distinct locations as New York City and Hawaii. Glover's inside look at Delta Airlines illustrates how mission translates into service when policy and practice are true to stated corporate values.

5. *Identification of culture as an asset to be managed for increased sales, quality, productivity and reduced operating costs*

Culture's impact on the organization is real and compelling. Service managers have the choice either of leaving its workings to chance or of channeling it toward constructive ends. They may treat culture as a bothersome enigma to be coped with, or they can learn about it and turn it to their advantage. World-class business strategists engineer customer-friendly social systems that capitalize on internal and external cultural diversity. JAL and its subsidiary, Nikko Hotels International, are examples of organizations that consciously orchestrate synergy through the creative blending of Eastern and Western values, management approaches, design, and technologies. While making the strategic decision to remain "refreshingly unique," they take great care to stay abreast of changing consumer preferences and competitors' offerings. Though they may choose to propagate a management approach that has yet to gain widespread acceptance in the West, they do so mindful that they are conducting a social experiment whose results will impact service quality. JAL uses its "Japaneseness," just as it uses its hosts' "otherness" to create a product that no competitor can imitate; internally it uses culture to engineer a social system able (according to Miura) to attain a service standard that no competitor can equal.

6. *Ability to transcend history and proactively shape the future*

There may have been a time when reactive organizations survived and proactive organizations thrived. Not anymore. In today's volatile and

186

competitive marketplace, the reactive organization doesn't stand a chance and even the proactive organization is at risk. The organizations that thrive in the twenty-first century will have transcended history and taken a hand in shaping the environments in which they operate. Michael Smith illustrates how organizations can tap into historical forces to strengthen their competitive position and ease the journey forward.

Marketing

1. *Ability to analyze each market's culturally shaped expectations, needs and tastes, and accommodate them whenever feasible*
    Each market segment a company targets constitutes a culture with its own unique perceptions, values and assumptions. Each customer arrives with expectations based on his or her particular cultural baggage. Market research capable of exposing the contents of that baggage is essential. The unbiased interpretation and use of its findings demands a high level of cultural awareness on the part of marketers and operations managers. The tendency to make attributions, judgments or assumptions may cause research findings to be misinterpreted or undervalued. Such tunnel vision, in the words of Klein, Lewis and Scott, "sets the stage for the provider to begin systematically disappointing the clientele." Foreign customers who cannot order a menu item to suit their national palate and dietary restrictions or make their difficulties understood by an organization representative are lost as repeat customers. The poor word-of-mouth publicity they generate will thwart the organization's attempts to develop its market. As Ferguson puts it, "Homework comes first in seeking business from abroad." When the culturally different customer enters a world-class operation, he or she finds enough that is familiar to feel at home and enough explanation and help to make the unfamiliar intelligible. Effective internal marketing makes every customer master of the service environment.

2. *Emphasis on retaining customers through personalized, culturally appropriate service rather than continually generating new markets*
    External marketing may bring the consumer in the door once, but it is internal marketing that makes a repeat customer. World-class service is the internalization of an effective global marketing strategy. Inside a world-class operation, all employees are empowered and motivated to act as marketers, ambassadors and hosts. The organization, through its employees, adeptly delivers the culturally adaptive product and service package its marketing department has designed and sold. Ferguson explains the relationship between international and internal marketing, and Sage illustrates it with the case of Sheraton's romancing of the Japanese market.

3. *The service chain as marketing technique*

World-class marketers string services together so that each comple-ments, "sells" and facilitates consumption of the others. JAL, for example, extended the door-to-door approach from air cargo to passenger service to create a travel service chain with the ease of a magic carpet for the consumer. SAS took the concept even further for the business traveler by providing not only door-to-door service, but training seminars to help the passenger have a more successful business trip. A well-designed service chain represents a complete and effortless service experience for the consumer and a logical and profitable form of diversification for the service organization.

4. *Adaptation of advertising, sales promotions and the direct-sales approach to each market*

In today's marketplace, even a world-class product does not sell itself. Consumers must be wooed until the organization establishes a service reputation—and then they must be cultivated, updated, reminded and/or cajoled thereafter. The culture of the consumers determines what means are used, what approach to selling is appropriate and what *works*. As Ferguson points out, the conventional sales practices of developed Western nations are by no means universal. For example, some nations show little responsiveness to advertising or respond adversely to sales pitches they interpret as a "hard sell." Common cross-cultural advertising faux pas include misuse of symbols and colors; inappropriate tone, role models or setting; and sales emphasis on the wrong needs and values. Klein, Lewis and Scott outline a procedure that enables marketers to understand the gaps in expectations and perceptions between service managers and consumers which cause these kinds of mistakes. Direct selling also pres-ents cultural challenges. The degree to which salespersons are expected to "sell themselves" along with their product, the amount of time they need to invest in cultivating customers, and the channels they may effectively use to make the sale are just a few of the numerous variables that must be considered. The world-class organization maximizes its sales force and budget by selling to the unique expectations, needs and values of distinct markets, using appropriate channels and images, and observing the protocol and mores of their target cultures.

5. *Differentiation of the organization's product by drawing upon the community's unique culture and resources*

In the search for ways to make one's product distinctive and more desirable to prospective consumers, marketers often overlook the possibili-ties at their own doorsteps. While not every property can or should claim to be "the most Hawaiian" (as White and Kanahele's Ka'anapali Beach Hotel does) or the most Greek or Irish establishment in a country, the business that reflects its host culture, without pretentiousness or empty

188

show, conveys an appealing sense of place that is fundamental to the travel experience. Of course, international travelers have come to expect certain standard amenities, menu items and facilities whose availability may be limited. By all means, if the company can afford to, it should give them what they expect—even if it means importing it from halfway around the world. The organization should be aware, however, that these generic facilities don't win business. They simply establish a base line. What will set the organization apart is its harmonious integration and creative use of the best its locality has to offer.

Human Resources Development

1.   *Acknowledgement of employee diversity and facilitation of its synergy*

Multicultural work forces are the norm in the hospitality, travel and tourism industries. These industries have long been a magnet for cosmopolitans, "corporate gypsies" and recent immigrants. Working alongside them are local personnel with parochial outlooks who, chances are, lack the awareness and skills to interact effectively with their culturally different coworkers. The organization that leaves employees to "figure one another out" not only risks workplace friction but also loses out on the potential synergy that the orchestrated mingling of cultures can produce. A number of progressive organizations, Hilton International among them, have introduced training programs to develop the ability of supervisors and managers to bring out the best in a multicultural work force.

2.   *Respect for the dignity of each employee—an understanding between managers and employees of the difference between service and servility*

The expectations of workers are on the rise in many parts of the world. Particularly in those Third World nations where the memory of colonialism, and even slavery, affects attitudes toward work, the dignity accorded the employee is a major issue. According to Flores, questions of human dignity are at the heart of most labor relations conflicts. As the hierarchical form of organization is still the norm in hospitality, travel and tourism businesses, resentment may fester among workers who are pinned down within a chain of command, uniformed, clocked, and closely supervised. Any incident perceived by employees to further violate their dignity may trigger a major crisis. The editors know of a case where a hotel coffee shop waitress accused a food and beverage manager of summoning her attention by nudging her with his foot. Incensed, she lodged a complaint with her union representative. Under the direction of the union, her fellow restaurant workers (thirty-five in all) walked off the job and staged a sit-in in the hotel lobby. Hotel management retaliated by firing the entire coffee shop brigade, an action that caused the rest of the hotel's work force to protest in sympathy. After more than two years, the battle is still being waged in the national labor court, and a number of employees continue to wear a swatch of red ribbon to commemorate the original protest. The reader can well imagine the forces working against service in this organization's climate. The point is this: self-esteem and faith in the integrity of one's employer are service-provider essentials. The servility stigma finds fertile ground in autocratic organizations. World-class service is possible only in high-trust organizations that make each employee feel important.

3.   *Provision for meaningful employee input into decisions*
During the past several years, service managers have been scrambling to get and stay close to the customer. Many have discovered how hard it is to do that without also getting close to one's employees and hearing them out. Frontline employees, in particular, hold a wealth of information and wisdom about customers and operations, but traditional organizations, for the most part, lack the means of drawing upon it. By denying employees meaningful input into the decision-making process, the organization is not only likely to make less than optimal choices but also risks demoralizing a work force barred from making the full contribution of which it is capable. Miura supports the former argument for employee input in his account of the creation of Nikko's participatory quality assurance program, and Smith supports the latter in his eloquent indictment of the traditional polarization of Bahamians and non-Bahamians. Rosen and Adamson caution against management fostering mass "learned helplessness" by confining decision making to the uppermost level of the organizational hierarchy.

4.   *Intercultural training as an important and integral part of the organization's training program*
Most organizations no longer need to be sold on the importance of the role of training in service. Many companies allocate considerable resources toward the training and retraining of their managers and employees. However, while technical, supervisory and customer relations courses have become standard fare, intercultural training is rarely found in industry programs or academic curricula. Service-related topics are presented *as if culture didn't exist*. Managers learn in a parochial mold and then are expected to lead a multicultural work force, cater to a global market, and relocate a number of times during the course of their careers. Corporate culture has been in vogue for the past several years as a seminar topic. Yet, even in the organizations where "culture is spoken," the discussion of national and ethnic cultural influences is nil. Resistance to intercultural training is diminishing as practitioners learn to document the astronomical costs of cultural illiteracy and to effectively market intercultural training to corporations. While a number of hospitality and

travel companies have dabbled in intercultural training, few have made a policy-supported commitment to it. SAS and Hilton International are among the few that have. In the case of SAS, their Intercultural Centre trains both company personnel and clients and is thus a profit center as well as an internal training facility. Hilton International, on the other hand, makes use of its existing facilities, programs and staff to achieve the same end—world-class service.

5. *Orientation and counseling of internationally mobile personnel and transferees to ease cultural adjustment*
Culture shock can be crippling to personal and professional effectiveness. While orientation and counseling do not immunize their recipients against culture shock, they do enable individuals to approach the experience positively and with realistic expectations, to diagnose and treat symptoms, and to remain productive throughout the adjustment cycle. Benefits to the organization are obvious—better job performance and working relations, fewer cultural faux pas, and a decrease in the extremely costly early returns of executives and their families from overseas assignments. Yet, many organizations continue to leave transferees to sink or swim in unfamiliar waters. World-class organizations recognize and attend to the special needs of their transferees and globetrotters. Hilton International provides both predeparture and on-site support to transferees and their families through an internally developed program administered by the company's own unit-level human resources development staff. SAS, in contrast, provides predeparture and reentry workshops through its Intercultural Centre. The workshops are designed and conducted by corporate staff and independent consultants.

6. *Integration of expatriate and local staff through team building and equitable management and promotion policies*
Team building has gained widespread acceptance in the hospitality, travel and tourism industries as leaders become aware of the importance of group dynamics and personal interaction processes in getting the job done. Multicultural work groups pose a particular challenge to the builder of teams because individuals bring distinct frames of reference, beliefs, values, assumptions and communication patterns to the task. While differences among members heighten the potential for synergy, they also increase the likelihood of misunderstanding, erroneous assumptions and prejudicial stereotyping. The team building intervention must address such differences, along with standard discussion of roles, goals, communication and decision making. Two essentials of intercultural team building are (1) the opportunity for close, stereotype-breaking interaction between culturally different members and (2) the development of team commitment to superordinate goals that all members may willingly embrace within their cultural framework. Naturally, once formed, the team will flourish

only within an environment that all members perceive as supportive and just. The organization that pays lip service to teamwork yet creates a privileged elite (for example, expatriate managers, managers of the same nationality as the organization's president, graduates of selected universities, etc.) stymies team formation. Likewise, as the findings of Rosen and Adamson's management training study suggest, companies that impose a rigid European/North American structure on aspiring managers from other countries will never have a synergistic management team. The world-class management team is a collectivity of mutually supportive and respectful individuals bonded by an organizational culture and committed to a common goal; the team consciously manages its differences and capitalizes on its diversity to orchestrate world-class service. Miura describes some of the steps taken by Nikko International to build synergistic, multicultural teams.

Customer Contact

1. *Ability of the organization's frontline employees to understand the nature of the service experience and to enter it empowered and predisposed to satisfy the customer*

An organization is only as good as its front line. The interface of service consumer and provider is a critical juncture. It is here the consumer forms a personal and decisive impression that will affect current and future patronage, as well as word-of-mouth publicity. The front line must be world-class: a team of customer satisfaction experts sensitive and responsive to the distinct expectations and needs of the markets they serve. Primed for proactivity and autonomy, the individuals on the front line are delegated the discretionary authority to satisfy most customer needs on the spot. Management and the organization culture encourage and support them in their service efforts. The SAS success story provides a classic example of, and makes a convincing case for, an empowered front line.

2. *Frontline employees who are at ease with culturally different customers and possess special skills for communicating with them*

As the findings of Glover, Shames and Friedman's study underscore, the service environment is a cultural meeting place where people of many backgrounds interact. People are not automatically comfortable or competent in dealing with others who speak and behave in unfamiliar ways. While they may not intend to be rude or discriminatory in their treatment, their discomfort and lack of intercultural skills may cause them to appear to be so. Service providers cannot act effectively within the service experience without in some degree being able to exchange information and feelings with the consumer. At a minimum the provider must ascertain the needs that bring the consumer to the service experience, express caring and good will, and confirm customer satisfaction with the service rendered. Even where considerable dialogue does occur, miscommunication may derail the interaction. Sage's example of Japanese customers' disinclination to complain when asked by a service provider, "Is everything okay?" illustrates one such derailment. Were the service provider a Japanese serving a fellow Japanese, he/she would probably know the answer without asking (by reading subtle nonverbal behaviors) or would ask the question in a more culturally appropriate way; the monocultural Western employees serving the same Japanese customer, on the other hand, will not know the answer without asking and will still not know it *after* asking. The likely result is a dissatisfied service consumer and a frustrated provider. Empowering an organization's front line includes preparing service providers to interact confidently and competently with the whole gamut of consumers they are apt to encounter. In globally attuned organizations, such as SAS, intercultural awareness and communication skills are a prominent component of customer service training.

3.   *Procedures that are customer-friendly and adaptive*
     Much has been written regarding the importance of making sure operating procedures don't interfere with the provision of effective service. Red tape can impair both the service providers' and consumers' ability to act within the service experience. The importance of simplicity and flexibility, which are desirable characteristics of customer service procedures, becomes even more pronounced as cultural differences are introduced into the experience. Ferguson's example of the gross inappropriateness of inflexible credit procedures applied to Japanese business travelers by some Western hotels suggests the need to evaluate practices market by market—what may be acceptable to one may be a hassle to another. An inflight service incident related to the editors by Clifford Clarke, an intercultural consultant, also argues for cultural specificity: arriving from Japan on a Japanese airline, Clarke raised the window shade in order to watch the landing. The flight attendant, offering no explanation, closed it as she passed. Clarke reopened it; she reclosed it. When Clarke, annoyed, questioned her about the window, she explained that landing procedures required that all window shades be closed to provide an orderly appearance. Her culture and that of the airline placed a higher value on form than on individual satisfaction—despite the fact that the individual in question happened to be a customer! Service on that airline may be meticulous, but—to the Western traveler—it is not customer-friendly. World-class service is not only friendly, but friendly *on the customer's own terms.*

4.   *Provision of literature, signs in the customer's language, and translators on the staff or on call whenever feasible*

Language barriers may interfere with the customer's mastery of the service environment. All customers have the right to full access to the facilities and services for which they have paid. Not only their satisfaction, but their safety and well-being depend upon it. By providing written and verbal orientation in the languages of all sizable target audiences, the world-class operation removes an increasingly common barrier to service. Sage describes how Sheraton helps Japanese travelers master the service environment.

5.   *Opportune and effective use by management of a variety of media to maintain a positive image in the organization's community and markets*

While the importance of face-to-face interaction between service providers and consumers cannot be overestimated, the influence of the media should not be underestimated. Favorable print and broadcast publicity complement the consistent delivery of quality service. The media may work for or against an organization's success; the proactive manager harnesses the media as a communication and public relations arm of the organization. Lett illustrates how the world-class manager, by understanding the medium's internal culture, may use television to enhance the organization's image, while Fennings illustrates how by understanding the culture and constraints of the larger environment, he may generate alternatives to standard media coverage.

Putting It All Together

The model organization that emerges is customer-driven, innovative and proactive. In fact, it is all the things current literature tells us a service organization should be. But it is *something more*: multicultural, synergistic and whole. Internally, a dynamic and managed social system focuses talents and energies on delivering world-class service. Open and connected to the larger environment, the organization maintains a symbiotic relationship with the surrounding community and an informed, cosmopolitan, adaptive presence in global markets. An engineered and tended corporate culture gives coherence and direction to the whole. The organization has a global identity, but one that employees and customers in distinct localities may make their own because of its resilience and flexibility. The world-class organization's product is set apart in the marketplace by its synergistic mingling of internal and external cultures—the competition simply cannot duplicate it. All of these factors give the organization an edge over culture-blind, tradition-bound competitors. World-class service is the passport to the global economy and service age.

Chapter 8

MAKING WORLD-CLASS
SERVICE HAPPEN

Even in the service age and with a global economy, the business of delivering service and turning a profit depends on, for the most part, ordinary people doing largely routine things. The grandiose-sounding "international service arena" is made up of mostly unremarkable places of business where people earn a livelihood, exchange goods, and share experiences.

Despite advances in technology and management science (or, perhaps, because of them), service managers continue to face the perennial dilemmas of low employee motivation, inconsistent service delivery, and customer defection. Rather than gaining mastery over the service environment, many managers feel they are increasingly losing control of their work force, budget and destiny.

One of the authors recalls asking his first boss and mentor, a veteran hotel manager whose career spanned twenty-five years and six continents, "Is it always like *this*? I mean, do things in an operation always seem to be slightly out of hand?" The resigned response: "Yes, this is typical. When you're dealing with people, you can never tell what's going to happen."

The truth is that service managers have never been in control of the service environment and never will be until they learn to manage social systems. Service managers *can* create and maintain social systems that predispose people to interact in mutually satisfying ways, *can* introduce adaptation and proaction into their operations as a living cultural practice, and, above all, *can* use culture management to deal with the day-to-day challenges of running a service business.

The Service Manager's Daily Bread

In the pursuit of service quality, managers must manage people, their cultures, and the social processes that regulate their interaction. Failure to take culture into account results in such common, interrelated dilemmas as employee apathy, high staff turnover, low productivity, elevated operating costs, dysfunctional technology, misdirected marketing, service inconsistencies, and unsatisfied customers.

Traditional approaches to dealing with these challenges only serve to keep these dilemmas coming back. Why? Because such approaches stop short of effecting significant, durable changes in the operation's social system. Rather than address the problem in its full context, they isolate and fragment it. Furthermore, they ignore the cultural influences present in the service environment working to perpetuate the status quo.

In contrast, management approaches that act on both the apparent object (be it the payroll, marketing plan, or a piece of equipment) *and* the social system make long-term improvement possible. When changes in procedure or technology are properly fitted within the framework of the operation's social system, cultural forces present in the environment work *for* the change and help sustain it.

Let's take a look at how a world-class service manager would deal with some of the most common service organization dilemmas.

The "Who Cares?" Dilemma

In a reactive service culture, it is quite common to discover that the motivation level of employees, supervisors and even managers is lower than it could be; in proactive service cultures, on the other hand, actual motivation more nearly reflects its potential.

Leaders of proactive organizations create and tend cultures characterized by two-way communication, participation and consensus, and a supportive climate of trust, security and sincerity. The tools they use include listening skills, consensus techniques, quality circles and ongoing employee recognition programs. The sequence of management interventions they might use to improve motivation would look something like this:

- Evaluate current levels of motivation using survey instruments, interviews and observation of staff
- Analyze the motivational influences in the organizational culture (what motivates? what demoralizes?)
- Identify variations in motivation among different staff segments (are all at comparable levels of motivation? are they motivated by the same factors?)
- Involve the receptive employees, or "doers" (ask for staff input and help)
- Develop a collective action plan reflective of staff diversity and keep communication lines open throughout its execution

196

- Evaluate results by repeating the survey, interviews and observation of staff

There may be easier ways to address motivation, but they will not permeate the social system to effect long-term change. It takes time to involve and listen to all organization members—particularly those outside the mainstream. However, the intervention will work only if it cuts across organizational levels as well as cultural, ethnic, racial and sexual lines.

In broad terms, people will become more motivated to perform their jobs when they are listened to, know what is expected, and are recognized and made to feel an important part of the social system. They need to be acculturated into the system and their affiliation reinforced through structured experiences.

Managers who fail to socialize employees and provide them with a sense of direction and belonging abdicate responsibility for employee motivation. Peer groups and informal leaders are quick to fill the gap, and their influence is rarely conducive to effective service delivery.

Take the case of the new waiter in the "problem" restaurant referred to in the opening vignette of "Service Environment as a Cultural Meeting Place." The waiter's manager and organization, by neglecting the employee's socialization, delivered him into the hands of disgruntled peers who wasted no time in teaching him to be apathetic and discourteous. Instead of setting the stage for the new employee to assume the desired role, management reacted to the script written by a hostile and unmotivated work group.

A world-class restaurant manager could have taken the situation in hand by, first, realizing that the existing social system was the cause of his employee motivation and service quality problems. The next step would have been to establish a dialogue with employees, through whatever means were acceptable to them. Distrust of management or cultural norms may have precluded face-to-face communication at the outset. The manager might have gradually established rapport by being careful not to react defensively or with anger to employee comments. By "checking" his cultural baggage and suspending judgment, he may eventually have come to understand the situation from his employees' perspective. He could then have analyzed the existing social system to determine motivating and demoralizing influences. Along with the "doers," he could have rewritten the script through participative methods.

The process would have taken time and would not have been without its conflicts. Social systems tend to resist change. Though the actors in the old system may have been unhappy in their roles, the script had become familiar. Changing scripts involves risk. The methods management uses for overcoming resistance must, again, be appropriate within the culture of the organization and the society from which its work force is drawn. At some locations, incentive programs may be effective; at others, use of informal leaders may be more appropriate.

Another obstacle to social system change is the conditioning of the manager responsible for it. Intimidated by social science theory, boxed in by the rational management paradigm, and pressured to show quick results, the manager may neglect or abandon outright the change effort before it takes hold. He would rather bail out than risk failure. As he reverts to managing "things," going to meetings with peers, and counting revenues, he leaves his people to form their own social system once again. Demoralizing influences invade untended social systems like weeds in a garden. Change must be maintained.

The Marketing Treadmill Dilemma

The world-class service manager defines marketing as anything and everything that must be done to bring customers to the business, satisfy their needs and expectations, and bring them back time and time again.

As consumer choices and consumption patterns are closely related to values, perceptions and actual experiences within the service environment, the customer's cultural programming is of paramount concern to the culture-savvy marketer. The successful marketer develops a multiple perspective, the ability to see and experience the product through the eyes of prospective buyers. He understands their expectations, attitudes and sensitivities. He can gauge their reactions to the express check-out, the complimentary headphones, or the oversized steak.

Culture influences every step in the consumer's decision process, from product awareness through postpurchase evaluation of the service experience. At each step, the customer filters information through cultural templates, evaluates impressions based on cultural norms and assumptions, and makes judgments and choices according to a cultural value orientation. In turn, the marketer, at each step, has the opportunity to use his knowledge of the customer's cultural programming to formulate selling points the customer can't refuse.

The following sequence of activities capitalizes on the cultural nature of consumerism to market a touristic product:

- Learn about your markets' cultures
- Cultivate close ties with tour operators, tourism and consular personnel, and other accessible and influential representatives of your target markets; enlist their aid as culture interpreters
- Learn about the "cultures" of decision-maker networks, including meeting planners and travel wholesalers
- Prepare your service environment to adapt to a diversity of customer

needs and expectations; empower frontline employees to interact effectively with all types of customers; empower all customers to master the service environment

- Introduce "total customer satisfaction" as a high-order cultural practice within the operation
- Constantly evaluate your success and check your perceptions of customer satisfaction/dissatisfaction

By using a holistic approach, the service manager avoids the treadmill effect created by luring customers to the business only to systematically disappoint them through maladaptive, inconsistent service delivery. Take the hypothetical case of the Sand and Sea Hotel referred to in chapter one. The resort's splashy advertising belied its hit-or-miss service environment. Customers rarely received what they thought they had paid for, so they checked out—*permanently*.

The hotel's reactive marketer responded by pouring more money into advertising and sales promotion. A world-class marketer would have focused on the hotel's internal marketing. Early on, he would have identified the hotel's divisive social system as a stumbling block to service delivery and championed an intervention to realign employee and management roles and objectives. He would have diverted some of those advertising dollars into employee relations and training. In short, he would have first brought the service environment under control and made certain he could deliver what he was selling. Then he could have iced the cake through enhanced market segmentation and product differentiation. The world-class marketer knows that, in the long run, the organization's profile in the marketplace is determined by satisfied customers, not by advertising and media hype. Customer loyalty and self-generating, word-of-mouth publicity are earned by consistently providing customers with positive experiences.

This truism was amply demonstrated by Delta Air Lines' 1987 brush with the media. When pilot errors were uncovered on several Delta flights, company executives proactively joined with the FAA to determine if the incidents were isolated or indicative of a serious flaw in the company's management. By cooperating with the media and government agencies, negative publicity was mitigated. In the end, the FAA's review found no fault with Delta's management.

The bottom line is this: no fall-off in passenger bookings occurred during the time the airline was the target of negative publicity. In fact, revenues and profits actually rose! Delta's customers were not influenced by the news reports. Why? Because their experiences, past and present, within the service environment neutralized the potential influence of the media stories.

Another specific illustration of using culture management to get off a marketing treadmill is the Sheraton Scottsdale Resort in Arizona. Five years ago this resort's owner agreed to participate in the American Hotel and Motel Association's "Quest for Quality" experiment. The second of seven pilot programs was implemented at the resort and it remains today as the most successful quality assurance system in the United States' lodging industry. The results are quite remarkable:

- A 25 percent average increase in sales over four consecutive years
- A doubling of the resort's number of rooms
- Recognition as a model of service management in lodging
- An average of $400,000 in documented savings and/or revenue gains for each year

Marketing is more than advertising and promotion at the Sheraton Scottsdale. The guests receive what they expect.

The moral? World-class marketing earns customer loyalty and profits.

The Back-to-the-Drawingboard Dilemma

Service managers look to automation as a means of containing labor costs while enhancing service delivery. Many have had the experience of purchasing and installing a shiny new piece of equipment only to have it crated off to a storeroom a few months later. Why? Because the technology didn't jibe with other ideological and social components of the system, and it didn't occur to anyone to take the time to make the adjustments in the environment that would enable it to take hold.

The world-class service manager avoids the costs associated with inappropriate and/or insufficiently interfaced technology by following a sequence of interventions such as this one:

- Describe the change sought in terms of ultimate enhancements to customer satisfaction
- Identify likely effects on the operation's social system
- Identify both driving and restraining forces present within the operation's culture, and devise strategies for harnessing the former and overcoming the latter
- Involve the doers among the employees in planning, executing and evaluating the technology interface; build feedback loops into the implementation process and ongoing operation
- Integrate the new technology's "culture" (jargon, implied values, time orientation, etc.) into the organization's culture. Make the new technology intelligible to those organization members not directly involved with it.

The careful selection and painstaking introduction of technological innovations protects the investment made in purchasing the equipment and safeguards the service environment against needless disruption. Unfortunately, many of the service managers who have come to favor this approach had to learn the hard way—through incidents like the one we are about to relate.

Once, the authors were discussing service problems in a quality circle meeting of restaurant waiters. As the discussion progressed, shared frustration with a new point-of-sale system recently installed in the restaurant became increasingly pronounced. One waiter lamented, "That new computer system was supposed to make our jobs easier. But, it doesn't. We work harder than ever now and have less time with the guests than before. To boot, our tips have gone down." The other waiters agreed. The new technology, heralded by management and the consulting company installing it as a major improvement, was apparently not working as anticipated. Another waiter offered this explanation: "We put the order in the machine out on the floor, but then we have to go back in the kitchen and tell the cooks what it was we input into the system. You see, the cooks can't read."

A classic case of haphazard, culturally insensitive technology selection and interface. The cooks, in the era before the new point-of-sale system, had received orders verbally from the waiters. The waiters did not have the extra, time-consuming task of inputting the order en route to the kitchen. When questioned, the general manager and other executives claimed to be unaware of the problems the new system had created.

In this case, the promising new technology, on balance, proved to be a setback rather than an advance. The old system took into account the cook's illiteracy, the social relations between the cooks and waiters, the waiter's priority of spending time with guests to finesse tips, and the customers' expectations of waiter attention throughout the meal. The new system, unfortunately, ignored the needs and expectations of everyone but the technology purchasers and vendors.

The world-class service manager would have done his cultural homework before committing the operation's monetary and human resources to an innovation of this magnitude. Yet, even had the cooks' literacy limitations gone undetected before the installation, the feedback built into implementation would have revealed this stumbling block early on. Unlike this restaurant's reactive manager, the world-class manager would have worked with his doers to find mutually acceptable ways of deriving optimum benefit from the system. Failing this, he would have, at least, gone back to the drawingboard a wiser manager of culture.

The "Who Owns Us Today?" Dilemma

No service business is immune to the takeover and merger wave sweeping industry. When two service organizations are combined through whatever means, each is subject to both positive and negative consequences of culture contact. When all the hoopla of consolidation and reorganization subsides, the outcome of the "marriage" may depend on culture management.

The world-class manager would adhere to the following tenets in taking over or reorganizing a service organization:

- Recognize that the existing managers and employees may already be doing some things right (don't change for the sake of change)
- Assess the cultures of both organizations to determine points of potential synergy and points of potential conflict
- Determine which aspects of the "old culture" are conducive to service delivery and should be preserved
- Obtain a consensus (with input from both organizations) concerning what the new hybrid culture should be (consider mission, values, relationships etc.)
- Begin the culture contact at points of commonality

The above sequence of events has not been the norm in past and recent corporate upheavals. More often, the first representatives of the acquiring company to make an appearance are not managers at all, but auditors and lawyers carrying sinister-looking notebooks and avoiding eye contact in the corridors. When the manager does finally appear, it is to hold a staff meeting announcing "the way things are going to be done around here from now on."

The climate at a soon-to-be-acquired or recently acquired company is one of insecurity, ambiguity, demoralization and gloom. Without a strategy to counteract them, these elements may seep by degrees into the service environment. People who feel like underdogs do not make the best service providers; acquiring managers who give their employees cause to feel like underdogs unwittingly sabotage their own service environment.

Take the case of the Grande Dame or Palace Hotel referred to in chapter 1. The hotel's new operating company took the property over without regard for its existing culture, employees or customers. Indignant, the oldtimers conspired to preserve the culture they had created and to retaliate against the arrogant, upstart management team intent on dismembering it. The employees attacked through union activity, labor suits, shoddy work and arbitrary opposition to all management initiatives; patrons loosed a barrage of complaints, letters to the press, and scathing word-of-mouth publicity. Reactive management responded by terminating dozens of managers and employees, hiring hotshot lawyers, and becoming increasingly stonefaced and inaccessible.

A world-class management team would have, first, looked for what the existing staff was doing right and recognized them for it. They would have taken measures to insulate the service environment against undue disruption while they set about managing the marriage of the two organizations. They would have done a lot more listening and a lot less "bloodletting."

Even the best-handled takeovers and mergers are not without hitches, but, by orchestrating culture contact, the world-class manager minimizes the loss of management and employee talent, patron and community goodwill, and profits.

Managing to a Different Drummer

> "As the world's largest industry, we have both an opportunity as well as an obligation to be the world's most responsible industry. An industry with a mission as well as a bottom line. An industry with a vision as well as a balance sheet."
>
> from the 1986 Resolution of the
> Tourism Association of Canada

The authors believe that a lot of people would like to change the organizations they work for. Few managers are satisfied with the results they are able to achieve through their people; few employees feel that their contributions are recognized.

As consumers, we are not generally satisfied with the quality of service we receive. According to the media, many people share these sentiments. They too would like to change the organizations whose services they purchase.

There are options to the way we currently deliver and consume service. A number of them are illustrated in the examples, anecdotes, and hypothetical cases presented throughout this book. We encourage readers to use them to begin a change process. In any departure from familiar ways, the first few steps are the hardest. For those setting out, we offer the following guidelines.

Rethink Your Philosophy

By the time most of us reach the ranks of management, our beliefs and assumptions about people and the way the world works have solidified. We have biases and perceptual blinders, and we think and behave within fixed parameters. We are likely ethnocentric. We may suffer from tunnel vision.

Breaking away from traditional, reactive practices will require a

203

change of philosophy. The new philosophy encompasses an appreciation of culture as an asset to be managed, a holistic perspective, and the valuing of diversity.

There are no magic formulas for taking on a new management outlook. However, you might consider the following suggestions:

- Read about culture and management (don't limit yourself to popular books)
- Identify your own cultural baggage and biases
- Take a course in cultural or applied anthropology
- Join international professional associations and attend international symposia

Vision is what separates ordinary managers from leaders. By casting off your cultural blinders, you will gain the ability to project a compelling vision to the people who look to you for leadership.

Expand Your Field of Action

As your perspective expands and you begin to view your organization and operation as open systems, you will feel increasingly confined within your office, department or outlet. You cannot manage service, culture or anything else by dealing only with people and reports that cross your threshold. Make yours an operation without walls. Through example, there is much you can do to promote system openness to both the internal and external environments.

You might begin by expanding your routine to include the following:

- Regular visits to the front line to talk with both service providers and consumers
- Active support of activities aimed at socializing employees (orientation sessions, social gatherings, athletic events)
- A high profile in community affairs
- Networking with peers within and outside the organization
- Shopping the competition
- Liaison with the academic community
- Affiliation with at least one group outside the realm of your profession and industry (for instance, a travel club, writers' workshop, or historical society)

The time spent away from your desk will pay dividends in fresh insights into the organization culture, a more penetrating understanding of your organization's mission and its place within the society, and inklings of opportunities that, if pursued, could result in profitable innovation.

Use Power Consciously and Constructively

As managers gain the ability to engineer social systems, they gain power in the organization. Every organization has a power structure, and every manager needs a share in it in order to make things happen within that organization. While the authors do not espouse "gamesmanship," they do heartily recommend that managers broker enough power to enable them to effect constructive change.

The service manager's style of wielding power will reflect on the service environment he or she engineers. An environment regulated through coercive power will stifle spontaneity and initiative and generate tension and frustration. The customer may receive a forced smile and efficient treatment but little help beyond the routinized procedures. In contrast an environment where consensus power reigns exudes energy, openness and harmony. Employees are more likely to take responsibility for customer satisfaction. The world-class service manager gains clout within the organization, then uses it to empower the service providers.

Managers may engage in the following activities to become more effective power brokers:

- Don't disregard the conventional formulas for gaining clout within an organization, but adapt them to the unique culture of your organization
- Capitalize on your superior understanding of the organization's culture to tap into the power structure
- In managing the people who report to you, use alternative styles of wielding power to effect constructive changes in the social system; gain influence with the people to whom you report by documenting your work in terms they value

A word of caution: depending on how it's used, power can propel or polarize. Handle with care.

Carry a Big Tool Kit

As the scope, complexity and competitiveness of your field increase, the size of your tool kit must increase proportionately. If you are like most contemporary service managers, your tool kit—as has been noted before—was packed in the school of service management as if culture didn't matter. The social sciences did not figure prominently in your curriculum.

Yet, in the past three decades, the social sciences have spawned numerous management disciplines, systems and methods with valuable applications to service environments. Among those that may particularly benefit the service manager are

- corporate culture analysis,
- organization development,
- intercultural management,
- business anthropology,
- quality assurance systems,
- social engineering,
- technology interface methods,
- change agentry,
- team-building methods, and
- consensus methods.

Although description of these tools is not within the scope of this book, management literature and resource persons abound to help the service manager learn more about them and put them to work. They are not intended to replace other basics like budgeting, staffing and controlling, but to take a place beside them as vital provisions.

Traditionally, management tools have been classified as either "hard" or "soft." Managers bestow the "hard" honorific on those laden with dollar signs; all the rest, whose bottom-line impact may be less obvious (though in fact equal to or greater than their hard cousins), are written off as "soft." Such myopic categorizing has contributed to and helped perpetuate the reactive cultures of most service industries.

This unfortunate double standard endures to this day. Culture management tools are already falling victim to the stigma of softness. The manager who uses them well, however, will find they are not soft at all, but essential tools—they are nothing less than the social lubricant that keeps the cogs of management turning.

Great Visions

In writing this book, we have stated the case for service management as if culture matters. Our aim is to raise the standard of service offered in today's service industries from poor or mediocre or even good to *world-class*. We propose culture management as the means for making it happen.

There's a potential world-class manager within every reader who scans this page. We invite you to break through to an alternative perspective and pioneer a new school of service management. Every service organization needs a visionary.

206

BIBLIOGRAPHY

Adler, N. 1986. *International Dimensions of Organizational Behavior*. Boston: Kent Publishing Company.

Albrecht, K., and R. Zemke. 1985. *Service America*. Homewood, IL: Dow Jones-Irwin.

American Hotel & Motel Association. 1985. *Quality Assurance I*. Lodging Reprints, April. East Lansing: The Educational Institute of the American Hospitality and Management Association.

American Hotel & Motel Association. 1985. *Quality Assurance II*. Lodging Reprints, May. East Lansing: The Educational Institute of the American Hospitality and Management Association.

Archer, B. 1976. *Tourism in the Bahamas: The Impact of the Tourism Dollar*. Nassau, Bahamas: Ministry of Tourism.

Aronowitz, S., and H.A. Giroux. 1985. *Education under Siege: The Conservative, Liberal, and Radical Debate over Schooling*. South Hadley, MA: Bergin & Garvey Publishers.

Bennis, W., and B. Nanus. 1985. *Leaders: The Strategies for Taking Charge*. New York: Harper & Row.

Bernstein, P. 1982. "Necessary Elements for Effective Worker Participation in Decision-Making." In *Workplace Democracy and Social Change*, edited by F. Lindenfeld and J. Rothschild-Whitt. Boston: Porter Sargent Publishers, Inc.

Blake, Brian F., Carl Dexheimer, and Nori Mercuri. 1986. "Disparity Analysis; A Double-Edged Sword." *Marketing News* (January): 34-35.

Booms, B.H., and M.J. Bitner. 1981. "Marketing Strategies and Organizational Structures for Service Firms." In *Marketing of Services*, edited by J.H. Donnelly and W.R. George. Chicago: American Marketing Association.

———. 1982. "Marketing Services by Managing the Environment." *Cornell Hotel and Restaurant Administration Quarterly* 23 (May): 35-39.

207

Brislin, R. 1981. *Intercultural Interactions: A Practical Guide*. Beverly Hills: Sage Publications.

Bryden, J.M. 1973. *Tourism and Development*. Cambridge, England: Cambridge University Press.

Burrell, G., and G. Morgan. 1979. *Sociological Paradigms and Organizational Analysis*. London: Heinemann Educational Books.

Carlzon, J. 1987. *Moments of Truth*. Cambridge, MA: Ballinger Press.

Carnoy, M., and D. Shearer. 1980. *Economic Democracy: The Challenge of the 1980s*. White Plains, NY: M.E. Sharp, Inc.

Casse, P. 1981. *Training for the Cross-Cultural Mind*. Washington, DC: SIETAR International.

———. 1982. *Training for the Multicultural Manager*. Washington, DC: SIETAR International.

Casse, P., and S. Deol. 1985. *Managing Intercultural Negotiations*. Washington, DC: SIETAR International.

Collier, D. 1987. *Service Management: Operating Decisions*. Englewood Cliffs, NJ: Prentice Hall.

Condon, J., and F. Yousef. 1975. *An Introduction to Intercultural Communication*. Indianapolis: Bobbs-Merrill.

Copeland, L., and L. Griggs. 1985. *Going International*. New York: Random House.

Cullen, Thomas P. 1981. "Global Gamesmanship: How the Expatriate Manager Copes with Cultural Differences." *Cornell Hotel and Restaurant Administrative Quarterly* 22, no.3 (November): 18-24.

Curtis, J. 1978. *Culture as Polyphony: An Essay on the Nature of Paradigms*. Columbia: University of Missouri Press.

Czepiel, John A. 1980. "Managing Customer Satisfaction in Consumer Service Business." Report No. 80-109. Cambridge, MA: Marketing Science Institute.

Dahl, R.A. 1985. *A Preface to Economic Democracy*. Berkeley: University of California Press.

de Kadt, E., ed. 1979. *Tourism: Passport to Development?* Oxford: Oxford University Press.

Deal, T., and A. Kennedy. 1982. *Corporate Cultures: The Rites and Rituals of Corporate Life*. Reading, MA: Addison-Wesley.

Dhir, Krishna S., and V. Chandresekar. 1984. "A Study of Consumer Subjectivity in Selection and Assessment of Restaurants." In *Hospitality: Profitability in an Era of Change*, edited by Robert Lewis. Forthcoming.

Drucker, P.R. 1954. *The Practice of Management*. New York: Harper & Row.

———. 1985. *Innovation and Intrepreneurship*. New York: Harper and Row.

Bibliography

Dubinsky, Alan J., and Michael Levy. 1981. "A Study of Selected Behaviors in the Purchasing of Consumer Services: Implications for Marketers." In *1981 Educators' Proceedings*. Chicago: American Marketing Association.

Duck, Steve W. 1973. *Personal Relationships and Personal Constructs: A Study of Friendship Formation*. London: Wiley.

England, G., A. Negandhi, and B. Wilpert. 1979. *Organizational Functioning in a Cross-Cultural Perspective*. Kent, OH: Kent State University Press.

Enis, Ben M., and Kenneth J. Roering. 1981. "Services Marketing: Different Products, Similar Strategy." In *Marketing of Services*, edited by J.H. Donnelly and W.R. George. Chicago: American Marketing Association.

Fay, B. 1987. *Critical Social Science*. Ithaca, NY: Cornell University Press.

Ferguson, H. 1988. *Tomorrow's Global Manager*. Homewood, IL: Dow Jones-Irwin.

Furnham, A., and S. Bochner. 1986. *Culture Shock*. London: Methuen.

Garland, J. 1986. *International Dimensions of Business Policy and Strategy*. Boston: Kent Publishing.

Glover, W. G. 1988. "Managing Quality in the Hospitality Industry." *FIU Review* 6, no.1: 1-14.

Glover, W. G., and O. H. M. Smith. 1982. "A Nation-wide Study of the Bahamian Tourism Product." Bahamas Ministry of Tourism, Nassau.

Glover, W.G., R.S. Morrison, and A.C. Briggs. 1985. "Making Quality Count: Boca Raton's Approach to Quality Assurance." *The Cornell Hotel and Restaurant Administration Quarterly* 25, no.1 (May): 39-45.

Gronroos, Christian. 1984. "A Service Quality Model and Its Marketing Implications." *European Journal of Marketing* 18, no.4: 36-44.

Gudykunst, W., et al. 1985. *Communication, Culture, and Organizational Processes*. Beverly Hills: Sage Publications.

Hagler, S.H. 1977. "Group Interview Not Hard, But Good One Is Difficult." *Marketing News* (July).

Hall, E. 1959. *The Silent Language*. New York: Fawcett.

———. 1976. *Beyond Culture*. Garden City: Anchor Press, Doubleday.

Harris, P., and R. Moran. 1987. *Managing Cultural Differences*. Houston: Gulf.

Heenan, D., and H. Perlmutter. 1979. *Multicultural Organization Development*. Reading, MA: Addison-Wesley Publishing Co.

Hofstede, G. 1984. *Culture's Consequences*. Beverly Hills: Sage Publications.

Hoopes, D., and P. Ventura. 1979. *Intercultural Sourcebook: Cross-Cultural Training Methodologies*. Yarmouth, ME: Intercultural Press.

Kanter, R.M. 1982. *The Change Masters: Innovation for Productivity in the American Corporation*. New York: Simon & Schuster.

Kelly, George A. 1963. *A Theory of Personality*. New York: W.W. Norton.

———. 1970. "A Brief Introduction to Personal Construct Theory." In *Perspectives on Personal Construct Theory*, edited by D. Bannister. New York: Academic Press.

Kelso, L.O., and P.H. Kelso. 1986. *Democracy and Economic Power: Extending the ESOP Revolution*. Cambridge, MA: Ballinger Publishing Co.

Kilman, R. 1984. *Beyond the Quick Fix*. San Francisco: Jossey-Bass.

Klein, D.M. 1983. Unpublished report to Sausman Hotel Group, Boca Raton, FL.

Kluckhohn, R., and F. Strodtbeck. 1961. *Variations in Value Orientations*. New York: Row, Peterson.

Lanier, A. 1975. *Your Manager Abroad: How Welcome? How Prepared?* New York: AMACOM.

Lehitinen, Uolevi, and Jarmo R. Lehitinen. 1982. "Service Quality: A Study of Quality Dimensions." Helsinki: Service Management Institute.

Lett, J. 1986. "Anthropology and Journalism." *Communicator* XL, no.5: 33-35.

———. 1987a. "An Anthropologist on the Anchor Desk." *Practicing Anthropology* 9, no.1: 2,22.

———. 1987b. "An Anthropological View of Television Journalism." *Human Organization* 46, no.4:356-9.

Levitt, Theodore. 1981. "Marketing Intangible Products and Product Intangibles." *Harvard Business Review* 58 (May-June): 94-102.

Lewis, Robert C. 1981. "The Positioning Statement for Hotels." *The Cornell H.R.A. Quarterly* (May): 56-61.

Lewis, Robert C., and Bernard H. Booms. 1983. "The Marketing Aspects of Service Quality." In *Emerging Perspectives on Service Marketing*, edited by L. Berry, et al. Chicago: American Marketing Association.

Liechty, Margaret G., and Gilbert A. Churchill, Jr. 1979. "Conceptual Insights into Consumer Satisfaction with Services." In *1979 Educator's Proceedings*, edited by Neil Beckwith, Michael Houston, et al. Chicago: American Marketing Association.

Lovelock, Christopher H. 1983. "Classifying Services to Gain Strategic Marketing Insights." *Journal of Marketing* 47 (Summer): 9-20.

Lynch, J. 1984. *Airline Organization in the 1980s*. New York: St. Martin's Press.

The Management of Hospitality. 1983. International Jubilee Conference on Hospitality Management. Oxford: Pergamon Press.

Markin, Rom. 1974. *Consumer Behavior: A Cognitive Orientation*. New York: Macmillan Publishing Co.

Matthews, H. 1978. *International Tourism: A Political and Social Analysis*. Cambridge, MA: Schenkman Publishing Company.

Melnyk, G. 1985. *The Search for Community: From Utopia to a Co-operative Society*. Montreal: Black Rose Books.

Bibliography

Mezirow, J. 1984. "A Critical Theory of Adult Learning and Education." In *Selected Writings on Philosophy and Adult Education*, edited by S. Mirriam. Malibar, FL: Robert E. Kriegar Publishing Co.

Morgan, G. 1986. *Images of Organization*. Beverly Hills: Sage Publications.

Murphy, P.E. 1985. *Tourism: A Community Approach*. New York: Methuen.

Nader, R., and W. Taylor. 1986. *The Big Boys: Power & Position in American Business*. New York: Pantheon.

NAFSA. 1981. *Learning across Cultures*. Washington, DC: NAFSA.

Naisbitt, J., and P. Aburdene. 1985. *Re-inventing the Corporation: Transforming Your Job and Your Company for the New Information Society*. New York: Warner Books.

Nightingale, Michael. 1986. "Defining Quality for a Quality Assurance Program: A Study of Perceptions." In *Practice of Hospitality Management II*, edited by R. Lewis, et al. Darien, CT: AVI Publishing.

Ouchi, W. 1981. *Theory Z*. Reading, MA: Addison-Wesley.

Parasuraman, A., Valarie A. Ziethhaml, and Leonard L. Berry. 1985. "A Conceptual Model of Service Quality and Its Implications for Future Research," *Journal of Marketing* 49 (Fall): 41-50.

Pearce, P. 1982. *The Social Psychology of Tourist Behavior*. Oxford: Pergamon Press.

Pedersen, P. 1981. *Counseling across Cultures*. Hawaii: University of Hawaii Press.

Perrow, C. 1986. *Complex Organizations: A Critical Essay*. (3d ed.) New York: Random House.

Peters, T., and N. Austin. 1984. *A Passion for Excellence*. New York: Harper and Row.

Peters, T., and R.H. Waterman, Jr. 1982. *In Search of Excellence: Lessons from America's Best-Run Companies*. New York: Harper & Row.

Phatak, A. 1983. *International Dimensions of Management*. Boston: Kent Publishing Company.

Piet-Pelon, N., and B. Hornby, 1985. *In Another Dimension: A Guide for Women Who Live Overseas*. Yarmouth, ME: Intercultural Press.

Rabin, Joseph H. 1983. "Accent Is on Quality in Consumer Services This Decade." *Marketing News* 17 (March): 12

Rosen, C., K.J. Klein and K.M. Young. 1985. *Employee Ownership in America: The Equity Solution*. Lexington, MA: Lexington Books.

Russell, L. 1973. *The New Service Society*. Harlow, England: Longman.

Sampson, P. 1972. "Using the Repertory Grid Test." *Management of Service Operations*. Boston: Allyn & Bacon.

Sasser, W. Earl, R. Paul Olsen, and Daryl Wycoff. 1978. *Management of Service Operations*. Boston: Allyn & Bacon.

Schön, D.A. 1987. *Education and the Reflective Practitioner: Toward a New Design for Teaching and Learning in the Professions*. San Francisco: Jossey-Bass Publishers.

———. 1982. *The Reflective Practitioner: How Professionals Think in Action*. New York: Harper Colophon Books.

Scott, Cliff, John Ford, and William Lundstrom. 1987. "Isolating Tangible Representations of Intangible Service Dimensions: An Extension of the Repertory Grid Methodology." *Services Marketing: Integrating for Competitive Advantage*. American Marketing Association.

Serrie, H., et al. 1986. *Anthropology and International Business*. Williamsburg, VA: College of William and Mary.

Shames, G., and G. Glover. 1987. "The Critical Juncture: Face-to-Face Service." *Travel Business Manager* (July): 2-8.

———. 1988. "Catching the Cultural Nuances." *Restaurant Hospitality* (April): 55-56.

Sheehy, G. 1981. *Pathfinders*. New York: William Morrow and Company, Inc.

Sherif, M., and C.I. Hovland. 1961. *Social Judgment: Assimilation and Contrast Effects in Communication and Attitude Change*. New Haven: Yale University Press.

Shostack, G. Lynn. 1977. "Breaking Free from Product Marketing." *Journal of Marketing* 41 (April): 73-80.

———. 1981. "How to Design a Service." In *Marketing of Services*, edited by J.H. Donnelly and W.R. George. Chicago: American Association.

Stewart, E. 1972. *American Cultural Patterns*. Yarmouth, ME: Intercultural Press.

Terpstra, V. 1985. *The Cultural Environment of International Business* Cincinnati: South-Western Publishing Company.

Thompson, A. 1982. *An Economic History of the Bahamas*. Nassau: Commonwealth Publications Ltd.

Toffler, A. 1985. *The Adaptive Corporation*. New York: McGraw Hill.

Tung, R. 1987. *The New Expatriates*. Cambridge, MA: Ballinger Press.

Turner, L., and J. Ash. 1975. *The Golden Hordes: International Tourism and the Pleasure Periphery*. London: Constable.

Ullman, Albert D. 1965. *Sociocultural Foundations of Personality*. Boston: Houghton Mifflin.

Vinson, Donald E., Jerome Scott, and Lawrence Lamont. 1977. "The Role of Personal Values in Marketing and Consumer Behavior." *Journal of Marketing* 41: 44-50.

Waters, S.R. 1986. *Travel Industry World Yearbook: The Big Picture*. New York: Child & Waters, Inc.

White, A. 1970. *Palaces of the People: A Social History of Commercial Hospitality*. New York: Taplinger.

Bibliography

Wilcock, K. 1985. *The Corporate Tribe*. New York: Warner Books.

Williams, C., et al. 1985. *The Negotiable Environment*. Ann Arbor, MI: Facility Management Institute.

Wyckham, R.G., P.T. Firzroy, and G.D. Mandry. 1975. "The Marketing of Services," *European Journal of Marketing* 9: 59-68.

Zeithaml, Valerie A. 1981. "How Consumer Evaluation Processes Differ between Goods and Services." In *Marketing of Services*, edited by J.H. Donnelly and W.R. George. Chicago: American Marketing Association.

INDEX

A

Albrecht and Zemke, 20
Alienation, 27–28
Aloha, 168–69

B

Bahamas, The, 25, 34, 60–71, 156–66;
    Bay Street Boys, 65-68; British
    rule, 64–65; Burma Road riots, 66;
    Hawksbill Creek Agreement, 68;
    Pindling era, 68–69; Progressive
    Liberal Party, 66
Bargaining, 95
Bay Street Boys. *See* Bahamas
Berger, F., 36
Borden, David, 57
Burma Road riots. *See* Bahamas
Business strategy, 4, 7, 11, 184–87

C

Caribbean resort, case of. *See* Sun
    and Sea Hotel
Carlzon, Jan, 77
Change agents, 62
Chaplin, Charlie, 18
Clarke, Clifford, 193

Client expectations. *See* Customer
    contact
Communication, 5, 27, 93–94, 103,
    145, 171, 192-93, *See also*
    Intercultural communication
Consumer. *See* Customer contact
Contracts, 95
Corporate culture, 13, 17, 20, 44, 78,
    87–89, 158-60, 190. *See also*
    Organizational culture
Cross-cultural, communication, 121
    (see also Intercultural communi-
    cation); environment, 79; man-
    agement *(see* Managing culture);
    misunderstanding, 80
Cultural, adjustment, 8; baggage, 2,
    172, 187, 197; differences, 79, 82,
    92, 105, 124-26, 137, 151-52, 160-62,
    191; faux pas, 127, 188; self-
    awareness, 148; sensitivity, 77,
    87, 106, 126
Culture, 2–4, 97, 126-27, 186; broker,
    6; management, 2-5, 14, 26,
    80–81, 103, 156, 159, 175, 177 *(see
    also* Multicultural manager); of
    dependency, 63; shock, 125, 191
Customer contact, 5, 9, 13, 77, 145,
    192-94 *(see also* Host-guest inter-
    actions); expectations, 89-90,
    98-101